VIRTUAL TERRITORIES

VIRTUAL TERRITORIES

TECHNOLOGY, REPRESENTATION, AND THE STATE IN A DIGITAL AGE

JORDAN BRANCH

OXFORD
UNIVERSITY PRESS

OXFORD
UNIVERSITY PRESS

Oxford University Press is a department of the University of Oxford.
It furthers the University's objective of excellence in research, scholarship,
and education by publishing worldwide. Oxford is a registered trade mark of
Oxford University Press in the UK and in certain other countries.

Published in the United States of America by Oxford University Press
198 Madison Avenue, New York, NY 10016, United States of America.

© Oxford University Press 2025

CIP data is on file at the Library of Congress.

ISBN 9780190063627

ISBN 9780190063610 (hbk.)

DOI: 10.1093/9780190063658.001.0001

The manufacturer's authorized representative in the EU for product safety is
Oxford University Press España S.A., Parque Empresarial San Fernando de Henares,
Avenida de Castilla, 2 – 28830 Madrid (www.oup.es/en or product.safety@oup.com).
OUP España S.A. also acts as importer into Spain of products made by the manufacturer.

CONTENTS

ACKNOWLEDGMENTS

FIRST, AN ENORMOUS THANKS TO Jon Lindsay, for generously read-ing the entire manuscript and providing exceptionally helpful feedback. Our conversations about these topics over the past decade have been both productive and enjoyable, and I look forward to many more. For comments and suggestions on earlier versions of this project, thanks to Peter Andreas, Mark Blyth, Adam Branch, Jonathan Caverley, Jeremy Crampton, Joe Devanny, Peter Dombrowski, Henry Farrell, Hein Goe-mans, Helen Kinsella, Ron Krebs, Sean Lawson, Helen Lee, Rose McDermott, Bryan Nakayama, Abe Newman, John Savage, Jacquelyn Schneider, Amit Sheniak, Max Smeets, Tim Stevens, my international relations and government colleagues at Claremont McKenna College, the editors and anonymous reviewers of *International Studies Quar-terly* and *International Organization*, the anonymous reviewers for Oxford University Press, and the audiences where versions of this work have been presented: the Mortara Center for International Studies at Georgetown University, the Judith Reppy Institute for Peace and Conflict Studies at Cornell University, the Watson Center at the Uni-versity of Rochester, the Centre for International Peace and Security Studies at McGill University, the University of Wisconsin, the Univer-sity of Minnesota, Cambridge University, the Norwegian Institute of International Affairs, the Naval War College, Yale University, King's College London, Marquette University, the University of Connecti-cut, Santa Clara University, the David Rumsey Map Center at Stanford

University, and the 2014 and 2018 International Studies Association meetings.

Excellent research assistance was provided by Omar Afzaal, Ercole Durini di Monza, Lindsay Lew, Kaitlyn Seever, and the staff at the National Security Archive. Generous support for the project came from the American Council of Learned Societies, the Keck Center for International and Strategic Studies at Claremont McKenna College, and the National Endowment for the Humanities (any views, findings, conclusions, or recommendations expressed in this book do not necessarily represent those of the National Endowment for the Humanities). Permission to draw on my earlier published work was provided by the University of Chicago Press, Oxford University Press, Cambridge University Press, and Edward Elgar Publishing.

Thanks to Dave McBride and the staff at Oxford University Press for enormous patience in awaiting the completion of this project, and great efficiency in moving it forward once I finally finished.

Finally, this book is dedicated to Helen, for everything.

I

Introduction

Technology, Politics, and Representation

TECHNOLOGICAL CHANGE HAS UNDOUBTEDLY ALTERED, and continues to alter, international politics. New weapons, communication media, surveillance systems, and more are increasingly interwoven into warfare, diplomacy, trade, and every other aspect of international relations. But *how*, exactly, do technological and political change interact? Answering this question requires stepping away from the search for a singular "effect" of technology and instead examining the diverse mechanisms that connect transformative technologies and the institutions, ideas, and practices of international politics. This book focuses on the essential but underappreciated mechanism of *representation*: how technologies and their capabilities are represented and how technologies produce or alter representations of the world. Three recent examples of this technology–politics interface reveal the importance of representations, suggesting how this book's focus can help us understand events central to international politics today.

2023: Lethal representations and representing lethality in the Israel-Gaza war. First, consider the Gaza war that started with the Hamas attacks of October 7, 2023. Although this conflict is rooted in long-standing issues, it illustrates the importance of representational

Virtual Territories. Jordan Branch, Oxford University Press. © Oxford University Press (2025).
DOI: 10.1093/9780190063658.003.0001

technologies in warfare today. For one, Israel's defense network and offensive capabilities rely not only on traditional military power but also on numerous cutting-edge technologies: surveillance systems, precision munitions, and—in a move widely seen as fundamentally novel—artificial intelligence (AI) target-selection systems.[1] Two machine-learning systems for choosing airstrike targets have reportedly been used, one for selecting structures that are sites of militant operations and the other for identifying individual Hamas or Palestinian Islamic Jihad (PIJ) militants. The latter system (known as "Lavender") was trained on data collected on known operatives of Hamas or PIJ, and then was used to look for similar patterns in the general population of Gaza after October 7. The system would then give each individual "a rating from 1 to 100, expressing how likely it is that they are a militant."[2] This technology proved essential for Israeli target-selection teams because the process used in previous conflicts—a lengthy process of "incrimination" where each potential target's profile was carefully examined before a strike—was impossible when the Israeli military decided after October 7 to label *all* Hamas military operatives as legitimate targets, regardless of rank. Reporting has suggested that human analysts often only played a rubber-stamp role, taking a mere twenty seconds to review an individual target, sometimes only to assure that the target was male. The demand for targets in vast numbers was simply too great for human analysts to fulfill in any other way.

This is a target-selection process that operates almost entirely through representations: conceptual representations of what features distinguish militants from civilians in Gaza, representations in data of those patterns, and then finally an output that reduces each individual to a numerical score of their likelihood of being a militant—a representation that often led to immediate lethal consequences. Reporting has highlighted critical issues with this reliance on representations. For example, the training data used with the system reportedly contained not only militants but also some Hamas-affiliated civilian workers, making their characteristics part of what defined the profile of a militant target for the system.[3] In addition, as one source reported, "the numbers changed all the time, because it depends on where you set the bar of what a Hamas operative is"—in other words, what numerical score output is judged to be high enough to be a "likely operative."[4]

That bar may have been changed in some cases simply to accommodate the daily demand for targets: if there weren't enough targets with a given threshold, then the threshold could be lowered.[5] In short, the AI system is trained by consuming representations; it then produces representations (using internal logic that is difficult if not impossible for the system's users to interpret, as with most large-scale machine-learning systems); and then airstrikes follow.

International attention and discussion of this technology and the conflict more broadly have also operated through representations, most prominently the enormous amount of photographic and video evidence made possible and distributed thanks to ubiquitous smartphones and the social media ecosystem. These visual representations of Hamas actions, Israeli responses, and civilian suffering are all deployed to shape how outside actors see and interact with this conflict.

In fact, Israeli AI targeting systems and their use are themselves subject to competing representations, particularly around the question of how legal or ethical such systems are. Defenders of the technologies have emphasized that they are simply a tool used by human analysts to help them select legitimate targets, making the system a neutral device used for military ends. For example, an Israeli military spokesperson "denied using artificial intelligence to incriminate targets, saying these are merely 'auxiliary tools that assist officers in the process of incrimination.'"[6] Yet claims that these are a minor addition to existing methods of analysis are belied by earlier rhetoric from the Israeli military, which had heralded its use of "AI war" as revolutionary since the 2021 conflict in Gaza.[7]

Moreover, commentators quickly pointed out that any efforts to keep an human in the loop are limited by time pressure, the tendency to believe what an information system outputs (i.e., "automation bias"), and other factors.[8] And even advocates for the system have at times highlighted how it replaces, rather than supplements, human judgment: "its influence on the military's operations was such that they essentially treated the outputs of the AI machine 'as if it were a human decision,'" in the words of one intelligence officer.[9] Others have justified the system as a better choice in the days after the October 7 Hamas attack, given that nearly all intelligence analysts would have lost someone close to them and thus would have their judgments clouded by grief or the desire for revenge.[10] Even the name given to the AI system for identifying structures to target suggests the enormous faith meant to be placed in it: "Habsora," translated as "The Gospel."

Much of the reporting on the enormous civilian harm of the Israeli response to the October 7 attacks has emphasized the unprecedented number women and children among the dead and wounded—individuals, in other words, who clearly fall outside the scope of even the most expansive definition of "Hamas operative." The sheer number of Israeli airstrikes, enabled by the AI targeting systems used, has been posited as a significant cause of those high casualties.[11]

2015: Territorializing the internet. In 2015, Secretary of State Hillary Clinton gave a major speech on how the United States was seeking to dismantle the Islamic State. Among the multiple approaches she outlined was the effort to combat the group's use of the internet for recruiting, propaganda, and coordination—an unsurprising tactic, given how central the internet was to Islamic State operations. As detailed in later reporting, this was a reference to Joint Task Force Ares, set up by US Cyber Command to carry out a variety of cyberattacks against the Islamic State.[12] Yet Secretary Clinton used a particular metaphorical language, arguing that the United States "must deny them [the Islamic State] virtual territory just as we deny them actual territory."[13] This language was by no means limited to Secretary Clinton: General Paul Nakasone, head of US Cyber Command, noted four years later that "to defend critical military and national interests, our forces must operate against our enemies on their virtual territory as well."[14]

Here, government officials are discussing the internet as "virtual territory" needing to be contested, defended, or occupied. Using such a simple label for a vast technological system allows policymakers to grasp what might otherwise be incomprehensible: the complex threats and opportunities created by the internet. Officials are then able to think about the internet's boundary-crossing implications through the familiar institutions of the territorial state, and use that framework to formulate, explain, and justify their actions. As Chapter 4 will show in detail, this kind of description, or representation, shapes how the internet is addressed by state actors, and thus its political consequences.

1995: Digitizing boundary negotiations. Multifaceted representational processes have also emerged in the use of digital tools for traditional diplomacy, even in some of the earliest examples. In 1995, the United States brought together the hostile parties involved in the Bosnian civil war in an attempt to broker a stable peace—a peace that would include the division of Bosnia into two autonomous territories. (These negotiations culminated in the Dayton Accords of November 1995.) A critical issue was the creation of a corridor of land connecting the Muslim enclave of Gorazde to the rest of the Muslim-Croat Federation. The US negotiators knew that the challenge would be finding a proposal acceptable to Serbian president Slobodan Milosevic. As Ambassador Richard Holbrooke later wrote:

> [US General Wesley] Clark and his colleagues had prepared well....
> Flying the land between Sarajevo and Gorazde endlessly ... they had
> found a route that could link the two cities. It was a small dirt track
> located halfway between the two roads, both now controlled by the
> Serbs, that had once connected the two cities.[15]

Conducting reconnaissance in preparation for negotiating a boundary was a long-standing practice, but this was, in fact, quite different. Clark was not actually above Bosnia in an aircraft. Instead he was "flying" over a digital representation of the territory, using a virtual terrain system originally created by the US military to plan bombing missions.

This system, which had been brought to Dayton as one component of an enormous set of cartographic support tools (discussed in detail in Chapter 3), was then used to negotiate the new boundary. It turned out to be a key factor in gaining Milosevic's agreement on this particularly contentious issue—the detailed terrain and immersive quality of the representations provided by the system were essential to achieving a negotiated solution. According to Clark:

> Milosevic was smart, but he wasn't a field soldier. He'd never walked
> that terrain [near Gorazde].... "You can see right here, Mr. President,
> here's the mountaintop on one side, here's the mountaintop on the
> other. You can't draw a line down the side of a hill like this and have
> it defensible." ... He could see this with real terrain; ultimately, he
> couldn't beat the argument.[16]

Of course, these negotiations did not take place over "real terrain," but over representations in a digital mapping system. In fact, while these systems and their successors are specifically designed to give the user an accurate and realistic view, incorporating three-dimensional terrain modelling, satellite imagery, and so on, the results are far from a photo of the real world. They are enormously constructed images, visual mosaics of vast amounts of spatial data, with the user's view defined by innumerable choices in coding and interface.[17]

Negotiations about borders nearly always take place over representations: it has been extremely rare for officials to draw a new boundary in the field. Diplomats have, for centuries, relied on systems of paper maps and overlays, modified with pens and pencils, thereby simplifying the world into a manageable abstraction. Yet digital mapping has come to represent spatial information in entirely new ways, including deploying the kind of far more realistic imagery and terrain modeling that was used at Dayton. This has changed negotiation in unexpected ways, including strengthening particular solutions over alternatives, as the US participants claim occurred in this case. In other words, the success of the negotiations relied at least in part on the representations made possible by the new technological systems.[18]

Yet there is also another representational aspect to this story, equally important to the outcome: how the technological systems and their outputs *were themselves represented*. Holbrooke's statement that Clark was "flying over Bosnia" and Clark's own contention that Milosevic had been convinced by "real terrain" are linguistic and narrative representations that shaped how those events played out. Of course, one could argue that those statements are merely metaphors, and that related ones have often been applied to traditional paper mapping. (In other words, the use of maps is often discussed as examining the territory or terrain itself, rather than an image on paper.) Yet metaphors can have enormous consequences (see Chapter 4), and the specific choice of metaphor here is revealing. Linguistic representations of traditional mapping have rarely if ever analogized to an *embodied* experience like flying over the actual territory involved, nor have they so clearly elided the distinction between the land and its artificially constructed representation (as Clark's phrase "real terrain" does). If the use of the digital mapping system was discussed and thought of more literally—for example, as manipulating and examining composite images on a display—the emotional and affective responses would have been weaker or absent and the technology would not have had the same effect.

Representation and Technological Change in International Relations

In all three of these examples, representations work as an important intervening factor in the connection between technological change and the transformation of political institutions, ideas, and outcomes. Technological systems alter how we see the world, and the way that we talk about those systems shapes their effects. This includes the possible reshaping of the territorial state in the face of novel technologies, particularly the expansion of information networks into nearly all aspects of social and political life. This book focuses on these representational processes, revealing new pathways by which technologies are changing international politics—and vice-versa. Technological systems create and transform the representations that define international politics, from the territorial state to core practices of international cooperation and conflict. Simultaneously, technological systems are represented in ways that fundamentally shape their political impact.

These representational aspects of technology have largely been overlooked in existing discussions in international relations (IR). Studies of the political effects of technology tend to focus on material features and resulting capabilities, rather than on how tools are represented. And theories that recognize the importance of representations largely leave out the role of technological systems in producing them.[19]

On representation in general, constructivist IR theory has demonstrated the importance of linguistic representations, including in the fundamental concepts of state sovereignty and authority.[20] Representations are essential to the "world-making" processes identified by feminist IR scholars and others, in which political rules and institutions are constituted in thought and speech.[21] Numerous examples have demonstrated how changes in these representations have reshaped political practices. For instance, metaphors from science and technology have guided military ideas and organization since the early modern period,[22] and changing scientific cosmologies, or "image[s] of the universe and the role of humanity in the cosmos," have made possible new forms of international order.[23] Representations, and their use by political actors, have reshaped both the motives and the means of international political interactions and domestic institutional change. Yet the specific interaction of representations and technologies has been overlooked.

This is not to say that IR scholarship has ignored the interaction of technological and political change entirely.[24] Nonetheless, most studies emerging from the dominant theories in IR have approached technology as a tangential component of broader, more explicitly political topics, such as trade or state security, or through an examination of a single technology like nuclear weapons.[25] Technological systems are then typically conceptualized either as causal factors or, often implicitly, as one component of the environment within which interaction takes place.

In that context, the role of technology has been interpreted according to two broad logics: instrumentalism and determinism.[26] The *instrumentalist* view sees technical systems as useful tools, put toward preexisting goals without reshaping the identities or interests of the actors using them. Technologies are thus understood to be "neutral" instruments, with their main political consequences emerging from their effects on capabilities.[27] On the other hand, the *determinist* approach assumes technologies to have certain—perhaps immutable—characteristics that determine what political actors can and cannot do with them. Actors' choices and goals, in other words, are less important than the features of the technologies themselves. Determinist accounts fall along a range, but all posit in some way that the effects of technological change are out of the control of human actors and thus amount to, in effect, inevitable consequences.[28]

When it comes to the question of what digital information technology means for the possible weakening, transformation, or persistence of the state—an issue central to the future trajectory of international politics—existing instrumentalist and determinist logics yield opposing positions.[29] Instrumentalism tends to support the argument that states are persistent and (relatively) unchanging, historically and today.[30] This includes both analytical assumptions of state persistence—neorealist IR theory, for example, largely assumes that state sovereignty and anarchy are fixed, with distributions of capabilities being the only form of systemic variation[31]—and empirical arguments aiming to demonstrate that states remain the sole locus of authority and power.[32] For these instrumentalist interpretations, technological change merely creates new sources of power or redistributes capabilities to different actors, without changing the nature of an international system that continues to be composed of sovereign states. States thus use new tools to pursue their existing interests in security, domination, wealth, or other ends.

On the other hand, a vast literature has drawn on an often-implicit deterministic framework to highlight the threats to state control or authority posed by technological change.[33] These threats range from direct vulnerabilities in areas such as cybersecurity to the more subtle dangers for state control when national identity and loyalty to state institutions are undermined by the effects of new technologies. Here studies emphasize the observable ways in which new technological capabilities are forcing states to share power or authority with other actors or organizations, the result being that technological change undermines the traditional notion of the state having a monopoly on authority within its territory.

In spite of these disagreements, however, instrumentalist and determinist approaches share a common assumption: nearly all IR theory treats technological change as *exogenous* to politics.[34] Technologies may be brought into the analysis as variables or causal factors, but the features of technological systems are understood to be outside the political processes being studied. For example, even when the instrumentalist position sees technologies being adopted for political reasons, the characteristics of what is being adopted are taken as given. This ignores the ways in which technological features and uses are interwoven into political processes, often resulting from the latter as much as shaping or driving them.

Recent scholarship has aimed to reverse this pattern, in two ways: first, by focusing explicitly on the role of technology in international politics and, second, by incorporating technological change itself as a process endogenous to political interactions. These studies are founded on an effort to increase conversation between IR and science and technology studies (STS).[35] STS scholarship, though diverse, suggests numerous adjustments to the standard approach to technology in IR.[36] Studies in STS have demonstrated the various ways in which technologies are inherently political, in their origins, in their effects, and even in their operation. In Langdon Winner's influential analysis, "technology in a true sense *is legislation*. . . . Thus, politics becomes (among other things) an active encounter with the specific forms and processes contained in technology."[37] In other words, like legislation or political rules and institutions, technological systems shape possibilities, constrain and incentivize actions, and—importantly—are simultaneously created and maintained by actors with specific purposes in mind.

Technologies and their politics are mutually constituted, in short, meaning that both instrumentalism and determinism leave out much of the politics of technological change. Technological tools and especially their uses are constructed through ideational and social processes as much as by material features. They can have effects on social and political phenomena, but those effects are rarely deterministic—instead, technologies shape the conditions of possibility for decision-making and interaction. This balance between the materially determined and socially constructed aspects of technology plays out differently at different spatial and temporal scales, but in nearly all circumstances, technology's "political consequences always remain *underdetermined*."[38]

In the face of this indeterminacy, the challenge is in delineating the specific connections between political change and technological innovation. A useful step suggested by STS scholarship is to focus less on the material *features* of technological systems and more on technologies' *affordances*, defined as "the set of possibilities for human action from any artifact."[39] This puts material technological features in their social and political context and asks what conditions of possibility emerge.[40] This also includes an examination of how technologies are used by political actors and organizations.[41] Affordances are shaped by specific circumstances, enabling instrumental uses in some situations and producing (somewhat) deterministic effects in others. The material features of a technology, in other words, only have political or social effects by interacting with their human context: institutional settings, ideational structures, systems of meaning, collections of practices, and arenas of political interaction.

Technological Representations

The fundamental argument of this book is that there are important technological affordances that have been missed in IR's conventional focus on technologies' material capabilities or features. Specifically, I concentrate on *representational* processes: how technologies enable particular representations and, simultaneously, how representations of technologies reshape their uses and effects. Focusing on representation usefully narrows the empirical scope and reveals new mechanisms connecting technological and political change.

The production, circulation, and consequences of representations have been considered by STS scholars, particularly when examining the role of representation in scientific research.[42] Since "objects can only be 'known' through representations,"[43] those representations will have consequences for how objects are understood and used. In other words, "graphic displays and other representations are not simply pictures of natural objects";[44] instead, those representations are part of how the objects and their affordances are constructed. STS studies of scientific research have emphasized the enormous range of consequential representations, in both devices and practices: "graphs, diagrams, equations, models, photographs, instrumental inscriptions, written reports, computer programs, laboratory conversations, and hybrid forms of these."[45]

In international politics, diverse representations provide the visual, linguistic, and conceptual "mediums through which the world comes to be known and understood."[46] They are, in short, essential intervening variables in political processes. Visually, techniques make possible the creation, distribution, and use of politically salient images, including photographs, diagrams, maps, and others.[47] Those visual representations are not simply communication devices: "visual artefacts do things. . . . They often shape politics as much as they depict it."[48] For example, how states have sought to "see" what they seek to govern has relied on representations like maps and censuses.[49] Linguistic and conceptual representations are also pervasive in international politics, including in narratives, discourses, and descriptions.[50] Ideas and concepts "are themselves forms of power through their capacities to produce representations,"[51] and available concepts and vocabularies have always constrained what actors are able to argue for and to do.[52] Other representational practices can be conceptual (how actors are classified in international law, for instance) or even emotional: particular affective responses can come to represent specific objects, ideas, or phenomena.[53]

While existing studies have identified these key representational processes in international politics, they have largely overlooked how such representations are shaped by material systems, particularly information technologies involved in creating, storing, and transmitting them.[54] Even affective representations interact with technological tools: What a technology "feels like," for example, is an emotional representation of something about that system, which can alter evaluations of risk and decision-making processes in particular ways.[55] As STS scholars have highlighted, moreover, material and ideational elements are closely interconnected: material systems create particular representational artifacts that can be used in political contestation.[56]

As illustrated by the three narratives above, understanding the interaction between information technology and international politics today requires a consideration of two sides of representation.

First, technological artifacts provide the *devices* or *media of representation*, making those artifacts' affordances highly consequential for what representations are possible and how they are used politically. This includes visual media and the material "surfaces" upon which linguistic representations are inscribed.[57] Which kinds of images, texts, descriptions, or models are made possible by a particular technology and which are discouraged? How does representing something with that medium shape the ideas that actors hold about it, or even make it identifiable and understandable as a thing?

Second, technologies themselves are often the *subjects of representation*, whether visual or linguistic—in images, diagrams, descriptions, or metaphorical comparisons. Complex technical systems in particular are nearly impossible to observe or understand without representational simplifications. Because those representations change the ways in which technological systems are understood, they shape the context of those systems' material features and thus their affordances.[58] Such representations constitute the myths surrounding technologies, myths that, in circumstances of rapid and dramatic innovation, serve to make novelty more comprehensible by rendering "socially and intellectually tolerable what would otherwise be experienced as incoherence."[59] How new technologies are understood is fundamental to how their features translate into affordances, and how those affordances reshape political interactions.

In short, these dual representational processes—representation *through* technologies and representation *of* technologies—act as essential intervening variables in international politics. Technological and political change interact through representations as much as through material capabilities, revealing transformative mechanisms missed by instrumentalist and determinist logics. As the cases in following chapters will demonstrate, representations are involved in producing novel ideas and concepts, making particular political arguments tenable or convincing, and foreclosing certain political choices or outcomes. These processes are essential to the core features of international relations, including the future of the territorial state and the international system—with diverse implications for the trajectory of institutional change in states today. On the one hand, state actors are able to deploy representations to make the implications of technological change comprehensible, and, for a time at least, manageable with current institutions and practices. On the other, the nature of key features of states like territorial boundaries are being redefined by novel representations and their uses. These consequences are revealed in the four diverse empirical areas examined in the chapters that follow: the technologies of nineteenth-century state-building and imperial expansion, digital geospatial technologies and territorial borders, cybersecurity threats and how states address them, and remote and possibly autonomous warfare through drones.

Methodology and Plan of the Book

Since my goal is to demonstrate the importance of a largely overlooked mechanism connecting technological and political change, and to do so through a series of distinct but related case studies, the book is not structured as a set of specific findings to be tested. Instead, following Rogers and Hill's study of drone warfare, it aims to "open up discussion and debate, in contrast to presenting a 'package' of exhaustive findings."[60] Thus the purpose of the case studies is to illustrate the complexity of representational processes around information technology, and to demonstrate their importance to how those technologies interact with states and their actions today.[61] Given that technological systems like the internet should be studied not as unitary entities but instead as "bundle[s] of mechanisms that we can in principle disentangle from each other" (as Henry Farrell convincingly argues),[62] this book takes one mechanism—representation—and seeks to demonstrate its prevalence, and consequences, across multiple important issue areas.

Technology is of course central to this argument, yet the very concept is difficult to define in an uncontested way.[63] Some definitions emphasize the materiality of objects or artifacts,[64] while others focus almost exclusively on the application of knowledge for a practical purpose.[65] Most useful for this book's analysis is a relatively broad definition, incorporating both material artifacts and the systems of knowledge and practice that surround those artifacts.[66] Existing studies of technology in international relations tend to take this expansive approach, defining technology as, for example, the "accumulation of knowledge and artifacts for the realization of human purposes in a specifiable and reproducible way."[67] This type of definition, while certainly wide-ranging, is useful in that it incorporates the breadth of ideas and objects that are intuitively "technological" and thus frame what types of representations should be examined.

Thus technologies—material and otherwise—are involved in the dual representational processes discussed above: representations *of* technological systems through images, language, conceptual frameworks, and other means; and how the world is represented *through* technologies when artifacts produce representations used by political actors. As the cases in the following chapters will illustrate, both of these categories of representations then have enormous political consequences, through deliberate use and by unconsciously framing interests, rhetoric, and contestation. Negotiators use representational tools like maps that they feel support their interests, often with only a limited awareness of the extent to which those representations shape the negotiation process—for themselves as much as for their counterparts. Bureaucratic contestation is channeled through the linguistic framework brought to discussions over resources, solutions, and even the nature of the problems posed by information technology. And ethical debates are shaped—or even created to begin with—by the ways in which lethal technologies and their use are represented, and by the visual imagery that emerges from those systems.

While these mechanisms can be observed across historical eras (as illustrated in Chapter 2), the digitization of information technology has accelerated and transformed these processes. The explosion of visual representation, the malleability of digital tools when compared to their predecessors, the ever-increasing complexity of the systems requiring simplifying representations, and the blurring of the material–ideational distinction[68] make the role of representational dynamics one of the most important, though neglected, mechanisms in the interaction between technological and political change today. Traditional frameworks that overlook representation—particularly in IR, where the focus is typically on institutions, ideas, interests, or material factors—are thus missing an essential part of the story.

The case studies in the following chapters demonstrate how the general mechanisms and dynamics of representation play out in different ways across technological and political fields. What politically consequential representations does a technology enable or suppress? How is a particular technology represented and understood? Who deploys those representations and why? How, then, do technologies and their representations drive or constrain changes in political ideas, institutions, and outcomes?

Chapter 2 demonstrates how the book's framework applies to the nexus of technology and politics before the digital revolution, exploring how information technologies and their representations shaped state-building and imperialist expansion in the nineteenth century. (This serves to expand and strengthen the theory in the book, rather than offering a detailed empirical study of what is a well-documented period.) Information technologies were integrated into governance in new ways, particularly through statistics, mapping, and telegraphy. These tools produced representations with political uses and effects, but they were also represented in particular ways that shaped their political impact. This chapter demonstrates that in addition to the conventionally emphasized changes in capabilities created by nineteenth-century technological innovation, representations were also a core element in the politics of technology during this transformative era.

Chapter 3 considers the ways that digital mapping is changing how states dispute, negotiate, and settle contested boundaries.[69] When compared to even the most accurate and detailed paper maps, digital cartography has a host of new affordances—including flexibility, layering, accuracy and certainty, realistic imagery, and three-dimensional modeling—and has also redistributed the capability and authority of mapping to new actors, ranging from individuals to corporations like Google. While this chapter focuses largely on the representations produced by digital cartographic tools, how those tools are themselves represented is also important, particularly in the expectation of accuracy in position-finding and the positive affective valence assigned to "realistic" imagery.

Chapter 4 examines the politics of linguistic and conceptual representations in cybersecurity. In such a novel and uncertain area, state actors first have to make sense of what the internet means for their security before they can seek to address the threats and opportunities that have emerged. This chapter focuses on how the United States, particularly its military, has discussed, understood, and sought to manage the internet's implications for state security. A detailed empirical study of US military strategy and doctrine traces the emergence and consolidation of terminology built on the "cyberspace domain," a metaphor that has strengthened specific ways to understand complex issues, provided discursive resources to some arguments over others, and shaped policy contestation and outcomes.

Chapter 5 addresses the use of drones by the United States in counterterrorism operations, demonstrating the importance of representational processes. This includes both how drone systems produce consequential representations and how drones and their use are represented. Those representations shape the policies pursued through drones, the debates about their use, and the possibility of future autonomous systems. This case illustrates the complex mix of instrumental and deterministic logics at work around novel technologies: drones and their representations not only provide useful tools—material, rhetorical, and ideational—but they also drive new policies and impose constraints on action.

Chapter 6 concludes the book by noting common threads that run through the chapters, including the interplay of diverse forms of representation and the role of affect and emotional processes in how technologies and their representations work politically. It also lays out how the book's framework and cases point toward new ways to conceptualize not just technology but also political institutions: representations are a core, unrecognized component of large-scale institutions like the modern state. Finally, it explores implications for how we might understand contemporary international conflicts, which are increasingly mediated by technologies and their representations.

International relations as a field has largely ignored representations, especially when it comes to technological change. Yet representations are everywhere in politics; they function as an intervening variable in innumerable processes and mechanisms. Those representational dynamics are only growing more complex with the continuing expansion and evolution of digital technologies, and this book provides an essential framework to understand their implications. The case studies in the following chapters demonstrate these processes, revealing the diverse ways that representations are essential to understanding the political implications of technological change, including how the sovereign state may be changing in an era of "virtual" as well as "actual" territory.

2

Information Technology, State-Building, and Imperialism in the Nineteenth Century

WHAT CONSTITUTES "INFORMATION TECHNOLOGY" BEFORE digitization? While the term tends to conjure images of computers, smartphones, and telecommunication networks, it can be defined broadly, revealing the presence of information technologies throughout human history.[1] Technology includes both material artifacts and applied knowledge, so information technology encompasses systems and techniques that change how information is gathered, stored, processed, and communicated. This includes everything from the earliest written or even spoken language to the digital computer of the twentieth century. This chapter concentrates on how information technologies and their representations have shaped political transformations before the contemporary era—focusing in particular on state-building and imperial expansion in the nineteenth century. Emphasizing representations brings overlooked questions to the fore: How were new information technologies represented? How did new technologies create or shape other, politically consequential representations? How did those two sides of technological representation interact in state-building and imperialism?

Examining a historical case through this lens serves to build out the theory to be applied to the book's three contemporary cases. Although

Virtual Territories. Jordan Branch, Oxford University Press. © Oxford University Press (2025).
DOI: 10.1093/9780190063658.003.0002

mechanisms connecting political and technological change are certainly structured by their context, there are generalizable elements that can be traced across historical settings. Thus, while the sense that today's digitization is fundamentally new and without precedent may be accurate in part, it misses recurring patterns in how technologies have always interacted with political ideas, practices, and outcomes.

Focusing specifically on nineteenth-century information technologies illustrates the two sides of representation introduced in the previous chapter. First, the nineteenth century saw new technological practices that produced representational artifacts: visual depictions, written descriptions, and other material means of representing political ideas, interests, and institutions. Nineteenth-century states and empires relied extensively on maps, statistical tables, geographic and demographic descriptions, and numerous other material representations of peoples, resources, and territories claimed or ruled. Second, technologies and their effects were understood—and thus made politically consequential—through how they were represented, using particular metaphors, analogies, conceptualizations, and other forms. For many nineteenth-century technologies, their political effects had as much to do with ideas about them as the material capabilities they provided. Examining the interaction of these dual processes also reveals a third form of technological representation, particularly important in nineteenth-century politics: technologies themselves can constitute ideational representations of political processes or institutions.

This chapter therefore explores these multiple interactions—among diverse forms of technological representation, between material and ideational processes, across states and empires—in nineteenth-century international politics. As with the three contemporary case studies in the chapters that follow, focusing on representations here provides a useful addition to the traditional emphasis on how the features of technologies provide new instrumental tools or impose new deterministic constraints. In particular, this chapter demonstrates how a focus on representations provides a new means of investigating the interaction of technological and political change, through an examination of a historical period with both parallels and genealogical links to today.[2]

Comparing Today with the Nineteenth Century

The nineteenth century provides an especially productive demonstration of the role of material and ideational representations in the interaction of technological change, imperial expansion, and the transformation of state institutions. There are four reasons in particular to focus on the nineteenth century.

First, while nineteenth-century state-building and imperialism followed some earlier patterns, they were also distinct—and distinct in ways that tie them closely with later developments. In the nineteenth century, for one, centralized bureaucratic states emerged across diverse settings. While earlier polities exhibited elements of what would become the consolidated national state in the twentieth century, only in the nineteenth century did state capacity and reach begin to resemble the highly regulative or authoritarian states that followed. This involved a dramatic increase in the capacity of states to enforce their rules,[3] an increase that was a significant—and distinct—element in the long-term emergence and consolidation of the state. In other words, the notion of a singular moment when "the state" as we know it appeared misses the various chronologies—and causal processes—involved in the diverse components that make up "state-ness": internal centralization and hierarchy, external formal legal equality, territorial boundaries and exclusive rule, and state capacity and authority to intervene in society.[4] The nineteenth century was when significant parts of the entire combination came together for the first time.

European imperialism in the nineteenth century—particularly in its latter decades—also diverged in significant ways from its predecessors. European powers increasingly reached into the interior of Asia and Africa, overcoming previously insurmountable barriers of disease and local resistance. Although some of the factors behind this expansion also appeared in earlier phases,[5] many others were novel—and the outcome in terms of near-total global domination was certainly new.[6] Moreover, the nature of twentieth- and twenty-first-century international politics owes more to the legacies of nineteenth-century imperialism than to early-modern developments.[7] Contemporary postcolonial international relations emerged in the second half of the twentieth century out of the end of nineteenth-century formal and informal imperialism.

Second, the later nineteenth century in particular suggests intriguing technological parallels with today. It saw a similarly rapid increase in global interconnection, built on new technological systems: in this case railroads, steamships, and the telegraph. The telegraph, in fact, has been heralded as creating a "Victorian internet," with near-instantaneous communication, global spread, and even technology-driven boom-and-bust business cycles.[8] Yet then as now, the interaction of technological and political changes went well beyond the ways in which the material features of new technologies created new capabilities, incentives, or constraints. By focusing on the dual nature of representation—representations *of* information technologies and *through* information technologies—this book draws new attention to a specific, and overlooked, set of nineteenth-century parallels and precursors to today's digital politics.

Consider, for example, the striking similarities in the two period's contemporary descriptions of new tools and their effects (as opposed to the very real differences in actual capabilities between the two periods).[9] Much of the rhetoric of the internet echoes late nineteenth-century discussions of the telegraph: the "death of distance," the end of time and space as constraints on human interaction, and predictions of dramatic political, social, and economic effects. For instance, after the public demonstration of one of the first US telegraph lines in 1844, "the *Baltimore Patriot* newspaper employed the same Washington-to-Baltimore line to report on a vote in the House of Representatives, concluding that the telegraph represented 'the annihilation of space.'"[10] These similarities in rhetorical representation—and, in some cases, a direct lineage that can be traced between the two periods' rhetoric—make the late nineteenth century a particularly useful period to examine through this book's theoretical lens.

Third, international relations (IR) scholarship is increasingly recognizing the importance of the nineteenth century both for shaping the contemporary international system and for defining how we study international politics today. The nineteenth century not only exhibits parallels to contemporary politics; it also contains the seeds of many of the central developments of the twentieth century.[11] The telegraph and the internet again suggest this dual connection. In addition to sharing some parallel features, the actual physical infrastructure of today's fiber-optic internet backbone often follows the paths first laid by nineteenth-century telegraph cables, especially when it comes to where undersea connections reach land.[12] The nineteenth century also saw the emergence of modern IR as an academic field, much of it connected with the defense of imperialism.[13] Recent research in IR has thus increasingly focused on this era, in nearly all cases looking beyond the straightforward aspect of new technologies giving imperial powers greater military capabilities and instead focusing on ideational changes, legitimation strategies, social networks, and other factors.[14]

Fourth and finally, there are important parallels between the nineteenth century and today in terms of the interaction between technological change, institutional transformation, and warfare—long understood to be a major driver of international politics. Like today, major wars among the so-called great powers were rare in the nineteenth century. Both then and now, however, war or preparation for war remained a prominent driver of technological developments and institutional transformations, and warfare was itself shaped by those changes in return. Within Europe, international politics were framed by a relentless preparation for war, even if few were fought on the continent. In imperial spaces open conflicts were limited among European powers, but force was regularly deployed or threatened against indigenous peoples and polities. The incessant "qualitative arms race" among great powers—that is, the need to keep up not just in terms of manpower or spending but also in weapon technology—began in the nineteenth century and has continued through today.[15] Thus, as today, preparations for war, the use of force by powerful states against distant targets, and efforts to diplomatically resolve the conflicts that did arise were important drivers both of institutional transformation within states and of changes in the international system. In all of these processes, information technologies and their representations have played an important and underexamined role—a role revealed by this chapter's reexamination of this key historical period.

Technology, Representation, and Historical Political Change

Systems and techniques for storing and communicating information have been integral to—though by no means determinative of—the development of political organization throughout human history. Major early transformations such as the emergence of sedentary societies or the creation of ancient state-like organizations have coincided with developments in informational systems.[16] In early polities, techniques such as writing were essential to expanding the spatial scale of rule: "The creation and imposition of a written code throughout the city-state replaced vernacular judgments and was itself a distance-demolishing technology."[17] In short, early forms of writing and early political organization were "co-produced," each shaping and being shaped by the other.[18] The subsequent increases in hierarchical complexity and scale of polities in the ancient world were paralleled by developments in various forms of information storage and communication, from new written media to larger and faster courier networks.[19]

Moving closer to the present reveals escalating interconnections between information technologies and changes in political organization. For example, the fifteenth- through eighteenth-century "global early modern" period exhibits multiple close interactions among technological change, representational practices, and state-building and colonial expansion. This period laid many of the foundations for nineteenth- and twentieth-century international politics: the first wave of significant political and economic interconnection encompassing every region of the globe, the increasing consolidation and centralization of authority within diverse early states, and imperial expansion in a variety of forms and scales. These processes were by no means exclusive to Europe: while this period did see the first wave of European colonialism, particularly in the Americas, it also saw expansionary strategies pursued by political centers in China and South Asia.[20] All of these processes made use of—and led to changes in—information technology. In the European case, this built on a broader set of changes in how the world was represented, "a new way, more purely visual and quantitative than the old, of perceiving time, space, and material environment."[21]

In state-building, the new emphasis on quantitative and visual representation manifested in numerous technical artifacts and practices, epitomized by mapping. Cartographic tools came to redefine how the state was both conceived and put into practice, with a shift toward linear territorial boundaries defining exclusive claims to rule—the spatial definition of the modern state, in other words.[22] The state as represented in maps came to redefine the state as practiced on the ground: throughout the early modern period boundaries were negotiated and demarcated, post-war settlements came to discuss claims exclusively in territorial terms, and non-territorial authorities over persons disappeared. The "map room" became a key site of governance, a "center of calculation" (to use Latour's term[23]) bringing together representations of territories near and far, at scales from local property lines to global territorial claims.[24]

The global wave of conquest and expansion in the early modern period—including by European powers in the Americas, China in East Asia, and the Mughal Empire in South Asia—likewise relied on information technology and representations. The Chinese imperial court, for example, made use of many of the same tools of visual and quantitative representation that European states were using in their own state-building efforts.[25] European expansion in the Americas relied on written and visual representations—ranging from travel narratives to navigational maps—to construct New World empires, including early attempts by Spain and Portugal "to accumulate and regulate all geographical knowledge" in their respective colonial institutions.[26] Spanish officials requested detailed descriptions and maps of colonies, with mixed results.[27] This produced a complex set of legal representations of colonial possessions, including legal concepts that were developed through new geographic descriptions and depictions.[28]

European expansion into Asia and Africa before the nineteenth century, in contrast, yielded far less direct conquest and was made possible not by superior military or transport technology but by the absence of conflict between Europeans' goals of dominating maritime trade and local powers' emphasis on territorial control on land.[29] This resulting emphasis on controlling trading networks was itself built on a host of visual and written representations, particularly the "oceanic" perspective of much of the period's cartography.[30] For Portugal, for example, geographic knowledge and representations were essential: "'Possession' was based not on territories occupied but on the monopolization of logistical and navigational information which established precedence in the creation of commercial sea routes and specific trading points."[31] The Dutch East India Company (VOC), similarly, saw maps "as an aid to clarify political, military, economic, cultural, and administrative particularities in order to make sound decisions" and deployed them as "forceful expressions of the absolute rule of VOC administrators."[32] Representations, in short, were essential to early modern state-building, colonial conquest, and competition over global trading networks.

Technologies of Nineteenth-Century State-Building and Imperialism

The nineteenth century saw a significant growth in the internal capacity and reach of states and a dramatic expansion of European imperialism. State transformation included not only the integration of smaller units to form newly united nation-states like Germany and Italy, but also a dramatic increase in the capacity of states to provide services and regulate everyday life. Nineteenth-century empires, similarly, involved not only an increase in scale, as vast areas of Asia and Africa were brought under European control for the first time, but also a change in the character of expansion.[33] The goals, ideologies, and tools of nineteenth-century imperialism were not simply an extension of earlier phases.[34] In Asia, European powers increasingly dominated local polities, including the creation of an explicit empire in British India, the imposition of unequal treaties on China, and the forced "opening" of Japan. In Africa, European empires put in place various forms of direct and indirect rule, and in nearly all cases the scope and scale of imperial control went far beyond the coastal enclaves and trading networks of early-modern colonialism. In sum, although some degree of diversity persisted,[35] there were across-the-board increases in internal capacity within states and in external domination and authority in empires.

Especially for the second half of the nineteenth century, state-building and imperialism have long been linked with a set of technological developments that emerged out of the industrial revolution.

New artifacts, systems, and knowledge across a number of domains were closely involved in state consolidation and imperial expansion: military technology in rifles, artillery, machine guns, and warships; medicinal advances against tropical diseases; rapid transportation via steamship or railroad; and increasingly dense communication networks through the telegraph, mail services, newspapers, and other means. Existing arguments emphasize, with reason, the ways in which new capabilities made it easier for European states to pursue to their longstanding goals of internal centralization and external conquest.[36] Yet there is also more to this story.

While increasing capabilities—to dominate militarily, to transport goods or people, to communicate at unprecedented distances—were important, so too were the ways that new technologies enabled and embodied new representations: representations of global connectivity, of empires, and of national states.[37] Asserting and effecting claims over distant places, or intensifying control of the entirety of a state from a capital, relied on a host of representational practices and devices, and the means to move those representations from the peripheries to centers of rule. Moreover, this was not only about new means of representation and rule. New justifications for expanded state capacity and direct imperial control also relied on ideas and techniques emerging out of information technologies. In the internal centralization drive of states, the "sense that national space was a realm of relatively simultaneous application of control" depended the perception that new transportation and communication technologies made such control possible—whether they actually did so in practice or not.[38] Representations of imperial possessions, similarly, had significant consequences not just for how spaces and peoples were understood but also for how imperial officials planned and implemented policies. British policy toward the Afghan frontier of India, for example, was fundamentally shaped by the "idea of Afghanistan," which "had a demonstrable impact on the manner in which Britain engaged with the country itself."[39] Those representations were often wildly inaccurate, yet they altered how the British sought to manage what they saw as the "unstable periphery" of their control of India.[40]

Once we concentrate on the interweaving of multiple forms of representation in nineteenth-century imperialism and state-building, specific mechanisms are brought into focus. First, of course, is the use of information-technology systems and practices as a means of representing rule—that is, as representational artifacts to be used for governance over territories near and far. This practice was certainly not new in the nineteenth century (as discussed above), but existing techniques and their effects were scaled up and transformed. The next section details the role of mapping and statistics, not only as means of gathering information about subjects territories or peoples, but also as tools for effecting control from the center. New forms of state and empire were put into practice through the use of representational tools. Simultaneously, arguments about the future course of imperial or state-building policy were made more convincing—or less—by how well they were able to work with dominant forms of representation. Representational media, while not determining outcomes, can provide a better fit with certain ideas and interests than with others.[41]

Second, nineteenth-century technological developments, including in informational systems, were held up by advocates of Western imperialism as justifications for their domination of other parts of the world.[42] In early modern European colonialism, there had been almost no reference to science, technology, or material differences to legitimize expansion; arguments had largely relied on religious or other cultural differentiations. In the eighteenth century, this began to change, as "scientific and technological gauges were playing a major and at times dominant role in European thinking about such civilizations as those of India and China and had begun to shape European policies."[43] In the nineteenth century, rapid industrial development in the West made technological differences between regions even more pronounced, and the notion of a "civilizing mission" as a justification for imperialism came to rest in large part on comparative evaluations of science and technology. This displaced or subsumed many other justifications for empire.[44] By late in the century, "colonial administrators and missionaries, travelers and social commentators increasingly stressed technological and scientific standards as the most reliable basis for comparisons between societies and civilizations."[45] Representations of peoples, in other words, came to be tied to representations of their technologies.[46] Thus Western technologies were deployed not only for their material advantages but also as symbols of superiority: in the US mission to forcibly open Japan in the 1850s, for example, technologies such as the telegraph were demonstrated for this very purpose.[47]

Third, there are ways in which information technologies have been central to affective or emotional representations of empires and states, strengthening or shaping state-building projects and imperial expansion. As will appear in a number of the cases discussed below, a "sense" or "feeling" of increased control or knowledge—rather than any actual increase—has often followed from the deployment of new information technologies in political contexts.[48] Likewise, the affective valence attached to a particular imperial space in discussions by officials can color their choice of policies, and that valence is shaped by the available representational tools and practices.[49] Representations of technologies and representations using technologies overlap in these affective evaluations.

Nineteenth-Century Technologies and Their Representations

New technologies proliferated in the late nineteenth century, from weapons to transport to telecommunications, and many of them were incorporated into international diplomacy and new forms of industrialized warfare.[50] For European states, changes in military technology led to a vastly increased scale of mobilization through railroads and increasingly destructive firepower. While this new style of warfare was relatively unused within Europe until 1914, states constantly planned for war and the use of new weapons. In imperial spaces, moreover, new military technologies fundamentally altered the balance of power between European forces and local authorities.

Again, however, this was about more than capabilities. Important effects also emerged out of what new technologies represented. Railroads, for one, had symbolic importance in addition to their practical uses for trade and military deployments.[51] For example, railroads were important tools for westward expansion by the United States, but they also embodied the ideas that motivated that expansion: "Continental and imperial visions . . . took on renewed life with the transformation of railroads from short lines connecting close cities to long roads that could knit together remote points. Territorial thinking assumed new promise and new dimensions."[52] In imperialist expansion, railroads were among the technologies that most clearly represented Western modernity—for both imperial powers and others—and were actively presented as demonstrations of civilizational superiority.[53]

Even in the case of military systems, it is useful to go beyond the traditional focus on technological capabilities. Like the railroad, new weapons not only served as tools of European domination; they also were held up as a justification for those outcomes.[54] In addition, the mass mobilizations of nineteenth-century warfare depended as much on organizational changes—including the increasing adoption of informational tools like mapping—as they did on mass conscription and the industrial production of weapons.[55] One of the most important of these organizational innovations was the creation of a permanent general staff.[56] While military planning had been important for centuries, the creation of a permanent institution dedicated exclusively to preparing for *future* wars was novel. This new type of planning required a vast array of representational tools, including maps, mobilization tables, and other artifacts. The rapid development of weaponry also called for future-oriented planning, as militaries knew that by the time the next war was fought it would likely involve new weapons. This increasing creation and use of representations for war-planning had implications well beyond the military realm, however, as many of the informational tools that emerged out of military purposes were later used for state-building.[57]

Three technologies—statistics, mapping, and telegraphy—are particularly illustrative of the nineteenth-century interaction between informational systems, representations, and state- and empire-building.[58] Each is examined in turn.

Statistics

The rapidly growing field of statistics constituted a key state-building technology of the nineteenth century.[59] While gathering data about populations and resources had long been a practice of both amateurs and government officials,[60] the nineteenth century saw a new "avalanche of printed numbers," in which "nation-states classified, counted and tabulated their subjects anew."[61] This involved the creation of state institutions such as statistical bureaus, which had been exceedingly rare just one century earlier.[62] It also went far beyond an increase in the scale of data gathered on populations, and instead changed the type of information collected and how it was categorized: the "real innovation" was in the "systematic *quantification*" of categories like ethnicity or race, and the shift toward recording all members of a population rather than just the productive members of households.[63] (The latter had been the focus of many earlier, taxation-oriented government surveys.) While there were differences between the projects carried out in different countries, the increasingly statistical representation of a state's population was an international phenomenon, with techniques shared or imitated globally.[64]

Statistical projects like censuses were both a tool of nineteenth-century state-building and an embodiment and representation of those efforts as well. On the one hand, statistics provided essential new capabilities for increasing the state's reach into society,[65] gathering more detailed information on populations and enabling increased state capacity and action (i.e., the ability to "govern from a distance"[66]). On the other, the statistical projects themselves both *represented* the expanding state and *embodied* it in increasingly complex material systems. The Weberian "rationalization" of the state during this period, in other words, involved not only the bureaucratization of rules in formal institutions but also a vast increase in informational material gathered, stored, analyzed, and used within those institutions. In Latour's apt phrase, this explosion of material meant that state rationalization occurred "in the files themselves" rather than in the minds of bureaucrats.[67]

The authority attributed to those files, and to the statistics recorded in them, emerged from the way that scientific knowledge was brought into statistical institutions, combining the legitimacy of the state with that of science.[68] That authority was then deployed to justify increasing state capacity and to represent the nation as a coherent entity, defined by the characteristics of its population.[69] A census or other official statistical project, in other words, was not simply a tool of state-building: "Census making is itself a practice of state formation, an assertion of sovereign authority over people and social relations."[70] That relationship continues to the present day, including in the lineage from various nineteenth-century informational techniques to the twenty-first-century surveillance state.[71]

The dual nature of statistics as both tool and symbol of state-building—that is, both a representation-producing system and a representation itself—appears across diverse cases. Prussia (and later Germany) saw extensive use of official statistics to define the nation and state, based on "the idea that the nation-state is essentially characterized by its statistics, and therefore demands a statistical office in order to define itself and its power."[72] In the United Kingdom, the nineteenth century saw a growth in both "administrative statistics"—meant to guide government activities—and "informational statistics," which were fundamentally about understanding and representing the nation. They were intended explicitly to "provide a unified picture of the nation—a picture even the public should be allowed to appreciate."[73] In Canada, the later nineteenth century saw an increasingly complex statistical census as an active tool of defining a national identity and placing the state in control of that identity.[74] In colonial spaces as well, statistics were deployed to gather information on, but also redefine, subject populations.[75]

The history of statistics in Italy in the nineteenth century illustrates these processes well. The statistical projects that were ostensibly intended to measure the Italian nation in fact "produced" that nation more than describing it.[76] Before unification, statistics were actively used to promote the idea of a unified Italy, as research projects "undertook to describe not only single communities and provinces, but also the condition of the peninsula as a whole, as if Italy were already a unified country."[77] This "work of representation" was an active effort to counter what were felt to be misleading foreign images of the Italian peninsula.[78] After unification, statistical studies were immediately deployed to support arguments for particular administrative policies in the new state, including the division into geographic regions.[79] These projects produced "one of the few truly 'national' manifestations of the country."[80]

In domains beyond state-building in newly unified European countries, statistical projects were also central to governance and even diplomacy. In nineteenth-century India, for example, various competing rulers all relied on their access to networks of informants to gather information on their subjects. The British (first in the East India Company and later through colonial officials) adjusted this approach, replacing the "statistically rich," single-purpose reports upon which indigenous rulers relied with "multi-purpose social data in conformity with the new European science of statistics."[81] When combined with the British ability to put vastly greater financial resources toward information-gathering, these techniques gave them an advantage over indigenous rulers.[82] Moreover, the purportedly more "scientific" character of the British statistics "had the effect of reinforcing Europeans' notions of their own historical superiority."[83]

The nineteenth century also saw the emergence of the use of statistics at peace negotiations, in a practice that would become common thereafter. At the post-Napoleonic meetings in Vienna, for example, disputes over how to re-divide conquered territories among the victorious parties relied on the new increase in numerical data, including statistical tables (of "souls") used to calculate a balanced result.[84] This changed the processes of negotiation by altering how outcomes were represented and thus evaluated: "the precise divisions of the statistical commission expanded the number of bargaining outcomes so that all the great powers could agree on one."[85] Statistical representations were the subject of negotiations, and their use lent an air of legitimacy and scientific accuracy to the overall proceedings.

Mapping

Like statistics, cartographic techniques were integral to nineteenth-century state-building and imperialism—an unsurprising parallel, given that the two sets of practices were increasingly interwoven. As Anderson puts it, in nineteenth-century projects seeking to define and create national identities, there was a "crucial intersection between the map and census."[86] Combining mapping with statistics brought together two increasingly technical forms of measurement and calculation, allowing further centralization of information-gathering and decision-making regarding even the most distant subject peoples or territories.

The importance of mapping in defining the state as a territorial entity (a process largely completed within European states by 1800) had two consequences for the development of nineteenth-century states and empires.[87] First, the new "avalanche" of numerical data could be gathered on and applied to a political entity now understood exclusively in territorial terms—a territorial state. In other words, the meaning and content of the boundary-defined state could now be filled in with statistical representations of its population. Second, nineteenth-century imperial expansion was carried out by European states whose territorial form was very different from that of their sixteenth- and seventeenth-century colonial predecessors. Thus nineteenth-century imperial actors took their idea that boundary-defined territoriality was the natural or even superior form of political organization and applied it to their expanding colonial claims. (In early modern expansion to the Americas, in contrast, complex "conglomerate states" constructed diverse forms of authority in colonial spaces.[88]) Nineteenth-century colonies came to be defined, then, in exclusively territorial terms—exemplified when non-European spaces were carved up with linear divisions on the ground *and* on maps. Policy-making, intelligence, and diplomatic activities were increasingly brought into governing institutions in the metropole or capital city, where knowledge and control from afar could be pursued, even if rarely fully achieved.[89]

The new, powerful combination of cartographic representation with the explosion of statistical information was directly enrolled in state-building projects. In Germany, for example, the spatial extent of German national identity was defined through ethnographic mapping, which drew on technical innovations in cartography and the increasing availability of statistical information.[90] Early in the century, ethnographic maps of German states were based on diverse, largely non-statistical sources of information, such as travel reports. They were treated not as accurate representations but instead "as idealized portraits of a thing that could be rather than as absolute reflections of something already in existence."[91] During the nineteenth century, however, the growth of statistical data—and the legitimacy and authority attributed to it—made ethnographic maps increasingly influential. By 1900 they served as "a powerful and believable force in public discourse."[92] This built not only on the growth of statistical information but also on improvements in the mass-production of colorful, detailed maps. Technical innovations "brought down the costs of production, made images more manipulable and allowed cartographers to use brighter colors in map design. As a result, representations of nationality became increasingly believable."[93] The resulting representations, combining statistical and cartographic techniques and authority, reshaped German political development and diplomacy. They changed "the practical application of nationalist ideology to everyday life," and were used in negotiations such as the 1871 Franco-German postwar settlement.[94]

In nineteenth-century imperial settings, mapping embodied the dual nature of technological representation, serving not only as a practical tool of information-gathering and control through visual representations but also as a symbol of, and justification for, empire itself. The British effort to map its empire in India, known as the Great Trigonometrical Survey, began early in the nineteenth century and continued for nearly seven decades.[95] On a practical level, colonial administrators sought to increase their knowledge of India through this survey, and to then use that information to exert closer or more effective control. Yet the effects of this project went far beyond those explicit goals. For one, the nineteenth-century mapping of India was one of the primary ways in which the subcontinent came to be understood as a single political space, as "India." This eventually changed how both British imperialists and Indian nationalists understood the region.[96] Second, the very project of mapping the region, using the latest cartographic technologies, represented for the British their own superiority and justified their rule over the indigenous population. "For the British in India, the measurement and observation inherent to each act of surveying represented *science*. By measuring the land, by imposing European science and rationality on the Indian landscape, the British distinguished themselves from the Indians."[97] The British thus saw themselves as rational, liberal, and scientific, as opposed to how they thought of the Indians as irrational, mystical, and despotic. This was a powerful justification for empire, never mind that the mapping project was not able to live up to its own ideals of perfect measurement and accuracy.[98] The symbolic power of nineteenth-century technologies as representational justifications for imperialism often had little to do with practical consequences.

Telegraphy

Among the many innovations of the nineteenth century, the electric telegraph stands out, in ways that make it an especially productive foil for the politics of information technology today. Although the direct parallels that have been drawn between the first decades of the telegraph and the expansion of the internet are probably overstated, telegraphy did represent something fundamentally new: the first means to move significant amounts of information separately from physical media—the "dematerialization" of information and information flows.[99] Focusing on what the telegraph represented, moreover, reveals its importance beyond new capabilities, in the symbolism and ideas that came to be attached to it.

Before the electric telegraph, the ability to communicate information was tied to transportation, with a few limited exceptions such as signal fires and, starting in the late eighteenth century, several increasingly complex systems of optical telegraphy (discussed below).[100] The electric telegraph thus did represent a new means of communicating, from afar, in a much shorter amount of time—though by no means instantaneously. After multiple proposals and prototypes, in the 1840s a few systems were inaugurated with varied technical and organizational features, but all relying on the same principles of electromagnetism. Telegraph networks soon expanded: "By the late 1840s, webs of telegraph wires were beginning to cover Britain, France, Germany, and the eastern United States, and were appearing in Italy, Austria, and even further afield."[101] In addition to these land-based networks, efforts were quickly underway to make telegraph connections across bodies of water using undersea cables. In the 1850s, for example, a cable was laid in the English Channel, as was the first—though only briefly functional—transatlantic cable. (A permanent cable connection across the Atlantic was inaugurated in 1866.) Rapid expansion of networks followed: for example, "by 1870 Great Britain was in direct communication with North America, Europe, the Middle East, and India."[102] (Britain would retain this dominant position in international telegraphy for the subsequent decades.) After the 1870s, reasonably reliable, albeit sometimes slow, networks had been extended to many parts of the globe, and the developments that followed were largely in terms of network density, speed, message volume, and other quantitative improvements rather than qualitative leaps.[103]

Although this can be read as a story of expanding communication driven by a singular technology, scholars have noted two important limits to the telegraph's impact. First, the increase in global interconnection was not built solely on telegraph networks; it also rested on other forms of communication such as mail service (itself dramatically improved by steamship and railroad) and the increase in mass printing of information sources like newspapers.[104] The telegraph constituted merely one component of a "larger modern information infrastructure."[105] In fact, for the vast majority of nineteenth-century people, long-distance communication was facilitated far more by improved mail than by the telegraph, which largely remained a tool for governments and elites.[106] As will be discussed below, one of the most important differences between the telegraph and other contemporary communication systems was in representations—how the telegraph was portrayed, what effects it was predicted to have, and the constantly reiterated vision of connectivity for all.[107]

Second, especially in imperial spaces, the most important information and communication networks remained largely nontechnological—that is, they relied little on nineteenth-century advances like telegraphy. In India, for example, British rule continued an indigenous tradition by which "Indian polities . . . were constituted to an unusual degree through their networks of espionage and information collection," working through local informants who also acted as "agents of persuasion and promise."[108] The informational infrastructure of British rule, like its Mughal predecessor, relied on "men on the spot" who functioned as, in Bayly's phrase, "the U2 spy planes of their day."[109] The strengths and weaknesses of these information systems were often unrelated to technical capabilities like the telegraph.

What did the development and spread of telegraphy—and the representations it carried and embodied—mean for state-building and imperialism? Especially for arguments focusing on the increased communications capabilities enabled by the telegraph, one conventional interpretation focuses on improving the ability to control events directly from the center of a state or empire. This point goes back to

Harold Innis' argument that the nature and extent of any empire is dependent on its available means of communication, including technological developments.[110] By this logic the telegraph, as much as advances in weapons and medicine, distinguished nineteenth-century imperialism from its predecessors. Telegraphy allowed for the increasing centralization of decision-making in imperial capitals at the expense of the independence of local agents.[111] One British colonial governor, for example, "called the telegraph 'a great Imperial binding force.'"[112] While the effects on decision-making were not necessarily improvements for efficiency—as many colonial and diplomatic offices were initially overwhelmed by the amount of daily information coming in—there is some truth to the argument that telegraphy increased the reach of imperial authority and that, in return, "the means of communication were, above all else, adjuncts of great power strategy."[113]

Nonetheless, this conventional focus on increased communication and control through the telegraph can usefully be supplemented.[114] Here I examine how the telegraph was perceived, described, and represented. The telegraph was held to represent civilizational superiority, closer integration of imperial centers and peripheries, and direct authoritative control from afar, and those representations had consequences for state-building and imperialism alongside—and sometimes beyond—the material capabilities the telegraph bestowed. The telegraph, in other words, was both "a model of and a mechanism for control,"[115] and in many cases the former outweighed the latter.

Contemporary discussions of the telegraph often began with over-the-top rhetoric about instantaneous communication and global interconnection.[116] Yet in reality there was a constant "tension between visions of frictionless communication and the stubborn materialities of physical entities."[117] In fact, "'Connectivity talk' . . . is better understood as an ideological formation" than as an accurate description.[118] But that ideology, built on representations of the telegraph as instantaneous and annihilating time and space, was consequential—even as, in practice, the ability of authorities to control distant events through the telegraph was decidedly mixed. The sense of increased or improved authority from the center was often more in the realm of giving officials a feeling of control rather than actually increasing capabilities. The idea that the telegraph helped "save" British rule in India during the 1857 uprising, for example, was more rhetoric than reality—but it was a deeply held belief among some imperial officials.[119]

The importance of representations and ideas to the deployment, use, and effects of the electric telegraph are suggested, on a smaller scale, by the development of its closest precursor: the optical telegraph.[120] These systems involved a series of towers or other locations where, weather permitting, visual signals could be passed from one site to the next, allowing at least small amounts of information to move more rapidly than physical media. While signal fires or other visual means had been used even in the ancient world, in the late eighteenth century several networks were developed to transmit a wider range of information (i.e., they could carry more than a single, pre-determined signal). Several US coastal cities had limited signaling to indicate the arrival of ships, the British admiralty also used a similar system, and in the 1830s a line of optical signals was even proposed to connect New York to New Orleans.[121]

The optical telegraph system created in France, however, was by far the most extensive and complex.[122] This network was begun during the revolutionary period and expanded under Napoleon. During the wars that followed it extended as far as Amsterdam and Venice; after France's defeat it was confined to French territory.[123] In other words—in a pattern reminiscent of many twentieth-century information technologies—a system originally built for military purposes was later turned toward state-building efforts. This was one of the first networks to avoid relying entirely on pre-coded messages, making it far closer to later electric telegraph code systems than earlier single-purpose networks. This was by no means a minor project: by 1850, a network of hundreds of stations extended over thousands of kilometers,[124] and it was still being expanded when the electric telegraph emerged and replaced it.[125]

While gathering information was certainly a purpose of this system, control by Paris over the outlying regions was always the dominant concern.[126] This can be seen in two features of the design of the system itself. First, it "was principally a hub-and-spoke system, with Paris at the hub."[127] Second, because there was only one message track to carry signals in both directions, protocols were needed to deal with "message collision" when signals arrived at a station from both directions. In that event, "a message from Paris . . . dominated a transmission to the capital."[128] In other words, administrative control (through messages outbound from Paris to the provinces) was prioritized over information gathering (through inbound messages). Like the much more extensive and international telegraph networks that followed, the design and operation of the optical system embodied the ideas that motivated its creation and use—in this case, control from the capital. In fact, in spite of the enormous practical challenges in making the optical telegraph function effectively, it "gave the nation's rulers a feeling of control,"[129] serving as an affective representation of state centralization.

Even this highly developed optical system, of course, was displaced by electric telegraphy, which had emerged, by the late nineteenth century, as a significant means of communication for governments, corporations, and individuals able to afford it. Focusing on how the electric telegraph interacted with representational practices reveals three areas in which it reshaped—and was reshaped by—political processes: diplomacy, state-building, and imperialism.

Given that diplomacy fundamentally relies on communication— between officials of different states, and between home offices and diplomatic representatives abroad—a means of communication as novel as the telegraph was bound to reshape diplomatic practices.[130] Practitioners anticipated that the increased speed would simply remove barriers to effective interactions, and few foresaw the possibility of new problems arising.[131] In fact, as with most new technological systems applied to longstanding practices, the effects were more ambiguous.[132] The autonomy of diplomats was undermined, with more centralized control now possible through rapid instruction and intelligence by cable. The speed of diplomatic interaction also increased, as capitals could communicate with their representatives much more rapidly.[133] Even the character of diplomatic institutions changed, as the telegraph's limitations as much as its capabilities—the demand for particular type of concision, the creation of new bottlenecks in information flows, and the high cost—promoted further hierarchy within foreign policy institutions.[134] Yet these effects were far from universal, as they varied across countries with different institutional cultures and preexisting practices.[135]

Significant aspects of the telegraph's effects, however, emerged not out of technical features but instead out of how those capabilities—and shortcomings—were understood and represented in ideas and discourse. In fact, there was often a significant gap between how the telegraph was expected to work for diplomacy and how it actually functioned. The expectation of immediate response from diplomatic agents, for example, drove more rushed decision-making, even as technical challenges sometimes slowed messages dramatically or prevented them from getting through at all.[136] The popular representation of the telegraph as instantaneous, "annihilating space and time," may have been wildly inaccurate, but that representation made diplomats sometimes feel as though they could—and should—move much more quickly. As early as the 1850s, diplomats during the Crimean War expressed a "sense of being hurried" by orders incoming by telegraph and felt the need to send immediate responses.[137] Even more dramatically, the diplomatic crisis that led to the First World War was shaped, in part, by the tension between expectations of immediate communication and the technical and sociological barriers to that—including the ways in which the older generation of diplomats was not ready for the rapid back-and-forth that, by 1914, had actually become possible.[138] This created a dangerous mismatch between the reality of the telegraph and expectations about it, shaped by how it had been represented (for decades by that point) as instantaneous and revolutionary.

On a more fundamental level, diplomacy itself is a matter of representation, "about making present what otherwise would be absent."[139] Those processes of representation were altered by the telegraph, and particularly by long-distance undersea cables. For example, after the laying of a reliable transatlantic cable, "the United States [was] made more directly present" in its diplomatic interactions with European states. With the telegraph, a diplomat could not only claim to speak for his government and thus give an authoritative response; he could also quickly present a direct confirmation of having done so.[140] Diplomacy with the telegraph altered this process of representation from afar but did not replace it—as diplomats' concerns that their role would be made superfluous were, in the end, unfounded.[141]

A second area in which the telegraph reshaped existing practices and institutions—not only by increasing communication capabilities but also through representations and ideas—was in the state-building projects of the late nineteenth century. Domestically, the telegraph did enable some improvement in surveillance and control from the capital over other parts of the state. As with the French optical telegraph, governments sought to use these networks not only to gather information but even more to implement their authority throughout their territories. Uniformly enforcing rule from the center to the periphery was a fundamental goal of state-building, and even the limited capabilities of the telegraph supported that project. Yet there were also symbolic aspects to the telegraph that dovetailed with state-building and even shaped the development and adoption of national telegraph networks. The expansion of the French network, for example, was driven in part by the network's symbolic purposes: "to keep France among the great powers in the realm of global communications."[142] Japan, likewise, pursued domestic and external telegraph construction for strategic, commercial, *and* symbolic reasons.[143] The Russian Empire, similarly, sought to regain their Great Power status and assert a "civilized" and European identity by building a telegraph network and joining international efforts to regulate and standardize telegraphy (including through the new International Telegraph Union).[144] In short, like detailed mapping or censuses, telegraphy was both a tool of state-building and a symbol of it, a component of the ideational construction of the state.

One of the most powerful symbolic aspects of telegraph networks during this period emerged when they were deployed as part of broader organic metaphors for nation-states.[145] The newly available symbolism of telegraphy provided additional support for the tradition of theorizing about a "body politic," a concept that had long been used to argue that a society or nation constituted a coherent entity, with diverse parts playing specific, and necessary, roles. If the nation was like a body, then the various new, state-spanning technological networks could be analogized to bodily systems. This included an analogy between railroads and the body's musculature, but even more prominently an analogy between the telegraph and the nervous system.[146] Numerous contemporary authors "saw the cables of the 1840s as nerves transmitting the impulses of a society."[147]

The telegraph-as-nerves metaphor was particularly prevalent—and convincing—because the period saw extensive conversation between

studies of nerves in biology and studies of the telegraph in engineer-
ing. In fact, many of the same scientists worked on both neuroscience
and telecommunications, often using similar electrical apparatus in
both fields.[148] This meant that the connections went beyond mere
metaphor: representations of the nervous system inspired particular
technological designs in telegraphy, and innovations in the telegraph
suggested new experiments in biology.[149] Thus "the scientists and engineers who designed nineteenth-century communications networks
viewed their growing webs as organic structures," with telegraph pioneers like Samuel Morse constantly referring to the telegraph in terms
of nerves.[150] Moreover, "this understanding of the telegraph as a nerve
network affected engineers' decisions about how to construct it."[151]

The result was a complex interaction between ideas of the state as
a body politic, new discoveries about the human nervous system, and
the development and expansion of telegraph networks. These interconnections provided rhetorical support to political arguments about
the organic cohesion of a society or nation, a key element in late-
nineteenth-century state-building efforts, particularly (but not exclusively) in newly unified states like Germany. As studies of metaphor
have repeatedly demonstrated, metaphorical arguments become more
convincing when they fit into a larger system or "cluster" of coherent
and mutually reinforcing metaphors.[152]

Examples of this rhetoric appear in any number of late-nineteenth-
century state-building projects. In 1875 a Japanese intellectual likened
the telegraph to "the nerve system of a country," explicitly drawing a
metaphor to Japan as a body.[153] A British author wrote in 1883 that
"science has given the political organism a new circulation, which is
steam, and a new nervous system, which is electricity."[154] This metaphor
was even used to draw comparisons between different states' telegraph
networks: a German scientist suggested that his nation's telegraph was
superior to those of rival countries because it more closely resembled
the comprehensive web of the human nervous system.[155]

Finally, the role of the telegraph in late-nineteenth-century imperialism is the third area in which changing capabilities and new representational ideas together reshaped political arguments and practices.
Contemporaries certainly viewed the telegraph as integral to empire, as
British officials in India, for example, saw "telegraphy not as a business

enterprise but as an instrument of British power" (in contrast to the British view of domestic telegraphy as a commercial tool).[156] That instrument was useful not only for its communication capabilities, but also for its role as a symbol of Western advancement and thus a justification for imperialism.[157] This aspect is again illustrated by the case of Japan, which sought to join Western imperial powers, not only in claiming and administering overseas territories, but also in gathering the symbolic trappings of being an "advanced" state. These "discursive efforts" to construct a Japanese empire in language and representations were buttressed by the deployment of telecommunications like the telegraph, part of a broader strategy of "techno-imperialism."[158] New communication tools made possible "the crucial milieu in which the new strategic visions of Japan's imperium took place."[159] The symbolic aspects of claiming an empire—and thus the symbolic aspects of deploying what were seen as important technological *tools* of empire—were particularly relevant to Japan, as its late development made it especially concerned with this "ideological dimension" of imperialism.[160]

A different interaction between representations of the telegraph and of empire appears in late nineteenth-century discussions of the British empire, especially in the growing debate about how Great Britain would relate to settler colonies.[161] The ideas about what type of imperial polity was possible—and the rhetorical power of arguments about those ideas—were reshaped by new transportation and communication links, especially the expansion of the British telegraph network throughout most of the empire by the 1870s.[162] These technologies "transformed the manner in which future political possibilities were (and could be) envisioned."[163]

The rhetorical consequences of the telegraph were particularly important in how they undermined previously popular and apparently unassailable arguments against a closer union of Britain with overseas colonies. In the early nineteenth century, for example, theorists had emphasized "the absurdity of attempting to govern effectively over vast expanses of space."[164] This argument, convincing for decades, dropped out of discourse after 1870.[165] The "possibility of a single global (federal) state ruling over a homogeneous worldwide nation . . . required as its condition of possibility the belief that distance had been dissolved, that the world had shrunk to a manageable size."[166] Such a "global polity" went from an extremely rare proposal before 1870 to a "common demand" after.[167] Britain's global telegraph network even made possible discursive efforts to construct the entire Anglosphere—sometimes even including former colonies like the United States—within a global-scale body politic, again relying on the metaphor between nerves and the telegraph.[168]

These arguments depended only loosely on the actual capabilities of the telegraph (and other improved communications through steamships and railroads) to tie distant parts of the empire together. Instead, it was the *perception* that the tight integration of distant places was possible, and maybe inevitable, that served as "a necessary but not sufficient condition for the imagining of a global state."[169] The representation of the telegraph as a globe-spanning, distance-annihilating, instantaneous communication network—no matter how inaccurate in practice—was essential to arguments for this integration.

Conclusion

In spite of having been overlooked until recently in international relations scholarship, the history of nineteenth-century international politics has significant implications for developments today, particularly in the interaction of technological and political change. As the recent resurgence in IR scholarship on the nineteenth century has argued, this period contains both parallels to contemporary issues and some direct precursors to today's ideas and practices.[170] In terms of information technologies and their impact, many of the similarities and connections are at the level of representations as much as actual capabilities. The very emphasis on the novelty and revolutionary nature of new technological systems has itself been a recurring feature of modernity since the nineteenth century. New technologies are initially hailed as dramatically altering life—often in exaggerated ways—and then have very different, and sometimes more significant, effects once they come to be seen as everyday devices.[171]

Across diverse issues, the interaction between information technologies and representational processes continues. Just as diplomacy was reshaped—often unexpectedly, and certainly not always for the better—by the telegraph, and just as arguments about the form and justification of empires relied on perceptions of the telegraph's capabilities, so too we will see similar processes in the coming chapters: the impact on boundary negotiations when new mapping tools are brought to bear, how linguistic representations through metaphors alter the pursuit of state security in novel domains, and the impact of diverse representations of and through drones.

3

From Dayton to Google
Digital Mapping and Negotiation

TERRITORIAL DISPUTES DRIVEN BY UNSETTLED boundaries, competing claims, or historical grievances have long been a source of international conflict. Although these are often presented as the most concrete of clashes—struggles over physical land and its contents—the representational politics of information technologies are closely involved in their origins, course, and conclusion. These disputes are shaped by cartography and other representational technologies that are used to visualize, negotiate, and settle territorial claims. While cartographic techniques and their politics have a long history (see Chapter 2), the past several decades have seen a fundamental shift in the tools used to represent and communicate spatial information. Digitization is improving existing cartographic capabilities, redistributing those capabilities to new actors, and making possible fundamentally new ways to represent territorial spaces—enabling novel representations and circulating them in new ways. Yet the representations *of* these systems are also central: how various parties to a negotiation understand and represent new mapping tools can be as important as the tools' actual capabilities.

In spite of immense attention paid to territorial conflicts by scholars and policymakers, the role of new representational technologies has

Virtual Territories. Jordan Branch, Oxford University Press. © Oxford University Press (2025).
DOI: 10.1093/9780190063658.003.0003

been largely overlooked.[1] Thanks to digitization, the world can be represented through technical systems in entirely new ways. These mediating representations fundamentally shape disputes and negotiations over territory, and when the tools change diplomacy is practiced differently as a result. The counterfactual scenario—negotiations without the mediation of digital tools—would yield different outcomes in terms of the nature of settlements, the processes to reach them, and even their downstream stability. These differences are not explained well by examining bargaining dynamics, power differentials, or discursive framings alone.

This chapter thus shifts the focus directly to technological change—specifically, the digitization of mapping—and the representational processes around new cartographic tools. How are those technologies and their representations interacting with how boundaries are disputed, negotiated, and implemented? The role of digital geospatial technologies in territorial disputes and their resolution has seen almost no direct investigation, and the limited existing answers to this question tend to fall into the two frameworks discussed in Chapter 1: instrumentalism and determinism.

First, instrumentalist approaches argue that new tools simply make the goal of achieving peaceful resolutions easier to reach. As one US State Department official has written, "a properly implemented GIS [Geographic Information System] can go far beyond a paper map and pencil to assist in the resolution of complex boundary problems." The "GIS advantage" is that it can "help clarify the spatial elements of a territorial dispute and its socio-economic and military implications."[2]

Second, implicitly determinist logics hold that new digital systems could enable or even create fundamentally new ideas about how conflicts may be resolved, making possible novel solutions rather than simply aiding traditional approaches. The Global Positioning System (GPS), for example, makes it possible to fix boundaries in oceans or in unreachable terrain without the need for physical demarcation (an approach taken in some recent settlements, discussed below). Digital tools make settled boundaries feasible where before they were impossible, thus potentially resolving previously intractable conflicts. These logics are not necessarily incorrect—digital tools do make some tasks easier and do enable new possibilities—but they are far from complete.

These two interpretations, ironically, are equally positive about the implications of new technical solutions to boundary disputes. Considering instead the ways in which technologies are politically constructed as well as politically consequential, however, might make us less sanguine. This book's approach reveals that new systems enable diverse forms of representation that can have ambiguous or contradictory effects on the peaceful resolution of disputes. Sometimes the representational processes around new tools can create new barriers to resolutions or even destabilize and escalate conflicts that were relatively settled. For example, one challenge that emerged at the 1995 Dayton negotiations—an early application of digital cartography to negotiation—related to how digital mapping tools had made it much easier to calculate the results of boundary proposals. As one US State Department official later described the situation, "the problem was that because the system could rapidly calculate the percentages of territory, the Serbs realized they were not getting their 49 percent"—the proportion of Bosnian territory that they had originally agreed to accept.[3] Digitization created an objectively superior mapping system— unquestionably faster and more accurate than relying on paper maps— but that system's improvements nearly derailed the negotiations, specifically because of the way the tools were represented as accurate and efficient. The positive and negative implications, in other words, are not mutually exclusive, as new technologies and representations are yielding ambiguous effects.

Any number of representational and position-finding technologies have been used at negotiations over territorial boundaries. This chapter focuses specifically on maps, defined broadly as "graphic representations that facilitate a spatial understanding of things, concepts, conditions, processes, or events in the human world."[4] While maps are used in many types of political interactions, the empirical scope here is limited to territorial negotiations, understood as attempts to negotiate a solution to a dispute concerning competing claims to political authority over a territory, often involving where a boundary—new or old— should fall.[5] This chapter considers how the processes and outcomes of territorial negotiation change when digital cartography is used instead of paper maps. It combines this book's focus on representations with an array of existing research—on mapping technology, spatial politics, negotiation and bargaining theory, and the role of emotion—to explore the broader array of possibilities, revealing exactly how the particular features of digital mapping interact to reshape specific processes of negotiation over territory.

Digital mapping provides tools that, while developing out of paper maps, present new capabilities, features, and representations: layering of different information, greater flexibility of content and image, increased accuracy and certainty, and the realism of photographic imagery and three-dimensional modeling. Digitization has also revolutionized who is able to create, distribute, and use maps, with much greater public participation and a dramatically expanded role for corporate actors like Google. These novel spatial depictions, map-production capabilities, and representations of them transform territorial negotiation in particular ways. The effects are context-sensitive, and thus a feature that makes it easier to reach an agreement in one setting can have a different effect in another. Therefore, this chapter focuses on mechanisms that have an impact on negotiation processes, not just outcomes. As the discussion below will demonstrate, new digital mapping tools shape the types of settlements available, alter the evaluation of outcomes, change the perceived value of particular territories, and bring new actors into the negotiating process.

This chapter thus examines the role of technologies and their representations in the specific context of resolving territorial conflicts. As the next section makes clear, this requires drawing on theories of technological change, decision-making, negotiation, and mapping, all in order to identify key mechanisms by which digitization interacts with negotiation processes and outcomes. Several case studies over the past three decades then illustrate the evolving and diverse ways in which digital mapping tools have been involved, and how representations are central to this process.

Digital Mapping, Territory, and Negotiation

In territorial negotiations, technological tools and other contextual factors structure the types of solutions available, the ways that outcomes are evaluated, and interaction practices and norms. Technologies interact with the process of negotiation—not just the probability of reaching an agreement. This section explores how technologies relate to negotiating and bargaining processes, to the evaluation of losses or gains, and to the role of emotion and affect in decision-making. In order to examine these complex interactions, the following combines the book's overall framework—which draws on science and technology studies (STS) and its application to international relations—with arguments and concepts from political geography, negotiation and bargaining theory, and political psychology.

As Chapter 1 outlined, research from STS has shown that technologies constitute and are embedded in political relations, interests, and identities. The structuring effects of technologies have a foreseeable impact on the possible range of political ideas, interactions, and choices—including the politics of negotiation and mapping. Historians and political geographers have shown that cartography is, and always has been, embedded in political and social relationships of power.[6] Maps are more than communication devices, transferring information from a mapmaker to a map user. Instead, mapping is a representational technology that embodies mapmakers' worldviews and that can reshape map users' ideas.[7] Digital mapping in particular should be understood as a set of technologies and practices that are deeply embedded in social and political relations, given the ways in which such systems are composed not of singular artifacts but of complex webs of hardware, software, data, and users.[8]

The characteristics, prevalence, and uses of mapping have changed dramatically over time. New tools have restructured political interactions—including negotiations over territory—and, simultaneously, political ideas and interests have altered the demand for maps and their characteristics. As Chapter 2 discussed, mapping played a central role in the early-modern emergence of the state and its consolidation in the nineteenth century. More specifically with regards to negotiations over territory, historical cases reveal that different mapping technologies yielded different negotiation processes and different outcomes. New tools gave rulers not only new capabilities in terms of the claims they could make but also new ideas about what types of claims they *should* make. For example, the shift from medieval political authority defined by personal bonds or feudal jurisdictions to the modern emphasis on clearly demarcated linear boundaries came about only after mapping had emerged as the dominant means of representing and interacting with political spaces—lines on maps became lines on the ground.[9]

Today, mapping continues to shape the conditions of possibility for how negotiations proceed and, potentially, for their outcomes. The following discussion—which draws on studies of negotiation as well as on concepts and arguments from related areas—is not aimed at reinventing the study of international negotiations. Instead, this chapter builds on existing scholarship by exploring how mapping technologies are reshaping specific negotiation processes. Of course, there are any number of potential obstacles to conflict resolution unrelated to technological factors, including strategic barriers to cooperation, incentives to keep information private, and political interests in prolonging the conflict.[10] Nonetheless, in negotiations over territory, processes and outcomes can also be reshaped by new mapping technologies.

The important outcomes of international negotiation include not only whether an agreement is reached but also the likely stability of that agreement and the efficiency of the distribution of benefits.[11] In addition, the process itself is consequential: "A given set of initial conditions will not regularly produce the same outcome, so that outcomes are affected not only by initial conditions but also by the process variables that intervene."[12] Technological systems are integrated into negotiation processes, from the formation of interests and demands, to the evaluation of proposals, to the implementation of settlements. Consider, for example, the interpretation of negotiations as cases of bargaining between self-interested actors.[13] This bargaining approach highlights the role of information: incomplete information may make a successful bargain harder to reach, and uncertainty about information can influence strategies and outcomes.[14] That information, however, exists only within the technologies used to record, store, manipulate, and distribute it. Thus, changes to those technical systems potentially reshape the information presented and its impact.

In the abstract, negotiators always have three general options: take a deal offered, stop negotiating and walk away, or engage in further bargaining.[15] Evaluating those options is fundamental to the process of negotiation, and decision-makers have been shown to make "distorted," or not strictly rational, evaluations. They overvalue concessions that were difficult to achieve, evaluate outcomes relative to a particular reference point, or overemphasize an intuitively more acceptable division like an even split.[16] Studies in political psychology have further specified these types of processes. According to prospect theory, for example, decisions are framed in terms of an initial reference point and not in terms of a final position.[17] Losses are then more heavily weighted than are equivalent gains, which leads to loss aversion: the tendency to overvalue what one possesses but might lose, including territorial holdings. Yet the definition of what territory counts as a loss versus what counts as a gain depends on how territory is operationalized, both in terms of material control and also in terms of depictions in maps and other technological tools. As a related issue, concession aversion holds that each party overvalues its own concessions above those offered by the other side (a product of loss aversion as well the "reactive devaluation" of another's offer).[18] In territorial negotiations, the types of concessions offered depend on how those concessions can be represented, a process that occurs only through some medium, whether it be verbal, written, or visual through the representation of a map. In other words, the material tools brought to bear shape the impact of well-documented psychological processes of decision-making and negotiation.

The importance of emotion and affect suggests additional ways in which technological tools might alter negotiation processes. Emotions are integral to all decision-making processes, not just deviations from rationality, and they may be particularly relevant to face-to-face interactions like negotiations.[19] Decision-making is particularly shaped by *affect*, defined as "positive and negative feelings evoked by a stimulus" or "general valence feelings toward something." In other words, "Instead of appraising objects, events, or people by cognitive analysis, we simply *feel* what these objects, events, or people mean to us and respond accordingly."[20]

During negotiations over territory, the relevant affective reactions may be in response to any number of factors, including the bargain being considered, the territory being disputed, or the technological tools being used—as well as to representations of them. For example, in "mood-congruent processing," information that fits an emotional state is privileged in judgments of reliability or certainty because "vivid and emotionally compelling facts and information hold greater impact" than other evidence.[21] In terms of disputes over territory, different areas—strategic places versus homelands, for example—will have different degrees of affective attachment,[22] with consequences for decisions or judgments. Finally, actors may have an affective reaction to the tools brought to the negotiations, which could alter how information provided by those tools is evaluated or recalled.

Applying these findings and concepts suggests new mechanisms by which technology interacts with negotiation processes. Conventionally, technology is treated as a background factor or "contingent variable," without an explicit consideration of technology's mediating effects.[23] Most scholarship that focuses directly on digital technology and diplomacy falls into one of two categories: studies of social media as a form of "digital diplomacy"[24] or studies of new communication technologies potentially replacing face-to-face interactions.[25] Both approaches build on historical cases of the impact on diplomacy of technologies like radio and the telegraph. One of the main findings, ironically, is that even today's new technologies have not significantly reduced face-to-face negotiation.[26]

Rather than examining the substitution of technology for face-to-face interaction, this chapter instead asks how technological changes transform the tools that negotiators use during face-to-face meetings. Although diplomatic practices have not replaced direct interaction with communication via technological means, the new tools brought to support negotiations do mediate and shape processes in consequential ways. The few existing studies that directly examine this interaction have focused on the much greater availability of information to diplomats, as well as their ability to communicate quickly.[27] When framed in these terms, new technologies tend to be portrayed as instrumental tools with unambiguously positive effects. For example, technological change has historically "made negotiation a more efficient and cost-effective tool."[28]

A few recent studies have considered the specific intersection examined in this chapter: the use of mapping in territorial negotiations.[29] Yet nearly all such studies build on an instrumentalist view of technological progress as making existing goals easier to achieve. They then follow a consistent line of argument: digital mapping systems are faster, more accurate, and more detailed, thus making it easier to reach set-tlements.[30] In mapping, technological change thus means connecting improved accuracy in cartography with improved outcomes in conflict resolution. "Accurate" maps, including those that make explicit ter-ritorial claims, are posited as an unproblematic basis for negotiators' discussions: "Most maps [used in negotiations] are largescale, prop-erly surveyed editions, quite unlike crude propaganda."[31] Moving from mapping in general to digital cartography, there is a clear expectation among practitioners that new technologies will provide better nego-tiating tools and thus will improve outcomes. Typically emphasized are the ease of computation and the reduction in time required be-tween mapping a territory, negotiating a new or altered boundary, and demarcating the updated boundary on the ground.[32]

As a director of the Office of the Geographer at the US State Depart-ment has argued, digital mapping tools like Geographic Information Systems (GIS) have become an important positive resource for conflict resolution.[33] "As the political map of the world continues to change, GIS tools could be used to make decision-making more transparent, analysis of options more thorough and the presentation of results more convincing—factors that could affect the future stability of those liv-ing in border regions."[34] In other words, better-defined borders can be good for stability, and GIS improves the definition process.

Part of this "GIS advantage" lies in the ability to "apply remote sens-ing imagery, terrain elevation models, and other digital data layers to visualise the extent of the area in dispute, the types of resources at stake, populations who might be affected, and other considerations."[35] Satellite and other remote imagery, in other words, provides a "rel-atively quick and accurate means to portray land features," building a more "objective" and uncontroversial base layer for negotiation.[36] Potential problems and hazards are raised, but they relate to parties not trusting each other—and thus not trusting each other's geospa-tial information—and have little to do with the new technological capabilities themselves.

Discussions of related issues reveal similar assumptions. For example, a study of the use of new mapping technologies in boundary demarca-tion (rather than in negotiation or delimitation) makes analogous argu-ments. New tools will "assist in ameliorating ongoing boundary-related controversies" and "help to put an end to measurement error and incongruities in the location of contentious borders."[37]

This view, in short, argues that digital mapping will increase the availability and accuracy of information, raise the speed of processing, and thus improve the chances for successful conflict resolution. All of these predicted outcomes are possible, but they are not inevitable. The implicitly instrumentalist framework leaves little room for other processes involved, or even unintended consequences. Not all uses of digital mapping will inevitably make negotiations easier or more efficient. This chapter instead asks if new technologies reshape the complex processes and outcomes of face-to-face interaction in unexpected ways. Studies of negotiation, bargaining, political psychology, and emotions have revealed important processes that interact with the conditions of possibility created by technological systems. Ignoring this mediating effect of technology leaves our explanations for the course and outcomes of international negotiations incomplete.

Implications for Territorial Negotiation

Although countless differences exist between digital and paper mapping tools, a few broad transformations—evident in publicly available technologies[38]—are particularly relevant to territorial negotiations. These include features of the mapping tools themselves and changes to the broader context of cartography. Each has implications for how territory is depicted, claimed, and contested in negotiations—implications beyond the conventional view that faster and more accurate tools make negotiating goals easier to achieve. These other implications play out through representational processes: representations of the world through new technologies and the representations of those tools themselves.

First, digital tools are far more capable of showing multiple layers of spatial information than are paper maps (which can be layered only up to a certain point while still maintaining readability). Layering has always been a strength of GIS, and it is also integral to user modifications of online maps such as Google Earth.[39] Digital tools also make it easy for readers to choose which layers to display.

When it comes to territorial negotiations, layering makes it easier to depict more complex types of territorial divisions, including distinct authority claims over different aspects of the territory (resources, settlements, or airspace, for example). Digital tools also simplify the ability to show a gradual transition—rather than a line—between two claims. With complex depictions more readily accessible, negotiators can more easily discuss and even accept different forms of territorial division.[40] Layering can also have an impact on the way in which options are evaluated in terms of reference or anchor points. Especially for claims made through maps, showing more options simultaneously can alter the strength of the anchoring effect and the resulting aversion to losses. Moreover, one proposed remedy for the challenge posed by the related issue of concession aversion is to offer a menu of concessions, giving the other party more choice in the result and thus overcoming the tendency to devalue particular proposals.[41] Layering makes it much easier to manipulate and to offer a menu of territorial options.

Yet layering can also complicate negotiations by making it harder to find focal points that coordinate expectations and anchor commitments to particular places or territories.[42] Consider the exercise discussed by Thomas Schelling in which two people were given the same simple map and asked where they would expect to meet, without being able to communicate with each other directly.[43] He found that most participants gravitated toward unique features: "A map with many houses and a single crossroads sends people to the crossroads, while one with many crossroads and a single house sends most of them to the house."[44] Something that appears only once on the map, in other words, provides a focal point. With the proliferation of information in a multilayered digital map, it becomes harder to find an obvious point for coordination—with enough information, there are few if any easily identified unique spatial features. In territorial negotiations, this can potentially keep opposing sides from recognizing that they have similar outcomes in mind: with many more features or lines to anchor one's interests to before negotiations start, it becomes less likely that both sides will bring the same proposal to the table.

A second feature of digital mapping is greater flexibility in both content and display. Of course, maps have always been altered—marked up with pen and pencil or updated and printed in new editions. On many digital maps, however, the ability to edit content is fundamental, albeit within limits set by the code. Moreover, unlike pencil marks on a paper map, alterations often become indistinguishable from the original information.

Quick changes can thus be made in territorial claims. This increased speed, highlighted by advocates, may sometimes make it easier to achieve a resolution in less time. Yet digital flexibility can also affect participants' assumptions about the permanence of lines on maps. Typically, mapping a disputed boundary tends to make the conflict more intractable, deepening functional and symbolic entrenchment.[45] The flexibility of digital mapping, however, allows for quickly changing depictions that do not become as politically fixed over time. And more complex effects are also possible, depending on the particular context. Shorter turnaround times between offers can make an impatient actor (one willing to settle for the current proposal rather than wait to bargain further) *effectively* more patient and thus more intransigent. This deadline effect is simultaneously objective and perceptual.[46] Time pressure is potentially altered when negotiators feel that the new technology allows them to exchange proposals rapidly.

Digital mapping also changes the precision and certainty of information—and representations of those qualities. First, accurate position-finding is much easier, thanks to ubiquitous GPS devices.[47] Second, digital mapping vastly improves the ability to perform spatial calculations, making existing ones like surface area faster and enabling complex computations that otherwise would be practically impossible. Rapid and accurate calculation can provide benefits for territorial negotiation. Principals often want to exchange territories of equal areas, and now measuring the results of new boundary lines is much easier. Instead of waiting while new calculations are made by hand, negotiators receive immediate results, thus speeding up the process and removing possible sources of friction.

When decision-makers are sensitive to losses, however, increased accuracy can also make compromises harder to reach. Many historical negotiations relied on ambiguity to reach acceptable agreements (for example, by allowing boundary commissions to work out significant details later). Ambiguity enables each side to feel that it has suffered fewer losses than its adversary and thus has gotten the better deal.[48]

With the precision of digital mapping, this strategy is no longer available. Of course, the utility of ambiguity is context-specific; sometimes negotiators favor exact delimitation for reasons unrelated to the ease of calculation. Yet when negotiators internalize the expectation that mapping tools will be exact—an expectation driven by the way that these technologies are represented as extremely accurate—ambiguity becomes increasingly unacceptable.

The most visually arresting new feature of digital mapping is the use of satellite imagery and three-dimensional terrain models, which present images very different from those of traditional maps. While satellite imagery obviously predates the development of digital mapping systems, it is only with the growing use of the latter that such imagery has become easily integrated into map use, both among government officials but also in the broader public.[49] The virtualization of territory has always been a feature of mapping, but the use of real imagery—or, more accurately, "realistic" imagery, given how constructed the end results are—gives that virtualization a distinct feel and has a stronger effect on users' perceptions. Information presented through imagery is often felt to be more accurate because of its photographic basis and the perception of greater realism. The power of mapping comes in part from the "you are here" effect of experiencing maps as windows onto the real world.[50] This effect is even more pronounced with realistic imagery, which blurs the line between being in a space and observing a representation of that space.[51] How these systems are themselves represented, moreover, reinforces a perception of realism: discussing the manipulation of on-screen images as "flying" through or over terrain supports the feeling that the user is inside a virtual space, rather than merely looking at constructed images on a screen.[52]

The perception of realism, however, is problematic. For example, virtual terrain models often exaggerate elevation change for visual emphasis, and satellite layers on mapping systems are almost always complex mosaics of multiple images. Raw satellite imagery requires significant interpretation to adjust for weather, time-of-day lighting, and other factors. Unlike other photographs, which would typically be discounted if they were known to be edited after being taken, heavily manipulated satellite imagery is still perceived as authoritative. This results from both the visually evocative nature of the imagery and the way in which it calls on broader "techno-scientific" authority.[53]

Thus, users express a preference for satellite imagery over traditional map representations, in spite of imaging's constructed nature and even though map-reading tasks are actually completed more efficiently without satellite imagery.[54] Moreover, the perception that satellite imagery and three-dimensional modeling are "more real" has consequences. Such a sense can make the image feel "experiential" rather than abstract and the resulting analysis more "value-laden" than calculative.[55] Those perceptions have made satellite imagery a powerful rhetorical tool, including in public diplomatic efforts.[56]

For territorial negotiations, photographic imagery, virtual models, and perceptions of them can expand the range of possible settlements. Negotiations can be conducted in three dimensions, and nontraditional solutions become more imaginable—and thus potentially more acceptable—when tools are capable of depicting them. The feeling of experiencing a space can give greater weight to the information being presented, potentially increasing the plausibility of a solution. This visual and experiential character also reinforces the impact of emotion or affect.[57] Three-dimensional visualizations "stimulate positive or negative emotional reactions in observers."[58] A negotiator's affective response toward a specific territory can thus change, altering the emotion-laden evaluation of particular gains or losses. Because the affect elicited could be positive or negative, however, the potential impact on negotiation outcomes is ambiguous. Depending on the context, one side could become either more intransigent regarding a particular territorial concession or more willing to see the other side's claim in a positive light.

Moving from the features of digital mapping to its broader context, two dramatic shifts have occurred in who creates, distributes, and uses mapping. First is the "democratization" of mapping capabilities, as a much wider public is now able to participate in making and distributing maps.[59] This shift builds on both the consolidation of GPS as a universal position-finding system and on the availability of digital systems for displaying and distributing maps.[60] Second is a transformation in the identity of the dominant mapping institutions—such as the rise of

Google as a provider of both mapping platforms and spatial information to the public but also to corporate and government clients.[61] The combination of these two trends has been consequential. For example, while many governments have long had access to satellite imagery, it has been made widely available to the public through digital mapping systems. Three-dimensional modeling of terrain and even buildings is now also integrated into "virtual globes" like Google Earth. Nongovernmental organizations use satellite imagery to monitor and expose human rights abuses, creating the possibility of new forms of "digitally enabled collective action."[62] This has empowered non-state actors to challenge states' "monopoly on the synoptic view of earth from space."[63] These trends specific to mapping build on the broader shift toward states being forced to engage with a wider audience in their diplomatic efforts, including using social media and other new tools.[64]

In territorial negotiations, the wider availability of mapping means that a broader public is capable of measuring and calculating gains and losses. "With the increased availability of both high-resolution commercial imagery and internationally recognized treaties . . . millions of people can now apply a new level of scrutiny to borders."[65] Since leaders' legitimacy is often tied to territorial claims,[66] more information in public hands can make losses harder to accept. This leads to a tension between the likelihood of reaching a solution and the stability of that solution. Wider participation and public pressure can make it harder to find a bargain acceptable to leaders on both sides, but once reached, the result might reflect more of the interests of the relevant publics and thus potentially be more stable. In short, the wider distribution of mapping capabilities reshapes the role of domestic political pressures in negotiations.

In another change in the context of mapping, the line between official government cartography and the activities of corporations or private individuals is increasingly blurred. Many governments have struggled to control the publicly available satellite imagery in tools such as Google Earth,[67] yet these relationships have also been cooperative. Private companies, for example, have removed images of sensitive locations and have often reserved the highest resolution imagery for military clients.[68] Google Earth itself has had customers in government agencies, and the publicly available GPS system was originally developed by the US military and only gradually transitioned to the everyday applications that we see today.[69] Although mapping has always brought together governmental and nongovernmental institutions, the ties between official and unofficial cartography have become increasingly complex. Even some state-to-state interactions are now shaped by maps and systems created and maintained by non-state entities, from corporations to activists. If what is depicted and how it can or cannot be altered is determined by nongovernmental mapping providers, then a significant piece of the framework for negotiation is outside of the direct control of negotiating parties or mediators.

This could be a boon to negotiation, especially when government cartographic resources are limited or unreliable. In place of official maps, "commercial remote sensing imagery can and should emerge as a key data layer for all boundary disputes."[70] This has, to some degree, already occurred: "Google's data-analytic supremacy and its incursions into the hard sciences have established it as a formidable distributor of 'fact,'" including in the area of cartography.[71] Thus, the idea of a neutral international repository of cartographic data for the resolution of disputes[72] may already have been achieved in the form of widely available commercial mapping. Yet much of the boundary data in "nongovernmental" maps are provided by government sources. For example, "fearing that boundary conflicts may arise from unwitting users of the web mapping program, the State Department decided to reach out to Google and offer up their authoritative boundary dataset."[73] The perception of Google and others as unbiased and unconnected to official positions, combined with the real links across the corporate–government divide, has complicated the application of these tools to territorial claims and negotiations (as the Costa Rica–Nicaragua case illustrates below).

Considered individually, many features of digital mapping are not entirely new. Mapping was never solely the province of official agencies, aerial imagery has existed for a century, all maps can be used to perform spatial calculations, and even digital features like layering are understood through physical metaphors. Nonetheless, taken together and combined with the radically altered context of mapping, these changes add up to a shift in what is made possible by cartographic tools. The result is a complex set of implications for territorial conflict resolution (summarized in Table 3.1). These are wide-ranging and sometimes

Table 3.1 Digital Mapping and Implications for Territorial Negotiations

Features of digital mapping	Implications for territorial negotiation
Layering: Digital maps can present and manipulate multiple layers of information simultaneously.	More complex divisions can be depicted and thus negotiated. Layering can reduce loss aversion by weakening the salience of any particular reference point. Presenting a menu of settlements can address concession aversion. Multiple layers can make focal points harder to find.
Flexibility: Users can easily change content and display.	More easily adjusted lines can reduce the intractability driven by mapped claims. Impatient bargainers become more willing to hold out for the next round of negotiation and thus become more intransigent.
Increased accuracy and certainty: Accurate position-finding is widely available; spatial calculations are precise and rapid.	Negotiators can calculate the results of proposed divisions immediately, speeding up the process. Representations create expectations of precision that remove the possibility of politically useful ambiguity.
Satellite imagery and 3D modeling: Photorealism and virtual terrain give a more realistic feel.	When calculating gains and losses, negotiators give greater weight to information in photorealistic imagery because of its representation as "real." Changes to affective attachments to territories alter concession aversion.
Wider distribution of mapping capabilities: Participatory mapping, volunteered information, GPS.	A wider audience can measure and calculate territorial losses and gains, narrowing the range of acceptable bargains. If an agreement is reached with public participation and approval, the settlement could be more stable.
Government-private interaction: Official and private mapping institutions share data and software tools.	The public ascribes authority on boundaries to corporate mapping institutions. The use of commercial tools limits government actors' ability to shape negotiations.

conflicting. Some point toward easier resolutions and some toward greater difficulties; some broaden the range of bargains that might be proposed or accepted and others narrow that range; and some increase the leverage of non-state actors while others strengthen the state. All of these implications—which are not accounted for by traditional theories of negotiation—emerge out of the novel means of representing territory provided by digital mapping tools, and the representations of those tools.

This survey has thus explored the full range of potential changes to negotiation processes and outcomes. The cases that follow, however, exhibit a narrower scope of specific implications. First, the Dayton negotiations illustrate the impact of using digital cartography in direct negotiation. Key features of digital tools were already present in 1995: layering, calculation, and realistic imagery and terrain modeling. Yet Dayton does not illustrate the significant changes in the broader context of digital mapping—the wider availability of mapping and the complex interweaving of state and non-state cartography. Instead, two post-Dayton cases reveal some of the complexities of more recent changes: the Eritrea-Ethiopia Boundary Commission (2000–2008) and the Costa Rica–Nicaragua border dispute flare-up of 2010.

Digital Mapping and Negotiation at Dayton

The November 1995 negotiations at Wright-Patterson Air Force Base in Dayton, Ohio, accomplished what had appeared to be an impossible task: bringing peace to Bosnia-Herzegovina. The talks were hosted by the United States with a team from the State Department headed by Richard Holbrooke, and involved the participation of the leaders of the three major parties to the Bosnian conflict: Bosnian president Alija Izebegovic, Croatian president Franjo Tudjman, and Yugoslav president Slobodan Milosevic (acting for the Bosnian Serb faction). The negotiations addressed a range of issues, including the territorial division between the Bosnian Serb entity (Republika Srpska) and the combined Croat and Bosnian Muslim territory (the Federation). Although this division was to be an administrative border within a formally unified state, it received the same attention that a new international boundary would have warranted.

Dayton is a useful case for exploring the impact of digital mapping because, in addition to being well documented, it "marked the first significant appearance of 'digital maps' in diplomatic negotiations."[74] Yet the maps used at Dayton were not entirely digital—paper maps were more popular among the negotiating principals—making it possible to compare the use of paper and digital mapping tools by the same actors in the same circumstances.

Of course, this case involves research challenges common to all studies of summits and face-to-face negotiations, including a need to rely on questionable first-hand accounts and an imbalance regarding which side the sources come from.[75] When examining the role of new technologies like digital mapping, further potential issues appear. The individuals using the new systems are often focused on their novelty, and thus they may tend to construct narratives emphasizing the technologies' revolutionary nature and implications. While this can this distort post facto recollections, it can also sometimes shape individuals' assessments of technologies during the negotiations themselves. This means that what might otherwise be an exaggeration of the importance of a new technological system could become a self-fulfilling prophecy. In other words, technical systems end up having an important effect because participants expect them to, based on representations of those systems.

Nonetheless, various processes that connect digital mapping tools and negotiations can be traced at Dayton. The following discussion explores the effects of digital mapping features like layering, calculation, and satellite imagery, first reviewing briefly the technologies used at Dayton and then examining their complex potential impact on the process of negotiation.[76]

While the three Balkan delegations at Dayton had their own map experts as advisors, the US delegation provided overall cartographic support. More than fifty staff members from the Defense Mapping Agency (DMA),[77] the Army, and contracted firms worked with GIS and other tools. The mapping applications can be separated into three categories: traditional paper mapping, the digital production of paper maps, and the direct use of digital systems.

Part of the US strategy involved providing paper maps as a means of controlling and shaping the discussions. The US delegation aimed to "flood the negotiation site" with American military cartography, including more than 100,000 printed maps from the DMA.[78] Some discussions involved even the most basic maps, such as hand-sketched diagrams exchanged between the principals. For example, in an episode of "napkin diplomacy," Milosevic and Bosnian Prime Minister Silajdzic sent back and forth during a meal a crude map drawn on a napkin.[79]

The negotiators also used digital mapping tools, largely in the form of systems for updating and printing new paper maps. Thousands of maps were produced on-site, in immediate response to requests or proposals.[80] These were used to discuss boundaries, consider territorial exchanges, and frame the overall situation. For example, at one point "more than one hundred 1:50000-scale maps [were arranged] into a floor-to-ceiling display of the entire country."[81] The production speed impressed the participants. The typical turnaround time—from negotiators marking up a paper map, to operators entering that data into the digital system for spatial calculations, to printing a new map—was only eighteen minutes, much faster than traditional methods.[82]

The most novel use of digital mapping at Dayton involved Power-Scene, the virtual terrain system brought by the DMA.[83] Originally designed for military target selection and mission planning, Power-Scene combined a three-dimensional model of terrain with satellite imagery to create a virtual space through which the user could "fly." Some of the boundary negotiations took place while the principals directly observed the manipulation of PowerScene by a trained staffer, with the results then transferred into GIS to produce treaty maps. The most widely discussed use of PowerScene was the incident detailed in Chapter 1: the negotiation of the road to the Muslim enclave of Gorazde—later known as either the "Clark corridor" (for General Wesley Clark's close involvement) or the "scotch road" (for the apparently liberal drinking by Milosevic and others during the all-night negotiating session).[84]

The dual naming is actually quite revealing. On the one hand, Clark and the American delegation used PowerScene to plan their proposal and then to show Milosevic the need for a corridor that would not leave the road vulnerable to Bosnian Serb attack. PowerScene proved to be a powerful tool of territorial negotiation—accurate, realistic, and convincing, useful for breaking through stalemated issues.[85] On the other hand, however, the "scotch road" designation points to a different feature: the degree to which nearly all parties enjoyed using the system and even engaged with it for recreation. "PowerScene also became one of the rare forms of entertainment for many at Dayton, who passed what little spare time they had 'flying' through Bosnia."[86]

Did these various uses of digital mapping have an impact? As noted above, there are significant challenges to directly connecting the technical tools brought to bear and the outcome of the negotiations, yet some inferences can be drawn. For one, the application of digital tools at Dayton offers some confirmation of the conventional, instrumentalist interpretation. Certain aspects of map use in negotiation were made faster, more efficient, and more accurate (e.g., the quick turnaround time and on-demand map production). The improvement was clear to the participants, who had attended pre-summit meetings "supported by a few people working primarily with paper maps and manual measuring devices."[87]

Nonetheless, while there is some evidence for this position of digital technologies as "mapping, only better," these technologies also had more complex effects—many of them related as much to how the technologies were represented as to actual "improvements" in capabilities. How, in other words, do the features in Table 3.1 operate in this case?

In spite of the presence of sophisticated digital mapping at Dayton, there is little evidence for the potential effects of layering and flexibility, for several reasons. First, the principals remained more comfortable arguing on paper; they "were used to paper maps, the crisp appearance of printed detail, and the flexibility of drawing on their map copy where and when they wished."[88] Moreover, complex forms of division were never really under discussion. Thanks to "a failure of the cartographic imagination," the negotiations were oriented exclusively toward drawing a traditional linear boundary between two territories.[89] Even the initial attempt to implement a more complex scheme for Sarajevo (a "Washington, DC, model") was pushed aside when Milosevic unexpectedly gave in on control of the city. This set off a furious round of negotiations with pencils on a paper street map.[90] In other words, complexity was abandoned in favor of a traditional territorial division.

The accuracy and certainty of digital mapping, on the other hand, were important since all sides were focused on the final land areas of the two territorial entities.[91] The initial Contact Group[92] agreement had delineated a 51–49 percent split (in favor of the Federation), and subsequent proposals were constantly framed in terms of percentages. For example, an early US memo reported that the Bosnian Muslim side was "increasingly hinting that they will demand more than 51%."[93] Eighteen days into the negotiations, through a series of agreed territorial concessions and adjustments, the ratio had reached 55–45, in favor of the Federation. When Milosevic discovered this discrepancy, he demanded a return to 51–49, in spite of having accepted the individual changes that had occurred. As noted at the top of this chapter, that discrepancy was revealed by the digital systems' ability to "rapidly calculate the percentages of territory."[94] The obsession with percentages, encouraged and made immediately relevant by the precision of digital mapping, was thus easily translated into a strong aversion to "giving away" four percent of Bosnia's territory, no matter the lack of strategic or demographic importance. The specificity of the calculations made the number itself much more salient. Ambiguity in the final settlement, in other words, was no longer an available strategy.

Yet digital mapping tools also made it easy to redraw the boundary quickly, giving territory in a relatively unpopulated area to the Bosnian Serbs and returning to the 51–49 division. The precise level of detail available to the principals let them focus on ensuring that important places, such as towns or religious sites, fell within their claim while still adjusting total areas. This can be seen as a means of offering a menu of options to each side, thereby ameliorating part of the aversion to making concessions. The speed of the process was also significant: "At one point, over thirty proposed tradeoff areas were digitized and calculated during a period of eight hours."[95] While this does not seem particularly efficient when compared to passing a paper map back-and-forth across a table, in this situation the entire point was to reach an *exact* territorial distribution, which would have taken much longer to accomplish manually. In spite of their occasional impatience with the process,[96] the principals often remarked on the speed of calculation, an evaluation that may have helped keep all parties invested in continuing the process. Yet the fact that a vague delineation by hand was not acceptable was due as much to the expectations of digital mapping's efficiency and speed—undergirded by how all parties described the tools in this way—as to an intrinsic interest in exact percentages. In other words, digital mapping helped to solve a problem that it may itself at first have exacerbated.

Mapping technologies at Dayton were also related to anchoring and reference points.[97] For example, Bosnian and Croat officials "agreed that the 1994 Contact Group map should be the baseline for any territorial negotiations," even though that map included several lost territories that were unlikely to be regained.[98] In other words, a reference point can be a mapped division, rather than the de facto status quo. Later in the negotiations, the US delegation tried to establish a new reference point by producing a new map, an effort evident in US memos: "We are preparing a US map which will make no one happy" and, several days later, "U.S. prepared summary map option and presented to both sides. Not formal US proposal, but has become basis for negotiations."[99] In this case, rapid map production capabilities proved useful for altering the anchor point for all parties.

Finally, the emotional resonance of mapping played a significant role at Dayton, further accentuated by the evocative nature of the digital systems. Throughout, negotiators reacted emotionally to maps. At a pre-summit meeting, for example, Holbrooke reports that "the mere sight of maps . . . 'energized' the Bosnians into a deeply emotional state."[100] On day eight of Dayton, a "six-hour map marathon" addressing territorial issues had an unexpected downside. Holbrooke noted that "up to that point, those people had been reasonably cordial to each other—but the sight of the maps drove them nuts."[101] Although these reactions have as much to do with the territories themselves as with their representations in maps, a deep connection exists between the map and the territory it depicts. A map gives a strong feeling of the territory and thereby serves in its own right as a symbol of—or threat to—national identity.[102]

The use of digital tools—particularly PowerScene—interacted with this emotional impact of mapping. First, there was the sense that PowerScene served as both a tool for negotiation and a particularly effective and intimidating symbol of "America's technological prowess."[103] Unlike other efforts to remind the parties of US power (historic warplanes on display, for example), PowerScene could be directly connected to the principals' own interests: possible targets, including some leaders' homes, were visible on an American military computer system. In fact, PowerScene had been used to plan bombing missions against Bosnian Serb targets—including the destruction of a bridge that erroneously still appeared in the virtual model, a mistake pointed out by Milosevic himself.[104] This intimidation would not lend a positive affective valence to the system, but even a negative reaction could make the information presented more vivid, compelling, and memorable. The appearance of realism could have a similar effect, increasing the likelihood that the information would be easily recalled. Thus, the evaluation of a particular solution could be altered by presenting that information in the form of a virtual flyover rather than as a straightforward map or text. Clark's successful use of the PowerScene system to convince Milosevic to approve the wider corridor to Gorazde suggests this dynamic.

Even the possibly fun aspect of using PowerScene could have played a role. In addition to perhaps being intimidated, everyone seems to have been impressed with the technology in a way that could have led to mood-congruent processing. After all, Clark made the case for the Gorazde corridor to Milosevic while they were enjoying themselves, drinking scotch and flying virtually over Bosnia. The sense that this was a remarkable system was noted by participants on various sides. Holbrooke describes it as "the magic of Powerscene,"[105] and another US official recalled afterward that he himself "was very impressed" and noted "the way that people from the Balkan delegations were impressed."[106] This positive feeling, which like other emotions can be "contagious,"[107] may have made it easier for Milosevic to accept the proposed territorial concession. Of course, his emotional response would probably be a contradictory mix of the positive (the system is impressive and enjoyable) and the negative (it had been used in the bombing of his side's interests).[108] Even the latter, however, would raise the profile of the information presented, potentially making it more convincing. The resulting concession on Gorazde may have involved only a small piece of territory, but it was an important breakthrough on a difficult issue. The following day Holbrooke reported that the session with PowerScene led to "the first movement on this issue in over 36 hours."[109]

Many factors are involved in even the most straightforward negotiation over territory, and Dayton had its share of additional complexities. Yet there are reasons to believe that digital mapping had a real, if limited, impact. PowerScene stimulated an emotional reaction in the negotiators, reshaping evaluations of outcomes and helping to overcome sticking points. The battle over the 51–49 split reveals the importance of digital detail and accuracy—easy, precise calculation first generated new challenges and then helped to overcome them. Unfortunately, however, it remains difficult to empirically connect a new technological system directly to an observable change in negotiation processes, let alone to the overall outcome of the summit in terms of the agreement reached. The limited amount of information directly pertaining to these systems and their use, as well as the challenge of observing key intervening variables like the principals' emotional states or affective reactions, makes it nearly impossible to draw that connection conclusively.

Nonetheless, there were multiple points at which the negotiations nearly ended in failure, only to be saved by a sudden, last-minute reversal. For some of those—such as the successful negotiation of the land corridor to Gorazde—digital mapping tools were definitely involved and likely had some influence. Thus, while the narratives underlying most post facto first-hand accounts (such as Holbrooke's) emphasize the importance of a few personalities and their negotiating strengths and weaknesses, the material tools brought to bear were also consequential. Counterfactually, in other words, without those tools other important factors would not have had the same effects, and our understanding of outcomes like this is incomplete if we rely only on bargaining or other models of negotiation.

Moreover, digital mapping's importance goes beyond the straightforward instrumentalist or determinist stories—that is, arguments that the tools simply provided actors with more accurate information more efficiently, or that the systems drove certain outcomes directly. Instead, more complex interactions between the technological systems, how they were used, represented, and understood, and the processes of negotiation played a role in moving toward a compromise. New mapping technologies likely did not serve as the decisive factor in getting Dayton to a signed agreement. Yet they did contribute in identifiable ways to the positive conclusion of the negotiations.

Digital Mapping and Negotiation Since 1995

Dayton was transitional in terms of the mapping tools available and their application. Three decades later, we would expect to see a closer integration of digital maps into negotiating processes and further refinements in technical capabilities—as well as some trends unforeseen in 1995. For example, negotiators are no longer likely to be amazed or intimidated by tools like PowerScene. Satellite imagery, terrain modeling, and virtual flyovers are now commonplace in Google Earth and other freely available online systems. Rather than being surprising, those features have come to be expected on digital mapping platforms.[110] The affective impact of their realism, however, will continue to shape evaluations of information and arguments—especially as imagery and modeling become even more accurate and convincing, and users internalize the expectation of accuracy. With the ever-increasing technological capability to place users inside virtualizations like Google Earth (such as in virtual-reality applications[111]), the activation of emotional processes by these depictions is only going to increase. Additional dramatic changes since 1995 include not only the growing availability of advanced cartographic systems to more governments and even to private individuals but also the increasingly complex interaction between corporate and government mapping institutions. This section examines two cases that illustrate some of these post-Dayton dynamics: the Eritrea-Ethiopia Boundary Commission (2000–2008) and the Costa Rica–Nicaragua border dispute of 2010.

The Eritrea-Ethiopia Boundary Commission

The Eritrea-Ethiopia Boundary Commission (EEBC), created as part of the agreement ending the 1998–2000 Eritrean–Ethiopian War, was mandated to settle the two nations' contested boundary based on international law and colonial divisions. In 2002 the EEBC released a delimitation decision, but neither side implemented the boundary. The EEBC's efforts illustrate some of the dynamics involved with digital mapping tools: their usefulness—and occasional insufficiency—in delineation, the increased interaction with the responses of a wider public, and the possibility for new means of demarcation.

Digital technologies were integrally involved in delineating the new boundary and showing it to the parties. US diplomats, for example, used a virtual flyover system to demonstrate to Ethiopian officials where the new boundary would lie.[112] Reports indicate that this evocative and realistic system was more effective than traditional mapping in showing the delimitation, and the virtual flyover triggered an emotional response from Ethiopian officials who recognized the villages being depicted. Yet new technologies could not overcome several typical delimitation challenges, including unreliable geographic information and ambiguous source material. For example, efforts to use GPS and other technological solutions to determine in whose territory specific villages were located were undermined by preexisting discrepancies in village names.[113] Likewise, the use of geographic descriptions in colonial treaties to settle the boundary was made problematic by "the variety of different local names" given to streams and other features during the colonial period.[114] Italian colonial maps, moreover, depicted the border in at least three different ways.[115] More precise technologies, in short, could not solve these problems.

A second issue was the role of broader public participation enabled by the internet. The 2002 delimitation decision was quickly examined and criticized in online forums, such as a Demarcation Watch website that addressed the Eritrean diaspora community.[116] The ability to report on an ongoing boundary dispute, using publicly available geospatial information and the internet as a means of reaching a targeted global audience, marked a significant change since 1995.

The EEBC's most controversial application of digital mapping was its decision to implement a "virtual demarcation." The commission released its delimitation ruling in 2002, followed in 2003 with maps for demarcation (the process of placing physical markers on the ground). Neither Eritrea nor Ethiopia was entirely satisfied with the decision, and neither went forward with physical demarcation. In 2006, the commission wrote that, in the interest of discharging its mandate, it was "obliged to adopt another approach to effect the demarcation of the boundary,"[117] based entirely on a list of coordinates and supporting documents, rather than physical markers. From the EEBC's statement:

> Modern techniques of image processing and terrain modelling make it possible, in conjunction with the use of high resolution aerial photography, to demarcate the course of the boundary by identifying the location of turning points . . . by both grid and geographical coordinates with a degree of accuracy that does not differ significantly from pillar site assessment and emplacement undertaken in the field. . . . Although these techniques have been available for some time, the Commission has not resorted to them because the actual fixing of boundary pillars, if at all possible, was the demarcation method of first choice.[118]

This attempted innovation is couched explicitly in terms of technologies making new practices possible—although not necessarily preferable. Moreover, the "degree of accuracy" is held as an appropriate standard for comparison; now that a virtual demarcation is as accurate as a physical demarcation, the virtual technique is equally legitimate. The commission also noted that physical markers should still be placed if the parties were willing to do so within the following year. No progress was made, and in early 2008 the commission declared that "the boundary now automatically stands as demarcated by the boundary points listed."[119]

The EEBC justified virtual demarcation by citing earlier cases in which no physical demarcation was implemented: a 1966 Argentina-Chile border delimitation in which aerial photographs served as "the sole authority," a 1993 UN decision regarding the Iraq-Kuwait border that relied only on a list of coordinates, and the recognition of maritime boundaries without any physical markers.[120] The reaction to the EEBC plan was predominantly negative, with both sides rejecting the idea.[121] The Ethiopian government specifically "contended that the Commission's virtual demarcation 'has no validity in international law,'"[122] a sentiment echoed in several academic analyses.[123] Critics noted the contradiction inherent in the concept of virtual demarcation:

> Demarcation is in fact a very simple idea: it is the physical marking out of the boundary on the ground. Any other meaning ascribed to it would be difficult to accept in the absence of usage justifying

such a variation. There is no escape from this by stating that "virtual demarcation" is but another method of demarcation.[124]

Demarcation, for such critics, is physical, making the very concept of a nonphysical demarcation untenable.

The general skepticism with which the EEBC decision was greeted reflects a significant level of "cognitive dissonance" among officials and observers,[125] a deeply ingrained reaction that probably undermined any possibility of virtual demarcation being taken seriously. Like the preference of the negotiators at Dayton for paper maps over digital tools, actors' mental frameworks can be a significant constraint on how technical capabilities are applied and how much they influence outcomes.

In the future, however, this nonphysical demarcation could become more acceptable as virtual forms of territory become more prevalent and institutionalized at the international level—and as specific practical objections are overcome. One of the purposes of physical demarcation is to remind individuals in the border region of the boundary's existence and location, a purpose unlikely to be accomplished by announcing and archiving a list of coordinates with annotated maps and imagery.[126] Yet as more individuals use GPS-based navigation devices like smartphones, a boundary marked with virtual points on the grid will become more "real" since it would exist on those devices and their representations. These technologies were far from ubiquitous in the largely rural contested parts of the Eritrea–Ethiopia border, but their capabilities show that the notion of a virtual demarcation could become more tenable.[127]

The EEBC's virtual demarcation at least represents an attempt—albeit unsuccessful—to apply new mapping technologies to an issue facing many third-party efforts to settle territorial disputes. In this case, virtual demarcation probably had little hope of success, given the intransigence on both sides. Nonetheless, the capability might one day be useful when the expense or complexity of physical demarcation—rather than political disagreement—is the major obstacle to a peaceful settlement. The result would be a greater chance for a stable resolution, made possible by the extraordinarily detailed representations provided by digital tools and the way that those images are increasingly represented as "real" as much as virtual.

Costa Rica–Nicaragua 2010

The unpredictable effects of the wide availability of digital mapping today are illustrated by a series of border incidents between Costa Rica and Nicaragua. While not involving the direct state-to-state negotiations seen in the cases discussed above, this dispute reveals the importance of public perceptions and of the involvement of nongovernmental map producers like Google.

The dispute between the two countries over a small border section had existed for more than a century, but hostilities flared up in late 2010 when Nicaraguan troops crossed into territory claimed by Costa Rica. Digital mapping initially appeared to have played an unexpected role: one Nicaraguan military official noted that the incursion was justified because Google Maps showed the territory as Nicaraguan.[128] Media coverage immediately focused on how the online map may have caused "the first Google Maps war."[129] Google quickly reminded users that its boundary depictions are unofficial, and the company soon corrected its maps to match the internationally accepted Costa Rican claim.

Yet subsequent analysis has revealed a more complicated picture. The Nicaraguan military official who mentioned Google Maps probably meant this "more tongue-in-cheek than most casual observers understood."[130] It was "a taunt" rather than a post facto justification, let alone the inspiration for the Nicaraguan incursion.[131] Yet a story about an official state action instigated by a boundary on Google Maps was believable, because of the authority ascribed to Google: "Google Earth and Google Maps have become the online cartographic resources of reference. . . . Google is often the arbiter of first recourse for borders and toponyms."[132]

What does the ascription of authority to Google mean for territorial disputes? It is true that, officially, Google's borders "have no government's imprimatur,"[133] but the majority of the boundary data in online maps comes from government sources.[134] In this case, the error was in Google's source: US State Department data. So there was a way in which the incorrect boundary line could be read as the position of the US government. That mistaken position would have been inconsequential, however, if it had not been easily available in a free online mapping platform, felt by many users to be authoritative. It is only because of its easy availability that the mistaken depiction served any purpose for

Nicaraguan claims, even if only a rhetorical one—and rhetorical power can be consequential for the outcomes of political contestation. The ubiquity of extraordinarily detailed online maps and high-resolution satellite imagery creates new opportunities for what might otherwise be minor mapping errors to contribute to actual political disputes.

The question of how Google functions as a mapmaker and map provider today extends beyond this one incident. The last decade is filled with examples of governments, individuals, and organizations challenging Google's depictions and place names. Unlike earlier controversies about an authoritative mapmaker giving a contested place one name rather than another, Google has been able to pursue an approach of being "agnostic" about competing claims: including multiple names in one image or serving different labels and boundaries to different users.[135] After the Russian annexation of Crimea in 2014, for example, different Google Maps sites (in Russian, Ukrainian, or English) showed different versions of the boundary between Crimea and the rest of Ukraine (as an international boundary, an internal administrative border, or a disputed frontier).[136] The ability to be agnostic in this fashion is made possible only by digital mapping's flexibility. In some ways Google has taken an even more democratic approach to place names, as the company's policy has been to reflect, at least in part, "local usage" in addition to the claims of states or the position of international bodies—but the final determination is of course entirely made by Google itself.[137] In the cases of large-scale corporate cartography today, non-state mapmaking can be every bit as opaque and autocratic as state cartography.

Conclusion

While digital mapping can sometimes provide faster, more accurate cartographic tools that facilitate conflict resolution, it can also produce more complex effects. Negotiators can consider a wider range of settlement types, emotional attachments to territory may be altered, and a broader audience has the capability to intervene into territorial disputes. While these effects do not necessarily impede peaceful resolutions, neither do they automatically lead to better outcomes. Dayton revealed this complex, contradictory dynamic through the increased salience of spatial calculations and the emotional reaction to realistic virtual terrain. Subsequent cases have illustrated the importance of new technical capabilities and their wider distribution in contesting or settling territorial claims.

The ways in which technologies represent political interests can thus transform how leaders negotiate or bargain. In the case of mapping, how territory is depicted and manipulated on paper or on a screen interacts with what it means to negotiate over territory on multiple levels. First, technical tools and related practices shape social knowledge and underlying ideas, giving a particular character to what is being negotiated. Second, tools are directly integrated into the mechanics of political interaction: maps are used in, and can alter, the process of negotiating over territory. Third, material technologies continue to influence the outcomes of those negotiations, as new mapping tools can enable or discourage particular means of implementing agreements or demarcating new boundaries. When compared to pre-digital mapping and other representational systems like statistics, digitization has both accelerated longstanding trends and pushed representational practices in entirely new directions. On the former, the speed and accuracy of digital mapping offer officials and negotiators capabilities that they have long desired. On the latter, the embodied and convincingly "real" experience of using virtual terrain and other digital systems has transformed negotiation practices and outcomes in entirely new ways, blurring the line between physical territory and its representation and working through unexpected affective processes.

Finally, digitization has revealed the complexity of how political interactions have also shaped technological tools. For example, while much is often made of the military origins of ubiquitous systems such as GPS or Google Earth, their trajectories have been reshaped by other social and political pressures. Although these technologies were sparked by early military investments or interests, their later uses and effects on political interactions have not been constrained by their origins, and the systems and their use are not inherently militarizing.[138]

What do these novel, complex interactions suggest, in practical terms? The particular ways that new mapping technologies reshape negotiations and other interactions are diverse, but they are identifiable.

First, without a representation capable of showing a particular boundary or division, that division cannot be negotiated, agreed to, or enforced. Thus, if we want to improve the chances of resolving seemingly intractable conflicts, we should encourage the use of new technical tools. Even territories that are understood as "indivisible" have often been constructed as such by political and social practice,[139] and different tools might, at the very least, make it possible to put different solutions on the table—or on the screen. Second, we also need to remain aware of the potential downsides to new technologies. Technical improvements often have unexpected consequences, and in cartography as well as in other areas, it is rare that new technologies are simply "better, stronger, faster" versions of what preceded them. Finally, how new technical tools are represented—in this case, how new mapping systems have been described and the expectations of absolute certainty, accuracy, or realism that have followed—can be as important to shaping processes as the material capabilities themselves. These representations can be barriers to peaceful resolutions or assist in successful negotiations.

These questions regarding mapping and other spatial analysis technologies are relevant to domains well beyond territorial negotiations. For example, "geospatial intelligence" is becoming increasingly important for countries like the United States that have global security interests.[140] Here, too, the line is being blurred between individuals, corporations, and government agencies in map production and spatial analysis. The satellite imagery used by US intelligence agencies is often as much from commercial sources as from government satellites, and other forms of private contracting in geospatial intelligence have offered governments a way to extend their reach at a lower cost.[141]

Moreover, the ongoing shift of spatial analysis into systems requiring enormous amounts of data, with a resulting increase in processing required, may undermine many of the supposedly democratizing trends of digital mapping—and of digitization more broadly. "Big Data sensors, tools and applications are in the hands of powerful institutions rather than ordinary people. Big Data may therefore be exacerbating inequalities and exploitation, rather than ameliorating them."[142] It will likely be the tension—or collaboration—between dominant corporate and governmental actors, rather than the involvement of everyday users, that drives the future trajectory of how spatial technologies interact with territorial politics.

The parallels between government geospatial analysis and corporate location-based services are, in fact, striking. The disclosure of NSA policy by Edward Snowden revealed a "collect it all" mentality about intelligence data: as one former US intelligence officer described NSA director Keith Alexander, "Rather than look for a single needle in the haystack, his approach was, 'Let's collect the whole haystack.'"[143] On the corporate side, a similar pattern emerges:

> When [Google Geo head] John Hanke approached Google co-founder Sergey Brin with a data acquisition proposal for Google Earth, Brin asked how much imagery was available. When he saw a chart of global coverage he replied, "Well, I think we should get it all."[144]

For both types of institution, digitization has made massive amounts of data available, and the dominant strategy is to gather all of it. Governments have long sought to collect and analyze data on their territories and populations, but the capabilities—and representations of them—have undergone a qualitative shift with digitization.

Complete global reach, with information as detailed as possible, is not a goal limited to mapping and spatial analysis. Related processes are playing out in how cybersecurity and drone warfare are being deployed, and in how those tools and systems are represented.

4

Metaphors and the Internet

The Cyberspace Domain

Cyberspace: A new universe, a parallel universe created and sustained by the world's computers and communication lines.

> —1991, *Cyberspace: First Steps.*[1]

Strategic Initiative 1: DoD [the US Department of Defense] will treat cyberspace as an operational domain to organize, train, and equip so that DoD can take full advantage of cyberspace's potential.

> —2011, *DoD Strategy for Operating in Cyberspace.*[2]

THE INTERNET HAS GENERATED, EVEN for powerful states, fundamentally new security vulnerabilities, including commercial espionage, data breaches, intrusions into government networks, threats to physical infrastructure, and online election interference. Yet the internet is also seen as a source of opportunities, including for militaries: a virtual space for carrying out actions remotely that previously required crossing boundaries physically, enabling "force projection without the need to establish a physical presence in foreign territory."[3] This potential was demonstrated on the day of the 2018 US midterm elections, when a US military operation reportedly shut down internet access at an organization in Russia believed to be behind election interference and

Virtual Territories. Jordan Branch, Oxford University Press. © Oxford University Press (2025).
DOI: 10.1093/9780190063658.003.0004

disinformation. According to one US official, "We showed what's in the realm of the possible"—that is, the ability and willingness to use cybersecurity tools within another state's borders.[4]

Cybersecurity as a state concern goes back decades, with a long history of attacks on United States government actors and networks, and US espionage through digital means.[5] Yet the 2018 incident reflected a significant shift that has occurred, where the US government now carries out self-described "offensive military operations" inside an adversary's territory. What explains the policies and institutional changes that US officials—and those in other states, reacting to US actions—have pursued in response to cybersecurity concerns? In other words, how do policymakers understand these rapidly evolving threats and opportunities, and how are states adapting to face them?

Answering these questions requires looking beyond the material features of technologies or the structure of geopolitical competition. Although threats or attacks on hardware create pressure for a policy response—for example, the 2018 US operation was itself a reaction to online election interference by Russia—the *form* of that response is underdetermined by material or strategic circumstances. Instead, it emerges out of the interaction of technical or strategic factors with representational processes, in this case the effects of language. How issues are represented linguistically defines the problems to be addressed, gives a scope to possible solutions, and assigns responsibilities to specific political actors. As the second epigraph above indicates, in the US government context the linguistic representation of online threats and actions has come to be framed in terms of something happening in *cyberspace*, a distinct *domain* of conflict.

Focusing specifically on changes in cybersecurity terminology used by state officials, this chapter makes theoretical, empirical, and explanatory arguments. First, by focusing on the politics of representation, I provide a novel addition to theories of language and policy. I distinguish between, on the one hand, explicitly stated analogies and metaphors and, on the other, foundational metaphors, constituted by using particular terms as labels. Foundational metaphors implicitly connect otherwise distinct conceptual fields, reframing policy problems and solutions and shaping the rhetorical resources available for political contestation. This chapter's approach combines theories about the

linguistic role of metaphor with the array of theoretical and conceptual tools discussed in Chapter 1—particularly international relations
(IR) scholarship on the role of language, discourse, and rhetoric and
IR engagements with science and technology studies. This suggests
new generalizable mechanisms by which language shapes outcomes.
It highlights ways in which the features of technological systems are
in part endogenous to political contestation, rather than deterministic
constraints or instrumental tools, external to politics.

Second, through an extensive study of primary documents, this
chapter provides a comprehensive empirical account of the cybersecurity language used by the US military. After several decades of evolving
terminology, by the late 2000s US doctrine defined cybersecurity in
terms of threats and opportunities "in cyberspace." Simultaneously, cyberspace was defined as a "warfighting domain," suggesting that it is
as militarily important as land, sea, air, and outer space. The combination of "cyberspace" with "domain" has constituted a foundational
metaphor implying that the internet and related systems have created a
virtual space within which actions take place.

Third, I explain how this foundational metaphor, implicit in the
"cyberspace domain" label, has reshaped US policy and institutions,
in two ways. First, as state agencies have competed for cybersecurity
resources and responsibilities, this language has reinforced the military's arguments for a dominant role. Second, in contestation within
the military, the metaphor has supported a specific institutional solution: the creation of US Cyber Command. These changes have altered
policy outcomes, including the nature and frequency of US military cybersecurity operations. Moreover, creating a command for action "in
cyberspace" has effects beyond the United States, as Cyber Command
operates across borders and as other states emulate—or challenge—US
concepts, strategies, and institutions.

These linguistic representations and ideational factors are largely
overlooked by the prevailing approach to cybersecurity in IR, which
has emphasized technical and strategic aspects—quite productively.[6]
Focusing on the rhetorical consequences of foundational metaphors
implicit in terminological labels reveals new connections between language and policy outcomes, including identifying why language is so
consequential in a complex field like cybersecurity.[7] Representations

of technical systems are central to how political actors and institutions grapple with those systems' benefits and vulnerabilities, making it impossible to understand state responses without bringing these representational processes into our analysis.

Metaphor Theory and Cyberspace

Metaphors involve "understanding and experiencing one kind of thing in terms of another,"[8] a transfer of meaning that is especially important for thinking through new or complex phenomena.[9] Metaphors, however, are not simply evocative comparisons. Instead they have complex effects through their *entailments*: follow-on concepts or ideas that reshape thinking, decision-making, and practical outcomes.[10] IR studies have explored the effects of metaphorical language, demonstrating that even instrumentally deployed analogies have pervasive, often unintended policy consequences.[11]

In addition to analogies and metaphors that are used consciously, other metaphors operate on a deeper level. These *conceptual metaphors* are "systematic sets of correspondences . . . across conceptual domains" that "reflect conventional patterns of thought."[12] This chapter introduces a specific subcategory, *foundational metaphors*: conceptual metaphors constituted by using particular terms as labels, metaphors that then provide the foundation for explicit analogies and arguments. Like other conceptual metaphors, they provide "mental models [that] guide our thoughts without us really being aware of them"[13] — reinforcing specific assumptions, suggesting particular analogies and discouraging others, and limiting which arguments can be made convincing. Foundational metaphors, however, specifically emerge when something is labeled with a term whose connotations imply answers to the most basic questions: What defines this as a "thing"? What are its fundamental characteristics? To what other things is it similar?

Whether chosen deliberately or intuitively, the label itself is often presented by speakers as commonsensical, not needing to be explained. This requires no assumption that speakers or audiences believe the implicit metaphorical correspondences actually *are* true or commonsensical. Instead, following Semino's discursive metaphor theory, we can analyze texts' metaphorical content, including how prevalent metaphors "come to represent the 'commonsense' or 'natural' view."[14] Nonetheless, whether anyone is aware of it or not, these linguistic representations yield metaphorical correspondences.[15]

While all metaphorical language can draw on similar correspondences, foundational metaphors do so in a specific way. Unlike explicitly stated metaphors or analogies, foundational metaphors' correspondences are implied by the connotations of terminology. Because they are implicit, identifying the correspondences of a foundational metaphor requires multiple steps: noting that a particular label is consistently used,[16] examining the range of metaphorical correspondences *potentially* implied, and then analyzing surrounding texts to see which of those correspondences—if any—are guiding the entailed descriptions, arguments, and explicit analogies and metaphors. In other words, the content of a foundational metaphor is shaped by surrounding language, as well as revealed by it. Explicitly stated metaphors and implicit foundational metaphors often work in conjunction, each reinforcing and structuring the meaning of the other.

This chapter focuses in particular on the effects on political rhetoric and argument, where foundational metaphors play a powerful and distinct role.[17] Rhetorical contestation takes place at all levels of international politics,[18] and even "rational" actors need to use acceptable "normative reasoning" to convince others.[19] In such arguments, language can be deployed to remove opponents' discursive resources—not changing their minds, but denying them the "rhetorical commonplaces" needed to convince audiences.[20] Metaphorical language in contestation ranges from intentional deployments to unconscious choices. Historical analogies, for example, are often selected instrumentally by decision-makers (albeit by choosing from those analogies resonant within a community).[21] By contrast, invoking foundational metaphors by using particular terminology is rarely so instrumental. Speakers may reach for a term because they believe it "works" as a label rather than because they think it will directly support their arguments. In fact, opposing arguments often use the same terminology and draw on the same foundational metaphors, the entailments of which then frame debate. Yet not all arguments are as readily supported by the metaphors implied by shared terms—foundational metaphors can make certain arguments more convincing and undermine others. Their use, in fact, has significant structuring effects on rhetoric and the relative power of opposing arguments regardless of the intention of speakers: as will be seen below, even when a speaker believes the language to be inaccurate or meaningless, the rhetorical effect remains.

As with other linguistic processes, foundational metaphors are simultaneously a resource, constraint, and context for political interaction.[22] Language can support the hegemony of certain ideas, setting the bounds of what is up for debate and what is not, what is considered possible and what is "literally unthinkable."[23] Like "dominant narratives" in foreign policy, foundational metaphors "do not fully smother contestation but channel it,"[24] setting limits on which arguments count as legitimate. The point at which terminology comes to be at least provisionally settled—that is, presented as unproblematic and commonsensical—constitutes an important critical juncture.[25] Contestation and argument continue, but within different bounds.

Metaphorical language is everywhere in cybersecurity, as designers, users, and policymakers rely extensively on analogies and metaphors—including terminology no longer even considered metaphorical (desktop, virus, firewall, etc.). Existing studies have focused on instrumental analogies and metaphors, whose effects are often unintended.[26] For example, the analogy of a "cyber" or "electronic" Pearl Harbor explicitly emphasized the possibility of a catastrophic attack on infrastructure to promote specific preventive measures, but it also unintentionally minimized the threat of continuous low-level intrusions and espionage.[27] Likewise, the "threat representations" instrumentally deployed by decision-makers to support their arguments also shape perceptions in unintended ways.[28] Yet the inherent complexity of the internet—an assemblage of hardware, software, data, protocols, users, and institutions—means that nearly any label will have implicit metaphorical correspondences.[29] These foundational metaphors, embedded by terminology, have received far less attention.

In this case, the word "cyberspace" implies a metaphor between the internet (and related systems) and some kind of space.[30] This implicit correspondence follows a common pattern: something "relatively abstract, complex, unfamiliar, subjective, or poorly delineated" (global computer networking) is understood by reference to something "concrete, simple, familiar, physical and well-delineated" (physical space).[31] Yet space can be understood and defined in various ways, and identifying the specific spatial metaphor implied by a community's use of "cyberspace" requires examining the associated arguments and analogies, especially when they form a coherent whole.[32] Although the implication that cyberspace is a "place" is almost never meant literally, implicit metaphors nonetheless shape discussion.

Where, then, did "cyberspace" originate? Author William Gibson coined the word in a 1982 short story, and the term reached a broad audience in his 1984 novel *Neuromancer*. On how he came up with the term, Gibson noted in several later interviews that he was simply brainstorming different terms for some kind of space inside computer networks. Relatively unfamiliar with computers at the time, he was less interested in their technical features than in using them as "a metaphor for human memory."[33] After the term had been embraced widely as a label for the early internet, he wrote that he had simply "assembled [the] word *cyberspace* from small and readily available components of language,"[34] and that "it seemed evocative and essentially meaningless,"[35] Yet there was a meaning embedded in the term itself, in its designation as a type of space—reinforced by the term itself and the specific language used to describe this "consensual hallucination."[36] His novels employ a combination of two types of imagery, both of them spatial: experiential elements like virtual landscapes, streets, and buildings and explicitly "Cartesian" or geometric foundations like "lines of light ranged in the nonspace of the mind . . . city lights, receding."[37]

Within a few years "cyberspace" had been adopted in the media and by technology companies. During the late 1980s, the term was often used in a restricted sense, not describing all online activities but instead referring specifically to virtual reality systems.[38] By the early 1990s, however, cyberspace came to be used to describe the broader online environment, superseding the earlier narrower application. This more all-encompassing definition is illustrated by two influential publications from 1991.[39] One, quoted at the top of this chapter, was *Cyberspace: First Steps*. This emerged from a 1990 conference involving computer scientists, artists, and even Gibson himself.[40] The volume's editor suggests conceiving of cyberspace as "a globally networked, computer-sustained, computer-accessed, and

computer-generated, multidimensional, artificial, or 'virtual' reality . . .
to which every computer is a window."[41] While this still refers to virtual
realities, it also contains the soon-to-be-dominant idea of computers
serving as windows to this informational space. Second, in September 1991 *Scientific American* magazine published a forum on "How to
Work, Play, and Thrive in Cyberspace." As the title indicates, this represented a use of the term to denote the entirety of online activities—even
as limited as they were at the time.[42]

By the mid-1990s, "cyberspace" was widely used to describe *where internet users were*, metaphorically.[43] This metaphorical framework was
embedded in political arguments about the internet, including John
Perry Barlow's 1996 "Declaration of the Independence of Cyberspace,"
written in response to the US 1996 Telecommunications Act.[44] Although many aspects of this short document seem naïve or even absurd
in retrospect, it was at the time "an utterly serious document" whose
"language and sensibility suffused Silicon Valley thinking."[45] Throughout, cyberspace is discussed as a space or place *within which* social
interactions occur. Late-1990s legal debates about regulating online activity also relied on "cyberspace" and its connotations: even opposing
arguments shared the metaphorical framework that online activity occurred "in cyberspace."[46] In fact, the elasticity of *possible* metaphorical
correspondences from a single term is demonstrated by the contrast between those two discussions, both of which were spatial in broad terms.
Barlow uses cyberspace terminology but draws on nonterritorial images, calling it "a standing wave in the web of our communications." The
legal debate, on the other hand, included statements like "Cyberspace is
a Place. People live there."[47] This difference reinforces the methodolog-
ical point above: identifying the foundational metaphor constituted by
a term requires looking to the surrounding texts.

The popularity of a spatial term like "cyberspace" was in part predictable. Spatial metaphors are often used to understand abstract
concepts,[48] and they have been widely applied to online activities—
internet users have long described their actions in spatial terms.[49] Yet
the embrace of this specific term was also, in part, coincidental.[50] Many
technologists had been interested in cybernetics and thus were likely
to find the *cyber* prefix appealing.[51] This may help to explain why
"cyberspace" was adopted instead of other terms from Gibson's novels

("the matrix" actually appears more often[52]) or neologisms from other sources (for example, Vernor Vinge used "the other plane" in a novella widely influential among internet and computer pioneers[53]).

In spite of its popularity, in the early 2000s the term declined dramatically in media and academic discourses.[54] Yet it was exactly in this period that "cyberspace" increasingly appeared in US military language, where the term has since become ubiquitous. Thus cyberspace "remains present in the ways that many powerful actors talk about, enact and regulate the internet."[55] How cyberspace is defined is mixed, with variation in emphasis on hardware and material infrastructure, software or informational content, and the "user experience" of being online.[56] Yet nearly all definitions rely on the idea, implicit in the term itself, that cyberspace is somehow separate or distinct from "real" spaces. Even though many discussions emphasize the connections between cyberspace and the "real world," conceptualizing networks or the logical and informational content made possible by them as some identifiable *thing* or *space* still sets cyberspace apart as distinct. The term is used even though authors often know very well where it originated—Gibson's definition of cyberspace is often quoted directly, usually more for flavor than as a functional definition. In other words, even when it is clear how odd it might be to adopt a term from science fiction to describe something so important to national security, it gets used anyway. And, as will be shown below, regardless of its origins the term has had important consequences.

Interestingly, among the government and policy communities, even the stand-alone prefix "cyber" has come to refer to computers and networks.[57] As noted above, the prefix came from *cybernetics*, a neologism coined by Norbert Wiener after World War II to describe his "general theory of machines." He was "inspired by the Greek verb *kybernan*, which means 'to steer, navigate, or govern.'"[58] And "cyber" has definitely meant different things at earlier points in time, even among military and policy authors. For example, an influential 1993 RAND publication on "cyberwar" defined "cyber" as referring to "information-related principles," explicitly *not* limited to computing.[59] By the mid-2010s, however, the prefix is almost exclusively linked to computers and the internet: for example, "cyberwar" is war using or targeting computer networks[60] and "cyber security becomes the security of 'cyberspace' in its broadest sense."[61] Moreover, as the below discussion traces, the spatial aspect of the "cyberspace" term becomes predominant and comes to shape discussion of the internet in military and security discourses.

"Cyberspace" is more than just a catchy or useful word. As the next two sections demonstrate, in the specific context of US security policy and military doctrine it has been an essential component of terminology—and implicit metaphors—used to represent and thus conceptualize the political and security implications of information technology. These metaphors have provided the foundation for specific arguments and policies deployed by the US government to manage cybersecurity threats. As other states have emulated, challenged, or resisted US actions, the language and policy of the United States have played a significant role in shaping the global response to cybersecurity issues.[62]

US Doctrine and the Cyberspace Domain

Since computer security first arose as a policy issue, US decision-makers have used an evolving set of terms. By the late 2000s, however, US military doctrine had come to rely almost exclusively on cyberspace-based terminology, further specifying that computers and networks constitute a "domain" of warfare. This dual conceptual framework has changed little since then and is now deeply rooted in how the US military talks about, and organizes for, cybersecurity. To uncover this pattern, the following draws on a comprehensive reading of public and declassified cybersecurity documents. They were not read for an exact count of terms, or to identify the first or last use of a particular word or phrase. Instead, I survey trends in dominant terminology and implied foundational metaphors (identified in surrounding texts). Focusing on this level of language reveals broad patterns that cut across variation in documents' arguments, author intent, or drafting processes.[63]

In the 1980s, cybersecurity was rarely addressed in major national security statements; when it was, documents discussed the security of "telecommunications" and "information systems."[64] The terminology changed by the mid-1990s, especially at the Department of Defense (DoD), where the term "information warfare" dominated.[65] This was a broad concept: the definition in an influential 1995 Air Force document includes not only computer-network attack and defense but also all operations targeting information, from propaganda to the physical destruction of informational hardware.[66] "Joint Vision 2010," released by the Joint Chiefs of Staff in 1996, reflects a similar emphasis on information warfare and operations.[67] Neither document uses "cyberspace" or cyber-prefixed terms.

At the same time, "cyberspace" began to appear in other government documents as something *within* which things happen. For example, a 1995 National Security Agency (NSA) document is titled "SIGINT and INFOSEC in Cyberspace,"[68] and in 1997 an outgoing NSA official argued that cyberspace is a distinct site of espionage and conflict akin to territorial spaces: "Almost every type of action that occurs in the physical world will have a corollary in cyberspace," and "The Future of Warfare is Warfare in Cyberspace."[69] Yet these documents continued to use "information warfare" language as well.

Published in 2000, the Joint Chiefs' "Joint Vision 2020" reveals an evolution of information-warfare terminology, while setting the stage for the important later shift to "cyberspace domain." Like its 1996 predecessor, this document continues to use information-based terms rather than "cyberspace." Yet it now defines information as a "domain of operations," noting that "operations within the information domain will become as important as those conducted in the domains of land, sea, air, and space."[70] In contrast, earlier documents had sometimes proposed an "area" or "realm" of conflict in which information plays a special role,[71] but the terminology was inconsistent and had not included the word "domain." While it is impossible to prove the complete absence of a term or usage, it is suggestive that it is not until at least 1999 that this usage of the term "domain" appears at all in the *DoD Dictionary*, a glossary of terms from military documents (JP 1–02).

In the mid-2000s, US military language took a decisive shift, joining "domain" with "cyberspace"—a combination that would prove crucial. For example, the Joint Chiefs' 2004 "National Military Strategy" uses "cyberspace" as a framework to understand the new domain ("the Armed Forces must have the ability to operate across the air, land, sea, space and cyberspace domains").[72] Soon thereafter, other documents consistently deploy cyberspace language in place of information terms. The Joint Chiefs' classified "National Military Strategy for Cyberspace Operations" from 2006 explicitly defines cyberspace—not information—as a domain and argues that "treating cyberspace as a domain establishes a foundation to understand and define its place in military operations."[73] Finally, a 2008 memo from the Deputy Secretary of Defense officially defines cyberspace as a "global domain" in doctrine,[74] a definition subsequently adopted across DoD documents.

The metaphorical correspondences implied by cyberspace terminology provided a consistent conceptual framework for discussing this new nonphysical domain—in other words, "cyberspace" gave "domain" a particular meaning. The earlier information-based terminology was ambiguous, with diverse connotations, and the relationship between information and physical spaces was never clarified. For example, the "Joint Vision" document from 2000 argues that information has a "multidimensional definition": "domain of operations" *and* "target, weapon, resource."[75] Given that information was essential to military operations long before the internet,[76] is the "information domain" actually new? Which aspects are new and require new strategies or tactics? These questions were difficult to address with information-based terminology.

By labeling this new domain "cyberspace," however, it could be designated as a domain *and nothing else.* Cyberwarfare involves "operating within or through [cyberspace]," while information operations aim broadly to "influence adversary decisions."[77] Essential to this discursive effort was the particular spatial metaphor implied by the combination of "cyberspace" with "domain." While each term has diverse possible meanings, when used together their definitions are narrowed. Without this further specification, "cyberspace" could be used in a way that emphasizes the "cyber" rather than the "space": in other words, focusing on the ability to control or govern from afar using informational means. Or, even if the emphasis is on the latter half of the term, its use could imply various types of space: political territory, a postmodern "space of flows," a notional space of ideas, or others. Likewise, "domain"'s multiple etymologies—ranging from mathematics to medieval political authority over land—imply diverse metaphorical correspondences. Yet because the two terms are deployed together in US military documents, the metaphorical implications of each are narrowed down to a correspondence between the cyberspace domain and the four physical spaces within which the military already operates.

Of course, separating out land, sea, and air was a longstanding organizational principle of the US military, institutionalized in the National Security Act of 1947. But it was only when the "new" space of information or cyberspace appeared that a label (i.e., "domain") was needed—the 1947 Act simply distinguishes among "operations on land," "operations at sea," and "air operations."[78] Thus, as noted earlier, "domain" does not appear until the late 1990s. The eventual designation of *a single label* for land, sea, air, space, *and* cyberspace may have been more important than the term "domain" itself—which has continued to remain undefined in the *DoD Dictionary*.[79]

The spatial entailments of the combination of the two terms are evident in the geographic or territorial analogies deployed in surrounding texts: "terrain," "high ground," "borders," "failed state," "ungoverned frontier," and so on.[80] These explicit comparisons reveal the characteristics of the implicit spatial metaphor, and they are simultaneously made more convincing by it. Interestingly, the implied characteristics of cyberspace sometimes contradict explicit definitions. For example, while US military publications define cyberspace in terms of hardware,[81] the same texts' spatial analogies present cyberspace as a "space between the hardware components . . . where interaction happens."[82] The implicit metaphor, not the formal definition, often frames further arguments and proposed solutions.

The foundational metaphor implied by "cyberspace domain" allowed convincing parallels to be drawn to physical spaces. Broad objectives "in cyberspace" can be framed with available concepts: for example, the 2006 Joint Chiefs document states that a key strategic goal is "to ensure US military strategic superiority in cyberspace" just as in air, sea, land, and space.[83] The rhetorical power of that statement follows from the metaphor implied by the terms: here is a new space, created by computers and networks, into which existing goals can be translated. While these statements sometimes discuss actions or goals "in cyberspace" without using "domain," in this community "cyberspace" alone has come to embody the combined meaning of "cyberspace domain."

DoD documents have subsequently argued repeatedly that cyberspace is a domain, distinct from the four physical domains but similar in that the US military needs to operate within it. For example, a 2009 "Cyber Warfare Lexicon" defines a host of cyber-prefixed terms as the versions of real-world phenomena taking place "in cyberspace."[84] Especially after 2010, the dual shift in terminology—deploying the "cyberspace" label and then calling it a "domain"—becomes pervasive in high-profile documents. The Pentagon's 2011 "Strategy for Operating in Cyberspace," for instance, frames cyberspace as a domain within and through which the US and its adversaries act.[85] Although this document actively argues that cyberspace should be treated as an operational domain, it simply asserts that there is something called "cyberspace" within which things happen.[86] This terminology was taken up throughout the US military, as service branches used cyberspace-domain language to analogize to their existing practices and concepts.[87]

By the mid-2010s, the idea of cyberspace as a domain of warfare was fully entrenched in US military language. For example, while the DoD's 2011 cybersecurity strategy explicitly argues that cyberspace *should* be treated as an operational domain, the 2015 and 2018 revisions simply assume that cyberspace *is* a domain and discuss how to operate in it.[88] The pattern is also clear in document series: for example, the 1997–2014 Quadrennial Defense Reviews (QDRs) shift from using no cyberspace terminology to consistently discussing cyberspace as a domain.[89] This terminology was not only directed at external audiences; it also informed internal DoD discussions. Classified memos use the same foundational metaphor, including, for example, a 2010 secret instruction on "counterintelligence activities in cyberspace"[90] and a 2013 document on "Human Intelligence (HUMINT) Activities in Cyberspace."[91] A 2012 Presidential Decision Directive authorizing offensive cyber operations also addresses threats and actions "in cyberspace."[92] Finally, internal Pentagon communications about disrupting the Islamic State's online presence discuss the need to "counter the Islamic State of Iraq and the Levant (ISIL) in Cyber Space."[93]

This terminology has become both stable and ubiquitous, demonstrating its rhetorical power and its ability to fit logically with existing military concepts and ideas. In other words, at this point there is little contestation among military authors about the language to be used;

the arguments are entirely about how to apply the cyberspace-domain concept to improve strategies and tactics. Even when the new domain is simply called "cyber," this continues to imply a spatial metaphor: for example, "cyber terrain" and "terrain in cyberspace" are often used interchangeably.[94]

This framework's persistence is striking, given the incentives to propose new terms. Military documents often note the importance of language,[95] and promoting new or different terminology can be one way to contribute to strategy or doctrine.[96] Since at least 2010, however, efforts to innovate have continued to discuss the "cyberspace domain."[97] Major changes in US strategy since 2018, such as the shift toward "defending forward" and "persistent engagement" (see below), are consistently discussed and justified using the language of the cyberspace domain.[98] Fifteen years after cyberspace was officially declared a domain, the public summary of the 2023 DoD Cyber Strategy remains couched entirely in the language of operating "in and through cyberspace."[99] This language persists, as does the way it shapes further discussion and contestation, whether authors use it deliberately or unthinkingly.[100]

While scholarly attention usually focuses on contested aspects of language and policy, the consolidation of terminology—and implicit foundational metaphors—can be equally important. Contestation continues, but the available rhetoric has been transformed. Tracing these linguistic processes reveals new aspects of cybersecurity policymaking, considered next.

Metaphors and Institutional Change

By the mid-2000s, a series of significant intrusions into US government and corporate networks had been uncovered, intensifying pressure on policymakers to respond.[101] Yet the nature of that response was far from preordained and was shaped by the foundational metaphor implicit in cyberspace-domain terminology. This metaphor gave particular arguments more weight and made it possible to present certain institutional solutions as commonsensical. In other words, linguistic representations have not driven policy directly, nor have they entirely constrained how speakers or audiences think. Instead, explicit and implicit linguistic framings have made some propositions more resonant with existing ideas, arguments, and interests, strengthening those positions in political contestation.

A critical juncture occurred in the late 2000s, with concurrent changes in US doctrine, institutions, and outcomes. The shift to an exclusive reliance on cyberspace-domain terminology allowed an implied foundational metaphor to be deployed—both instrumentally and unintentionally—to support particular institutional and policy changes. While there is a role for these linguistic effects at the state–society level of contestation—that is, regarding the respective cyber-security roles of the state vis-à-vis corporations, civil-society groups, individuals, and so on—this chapter focuses on two forms of contestation within the US government.[102] First, as state agencies have competed for cybersecurity responsibilities and resources, this language has been successfully used to argue for increasing the role of military over civilian institutions. Second, within the military, it supported the creation of US Cyber Command, a single organization for military operations "in cyberspace."

The resulting institutional changes have had significant downstream effects, including enabling an increase in offensive cybersecurity actions by the US military. Given the ambiguity of many cybersecurity tasks—which could be framed in terms of commerce, law enforcement, homeland security, or national defense—these outcomes were not simply the most effective or rational responses. Even within a narrower category such as "cyber defense," possible actions range from preventing intrusions into military systems to countering online disinformation.

Policy outcomes in cybersecurity also emerge out of numerous other processes, of course, but many of those interact with the rhetorical effects of language. For example, DoD funding procedures can make it difficult to mainstream solutions to new problems, that is, to add a new task across existing organizations.[103] Overcoming that challenge by creating a new organization, however, depends on the availability of rhetorical resources to support such an institutional change. Similarly, while the militarization of cybersecurity may reflect general post-9/11 trends,[104] the metaphors implied by cyberspace-domain language have made it possible to present this as a commonsense solution. In other words, even though the military may enter these bureaucratic contests with inherent advantages—significant existing budgets, a wide array of accepted tasks, and a claim over the core national-security purposes of the state—linguistic and rhetorical resources have nonetheless been essential.

Moreover, although institutional and policy shifts have coincided with broader contextual changes—technical innovation, more skilled adversaries, turnover and learning among policymakers—the effects of those factors are, on their own, indeterminate. For example, given that there is rarely a single optimal policy, learning alone cannot explain which specific solution is chosen.[105] Instead, how officials revise strategies, respond to adversaries, and understand novel threats have all been framed by the terms, rhetoric, and ideas that predominate within the military cybersecurity community, including by the metaphors implicit in "cyberspace domain." Thus, at key moments, bureaucratic competition over cybersecurity has been shaped by this language—probabilistically, not deterministically—as cyberspace-domain terminology favored certain arguments over others.

DoD officials have actively used this framework to denote cybersecurity as a military rather than civilian concern, attempting to close the controversy around the nature of the problem and its solution. The early-2000s shift from "information warfare" to "cyberspace domain"—with its implied spatial metaphor—made it rhetorically easier to present cybersecurity activities taking place in something analogous to air, land, sea, and outer space, all of which involve civilian issues and concerns but, simultaneously, are spaces in which the military legitimately operates.[106] For example, in 2010 the Deputy Secretary of Defense wrote in *Foreign Affairs* that "the Pentagon has formally recognized cyberspace as a new domain of warfare . . . just as critical to military operations as land, sea, air, and space."[107] Officials at other agencies "were as much surprised by the article as some foreign audiences,"[108] and they immediately protested this designation.[109] Information-warfare concepts had not inspired such a direct reaction, but the cyberspace-domain framework suggested a more expansive—and bureaucratically threatening—claim.

This language supports military arguments, while also having an intrinsic appeal to military actors. As Michael Hayden (retired Air Force general and former NSA and CIA director) put it in 2011:

Like everyone else who is or has been in a US military uniform, I think of cyber as a domain. It is now enshrined in doctrine: land, sea, air, space, *cyber*. It trips off the tongue, and frankly I have found the concept liberating.[110]

That Hayden finds this language liberating reflects how the implied spatial metaphors are simultaneously useful in policy arguments *and* appealing as a metaphorical framework for understanding a complex and challenging area.[111] As noted earlier, they allow policymakers to apply existing ideas to new problems. The relevant questions are then straightforward—how do known strategies apply "in cyberspace"?—and less likely to require entirely new concepts or models. The ability to draw from other domains has been essential to military staffing, since many senior cybersecurity positions were initially filled by individuals who began in traditional "kinetic" operations.[112] In short, this terminology was adopted because it intuitively fit as much as because it was instrumentally useful.

While few argue that the military should play no role in cybersecurity, the DoD's gradual expansion of its remit is potentially reshaping US civil–military relations, which are defined by such "haggling over prerogatives."[113] Beyond the core problem of civilian control—formally settled in the United States—factors like the balance of funding affect how power within the state is distributed and who is perceived by the public to be "in charge" in a particular policy area.[114] Contestation thus affects the relative primacy of civilian goals, the choice of solutions to new problems, and how problems are defined to begin with—especially with novel or ambiguous issues. If the military's definition of cybersecurity problems comes to be accepted as commonsensical and beyond debate, that definition will frame which solutions are in or out of bounds. Cyberspace-domain language has been essential for normalizing the close involvement of the military. For example, when asked about the appropriate role of the miliary, former CYBERCOM commander Keith Alexander argued that the US Constitution "says that the purpose of the Union is to provide for the common defense. There is no parenthetical that says 'except in cyberspace.'"[115] The recent expansion of the military's role, and the consolidation of that role, thus represents an important shift in how the US government approaches cybersecurity.[116]

Within the Defense Department as well, there has been competition over cybersecurity roles and resources.[117] Diverse elements within the DoD have attempted to claim cybersecurity as "their" issue area, with the Air Force most prominent among the service branches. In the 1990s, for example, Air Force documents argued that the "information realm" was most similar to air,[118] and in 1995 it created one of the first "true combat" units for information attack.[119] A decade later, Air Force officials drew on emerging cyberspace language to propose an Air Force Cyber Command, describing its core mission as "to fly and fight in the Air, Space, and Cyberspace."[120]

Yet it was officials advocating for a joint approach, particularly within the Office of the Secretary of Defense, who successfully deployed the cyberspace-domain framework. Had the discussion simply been about cyberspace—that is, had cyberspace not been designated as a domain—Air Force arguments could have been more convincing: cyberspace is complex, and operating there shares features with maneuvering in air and space more than with acting on land or sea. Framing cyberspace as *one of five domains*, however, implies that each domain, while distinct, shares certain characteristics (i.e., those making it a domain), supporting the need for parallel organizations. This fits better with building a joint force for cybersecurity than with subsuming cyberspace under the Air Force, a service already dedicated to a "traditional" domain. In a similar pattern, in 2019 space operations were upgraded from an Air Force command to a standalone Space Force, a move also promoted with "domain" language. For example, in 2017 the future head of Space Force argued that "space is . . . a war-fighting domain and we need to treat it as such."[121] *Domain* language favors the separation, not merging, of roles.[122]

In 2008, Air Force Cyber Command's permanent activation was denied. Instead, in 2009 the relevant tasks were newly combined in US Cyber Command, one of the most significant organizational changes in US cybersecurity policy in the last two decades.[123] Creating an independent command for both defensive and offensive cyberspace operations represents a combat-focused "military paradigm" that favors specific "legal and policy choices,"[124] supported rhetorically by the foundational metaphor implied by cyberspace-domain terminology.

Unfortunately, the explicit analogies that have followed (e.g., maneuver or deterrence in cyberspace), while succinct and evocative, may compromise key cybersecurity goals.[125] Military institutions are always guided by more than official mandates or rational decision-making processes, and foundational metaphors shape outcomes in ways similar to organizational procedures or service "personalities."[126]

While distinct from the service branches, Cyber Command has been tightly linked to another military organization: The National Security Agency (NSA). Its commander is dual-hatted as NSA director, and both organizations are headquartered at Fort Meade. These connections reflect the Command's need to coordinate with NSA signals-intelligence activities—and, even more, to draw on NSA resources and expertise. Linking the two could be presented to the Joint Chiefs as "offering NSA's resources to enhance DOD cyber-combat power at little cost to the services."[127] While this practical explanation is compelling, the rhetorical effects of language may have played a role as well. One analyst notes that NSA declassified a host of cybersecurity documents in 2012, once Cyber Command was operational and PPD-20 had authorized offensive cyber operations.[128] Included were the mid-1990s NSA documents discussed above, which do not use "domain" but do discuss "cyberspace"[129]—suggesting at least the possibility that NSA sought to demonstrate its own lineage "in cyberspace." Yet such a rhetorical move was unlikely to succeed at asserting NSA dominance: by 2012 cyberspace-domain language was well established as a rhetorical resource to support Cyber Command's assertion of a combat role in this "warfighting domain," over the exclusive claims of an intelligence agency.

Thus the Command is organizationally separate, with authority to conduct combat operations rather than espionage. This distinction has enabled actions that would have been extremely unlikely to emerge from an intelligence organization, including Cyber Command's growing number of "offensive operations."[130] Revealing capabilities by engaging in attack or disruption runs contrary to the goal in intelligence collection to keep capabilities secret—and thus usable—for as long as possible. Overall, both organizations have likely seen advantages as well as disadvantages to this arrangement.[131] Thus, while the dual-hat can certainly be read as NSA "winning" a bureaucratic battle, the expansion of Cyber Command's combat-oriented activities—supported by the DoD's dominant cyberspace-domain language—suggests a limited NSA victory at best.[132]

Cyberspace-domain language provided essential rhetorical tools for those advocating for the new command. For example, the 2009 memo establishing Cyber Command emphasizes various threats "in cyberspace" and the need "to secure freedom of action in cyberspace."[133] In 2010, the Deputy Secretary of Defense argued that, because "the military must be able to defend and operate within [cyberspace] . . . the Defense Department needs an appropriate organizational structure."[134] Which institutional solution is deemed "appropriate," of course, is conditioned by how problems are framed—here, entirely in terms of operating "in cyberspace," making Cyber Command the correct solution. The Command's mission statement also draws on implicit spatial metaphors: the Command will "ensure US/Allied freedom of action in cyberspace and deny the same to our adversaries."[135] In later documents and testimony related to Cyber Command, cyberspace-domain language continues to be essential to further argument—and goes largely unremarked.[136]

Even when later statements explicitly emphasize new threats—requiring new responses—discussion continues to rely on the same terminology and spatial analogies. For example, the 2018 "Command Vision" outlines a significant shift in strategy toward a more offensive posture through "defending forward" and "persistent engagement," repudiating the more reactive 2011 strategy.[137] Cyberspace-domain language helps to legitimize the new posture—including potentially controversial elements like "operating outside our borders, being outside our networks."[138] Operating in another state's territory could be interpreted as a form of aggression, or raise concerns about possible escalation.[139] Those concerns, however, are undercut by arguments in favor of the new posture which draw on spatial metaphors. For example, in 2019 Paul Nakasone, the head of Cyber Command, wrote:

> We must "defend forward" in cyberspace, as we do in the physical domains. Our naval forces do not defend by staying in port, and our airpower does not remain at airfields. They patrol the seas and skies to

ensure they are positioned to defend our country before our borders are crossed. The same logic applies in cyberspace.[140]

The Command's new posture thus involves activity "in cyberspace" analogous to uncontroversial actions in the physical domains. Of course, the idea that these all follow the "same logic" depends on the underlying foundational metaphor that connects cyberspace to physical spaces, especially to global commons like the high seas.[141]

Nakasone's statement, moreover, operates at multiple levels of contestation simultaneously. It explicitly defends Cyber Command's new proactive posture. It justifies the Command as the military's centralized cybersecurity organization—if the high seas have the Navy and airspace has the Air Force, cyberspace requires Cyber Command. Finally, it implicitly promotes the broader role of the military: Civilian agencies do not contest the DoD securing physical domains, so why should they protest the "same logic" applied to cyberspace? All three arguments rely on the metaphor implied by "cyberspace domain." The use of this metaphor has been effective: media reporting on Cyber Command's new posture has drawn on the same analogies.[142]

Within the US military, this language appears to be firmly consolidated. It was first explained and advocated, then officially declared as doctrine, and finally taken as given. Cyberspace-domain terminology continues to justify the existence of Cyber Command, and, at the same time, the institutionalization of this language in the Command's mission—and even its name—makes it increasingly difficult for an alternative framework to replace it. In fact, while some discursive communities outside the government have resisted this terminological framework—rejecting "domain," "cyberspace," even the "cyber" prefix[143]—the military's terms and implied foundational metaphors have spread into broader discussions across the federal government.[144] Analysts have critiqued the implications of calling cyberspace a domain, but almost none—within the military and related discussions, at least—have contested the idea of calling the internet and related systems "cyberspace."[145] This terminology has shaped policy outcomes, not just rhetoric: the 2019 National Defense Authorization Act expanded Cyber Command authorities to respond to a wide array of threats "in cyberspace," resulting in a significant increase in offensive actions.[146]

Other Metaphors and Their Effects

How might different language have led to different outcomes? Without the foundational metaphor implied by the combination of "cyberspace" with "domain," cybersecurity debates would have played out differently. Essential here is the conjunction of the two terms and how that specified and strengthened the particular metaphorical implications that emerged: namely, that the internet has created a virtual space with territorial features, within which military ideas, strategies, goals, and actions apply. Without the specification as a domain, "cyberspace" could have continued to be associated with a wide range of spatial ideas and implications—in fact, before the military adopted this term, some of its prominent political uses were explicitly nonterritorial.[147] Likewise, "domain" could have a wide array of connotations, drawing on the term's use in any number of fields.

With the combined terminology, however, arguments for increasing the military's cybersecurity role had a powerful rhetorical resource, and counterarguments by other agencies have been undermined. Consider, for example, a published back-and-forth between officials from the DoD and the Department of Homeland Security (DHS).[148] In response to the DoD's assertion that cyberspace constituted a "domain of warfare," the DHS officials first deployed a nonspatial concept: "cyber-ecosystem—not just technology, but also policy, procedure, practice, and law." Yet the "cyberspace" term could not be ignored, so the DHS response also tried to redefine it: "cyberspace is fundamentally a civilian space." But land, sea, air, and space are "civilian spaces" and "warfighting domains" *at the same time*. The related assertion by the DHS authors that "cyberspace not a war zone" misses the distinction between a warfighting domain (where military operations are possible and sometimes necessary) and a war zone (where conflict is inherent and ongoing). The "domain" half of the term is such a powerful rhetorical tool for military arguments because of that distinction. It specifies exactly what the DoD means by "cyberspace" and makes it possible to weaken counterarguments that use cyberspace language. Without this ability to set the terms of the debate (literally), the DoD position would have lacked a key rhetorical advantage it has enjoyed against civilian agencies' arguments.

We can also ask what might have happened if Gibson had not coined the specific term "cyberspace" to begin with. It is certainly possible that a different term implying a spatial metaphor could have emerged and become widely adopted.[149] That could in theory have constituted similar rhetorical resources, if it was combined with "domain"—or another term, perhaps. (I am agnostic about how essential the specific term "domain" has been, rather than early alternatives like "realm." As discussed earlier, the crucial step was consistently applying *a single label* to land, sea, air, space, *and* cyberspace.) Yet not every candidate term with spatial connotations would have worked as effectively. For one, "cyberspace" does not just connote a space, it literally contains the word "space." And the term is syntactically efficient: speaking about events or actors "in cyberspace" is more succinct than many alternatives. (Compare, for example, "operating in the information domain/realm" with "operating in cyberspace.") Without the specific word "cyberspace," it is unlikely that arguments supporting the role of military actors and interests in this domain would have been so convincing.

Without cyberspace-domain language, nonspatial terms and implicit foundational metaphors might have become more prominent in these cybersecurity debates. For example, when "the internet" is used as an overall label for networking and computing,[150] it can imply a set of metaphorical correspondences to *networks* rather than *spaces*.[151] The resulting emphasis on network features (e.g., nodes and connections) rather than operating in a virtual space yields different interpretations of cybersecurity problems and solutions.[152] Consider, for example, the implications the two metaphors have for political control. In a spatial model, control can be most efficiently exerted through drawing boundaries, as states do in physical territory. In a network model, control might involve exercising power over network nodes or structuring the connections between them, not through boundary delimitation.[153] Biological terms and metaphors like "ecosystem," similarly, might be more prevalent in the absence of cyberspace-domain language, yielding different rhetorical resources.[154] While these and other terminologies have come in and out of use,[155] few have become as firmly consolidated within a community—and thus as consequential—as the US military's use of "cyberspace domain."

The effects of the DoD's cybersecurity language are further illustrated by a comparison with how different terminology has worked within other agencies—and by considering how those terms could have altered outcomes at DoD. For example, since its creation in 2002, the Department of Homeland Security (DHS) has not characterized cyberspace as a spatial domain but has instead discussed cybersecurity in terms of protecting "critical infrastructure." More than a description of internet hardware, "critical infrastructure" implies a metaphorical correspondence between the internet and other communication and transportation systems.

This terminology first became prominent in a 1997 presidential commission report that focused on "cyber" threats to civilian infrastructure, without framing them as threats *within* digital spaces and without using "cyberspace" at all.[156] This represented a significant departure from earlier framings,[157] which predominantly saw computer network technology as an asset and source of US economic and military power,[158] or at most were concerned with the security of specific military systems.[159] The 1998 Presidential Decision Directive NSC-63, which followed the commission report, uses similar language.[160]

Later, DHS documents continue this trend. For example, the 2011 "Cybersecurity Strategy for the Homeland Security Enterprise" entirely avoids the domain-based language or spatial metaphors of the military.[161] Although it contains the term "cyberspace," it is used as a blanket term for anything do to with the internet or informational infrastructure. The document even defines cyberspace in the glossary as "the interdependent network of information and communications technology infrastructures," not as a domain. In fact, the core difference between official DHS and DoD definitions of "cyberspace" is the DoD's use of "domain"—the two definitions are otherwise nearly identical.[162] DHS's mission focus on protecting critical infrastructure relies on noting the connections between information systems and physical infrastructure—something that is not clarified or emphasized by the idea of a spatial domain. Thus the metaphor of operating in a virtual space is absent.

The contrast between DHS and DoD language has had observable consequences. The two have reacted differently to major cybersecurity incidents, with each organization's response guided not only by its mission but also by its foundational metaphors. How an agency's mission is translated into policy priorities, organization, and action depends on how key tasks are framed, including in language.

In 2016, as evidence of Russian interference in US elections surfaced, the DHS largely stayed within the frame of monitoring, preventing, and mitigating direct attacks on election infrastructure.[163] The department's institutional response was then to reorganize its relevant components as the Cybersecurity and Infrastructure Security Agency (CISA). The DHS Secretary argued that this change "allows us to confront the threats of today."[164]

The Pentagon's response to 2016 election interference, on the other hand, involved a command whose mission is entirely framed in terms of operating "in cyberspace," defined as a military domain. Russian actions were thus labeled as "cyberattacks," and threats to the territory and sovereignty of the United States.[165] In March 2018 comments on Russian interference, for example, the head of Strategic Command argued that "Cyberspace needs to be looked at as a warfighting domain . . . and if somebody threatens us in cyberspace, we need to have the authorities to respond."[166] The response by US Cyber Command then focused on operating proactively "in cyberspace" to prevent or disrupt future interference, including the 2018 election-day operation discussed earlier.

How would the two organizations respond differently if their terminologies and metaphors were reversed? If the DoD were to use "critical infrastructure" as a cybersecurity framework,[167] its response to foreign interference would likely be framed by its existing definition of "critical infrastructure protection" in general:

> Actions taken to prevent, remediate, or mitigate the risks resulting from vulnerabilities of critical infrastructure assets. Depending on the risk, these actions could include changes in tactics, techniques, or procedures; adding redundancy; selection of another asset; isolation or hardening; guarding, etc.[168]

None of this is about defending those assets by operating in adversaries' territory and interfering with their corresponding systems. Actions like the 2018 cyberattack on Russian sources of election interference would not easily fit in this frame, making them more difficult to present as commonsensical and proportionate responses. In fact, a "critical infrastructure" rather than "cyberspace domain" framework might alter the "cybersecurity dilemma," whereby cyber actions are potentially destabilizing.[169] When defensively oriented intrusions are detected, cyberspace domain terminology analogizes them to territorial violations rather than to espionage, increasing the possibility of escalation.[170]

Likewise, DHS would pursue different policies if it relied on spatial terminology and metaphors. While using "domain" would be unlikely—since that term emerged from a specific context at DoD—a spatial model on which DHS could conceivably draw is an analogy to border protection (one of "six overarching homeland security missions").[171] This would place less emphasis on vulnerability and resilience in core infrastructure and more on preventing intrusions at network locations analogous to territorial boundaries (i.e., away from election hardware itself).[172] Yet DHS's long reliance on critical infrastructure language, which predates the department itself, appears to undermine other frameworks—just as DoD's cyberspace-domain terminology has, thus far at least, remained impervious to alternatives.

Cyberspace Beyond the United States

While this chapter has focused on the United States, cybersecurity language and metaphors also shape contestation in other contexts.[173] For one, US terms—and implicit metaphors—have appeared in documents from other states, particularly among US allies.[174] NATO documents have also drawn directly on US concepts,[175] and even US adversaries have, on occasion, used US language.[176] While the military, economic, and diplomatic power of the United States explains why US language has sometimes been emulated,[177] the consequences of that emulation result from the content of US terminology, including its implicit foundational metaphors.

Those consequences are evident in debates around how international law applies to cybersecurity—especially debates that have drawn directly on US language.[178] For example, the two *Tallinn Manuals* were written by a group of experts (largely from NATO states) seeking to codify how state practices reveal customary and treaty-based international law of "cyberwarfare" and "cyber operations."[179] The *Manuals* build on the spatial concepts in US cybersecurity language, even quoting from a US document that "international norms guiding State behavior . . . also apply in cyberspace," and defining terms like "cyber operations" and "cyberspace" very similarly to US terminology.[180]

Although the *Tallinn Manuals* only rarely refer to cyberspace as a "domain," the way that US "cyberspace" language has been imported nonetheless draws on the now-consolidated territorial metaphors implied by the combination of the two terms. In other words, because this discussion draws directly on the *specific* framing of cyberspace in US language (as a domain), the use of "cyberspace" alone has continued to territorialize these discussions, even without using the "domain" term.

The spatial metaphors implied by this terminology can complicate— maybe unnecessarily—the application of international law. Because the *Tallinn Manuals* discuss cybersecurity actions as occurring *in* or *through* cyberspace, nearly all issues are framed in terms of territorial sovereignty, defined as control over or independence of "a portion of the globe."[181] This is unproblematic for analyzing states' rights and responsibilities with regard to physical internet infrastructure (states have a clear claim over hardware within their boundaries) or actions that involve physically crossing a border. Yet there is more to cybersecurity than direct control over hardware, which is one "point of leverage" over internet activity[182] but a crude tool of internet governance and rarely sufficient on its own.[183]

The *Tallinn Manuals*, therefore, also attempt to classify actions that rely exclusively on informational or nonphysical means, especially actions that intentionally cross state boundaries. This ranges from using "remote cyber operations" to effect damage inside another state[184] to sending "cyber weapons" through the infrastructure of a neutral party.[185] The spatial metaphor implied by cyberspace terminology has complicated this analysis, preventing consensus within the *Tallinn* group of experts: some treated cyberspace as a spatial extension of state territory (and thus subject to the same rules, metaphorically translated "into cyberspace"), while others treated cyber operations as informational actions that should not be understood through spatial analogies. With progress unlikely on any treaty-based international law for cybersecurity,[186] even nonbinding discussions like the *Tallinn* process will guide further developments in international law and norms, including by framing questions with largely unexamined terms and implicit metaphors.[187]

In other international settings, less dominated by US interests, the interactions across diverse languages, terminologies, and metaphors have been more complex. For example, in two UN cybersecurity bodies—the Group of Governmental Experts (GGE) and the more recent Open Ended Working Group (OEWG)—US language has not predominated. In consensus reports in 2013 and 2015 (hailed for demonstrating a surprising degree of international agreement), the GGE framed its work as developing norms regarding the use of "information and communication technologies" (ICTs) and the "conduct of ICT-related activities"[188]—not actions "in cyberspace." It is possible that agreement was enabled, albeit temporarily,[189] by the broad language being used: "ICT activities" favors neither the US cyberspace-domain concept nor the very different language of "information security" used by some other participating states, including Russia and China.[190] The OEWG consensus report of 2021, similarly, avoids the use of "cyberspace" language almost entirely.[191]

Outside of international forums, there are other pathways by which US language may have global effects. For example, important aspects of internet governance could be reshaped by an unintended correspondence between US terminology and authoritarian governments' internet policies. The metaphors implied by cyberspace-domain language in US doctrine may inadvertently legitimize controls like China's "great firewall"—the US's spatial metaphors naturalize the idea of boundaries and state authority "in cyberspace." The Chinese government's claim of sovereignty over the internet within its borders has even been justified with reference to the *Tallinn Manuals*.[192] In other words, the cyberspace-domain concept and the resulting spatial metaphors could implicitly support "internet fragmentation," especially the "alignment" of internet controls with state boundaries.[193]

Conclusion

This chapter has demonstrated how cybersecurity has been constructed by linguistic representations, rather than only by technical features or strategic considerations. In particular, foundational metaphors, implied by widely used terminology, have shaped arguments, policy responses, and institutional changes. In US military doctrine and strategy, the "cyberspace domain" label has constituted a set of underlying spatial metaphors since the mid-2000s—providing instrumental rhetorical tools and, simultaneously, structuring the arguments, analogies, and policies brought to bear. This linguistic representation has shaped contestation within the United States government, supporting militarization and the creation of a unified Cyber Command. In circumstances of rapid technological change, uncertain consequences, and novel vulnerabilities—conditions clearly present in cybersecurity—how issues are framed in terminology and then institutionalized can have significant effects.

Given that cybersecurity metaphors are likely to persist (it would be nearly impossible to avoid them entirely),[194] we should at a minimum be aware of how the metaphors implied by terminology shape arguments in policymaking—and in scholarship. Research in IR and Security Studies often uses cyberspace terminology, asking whether and how conflict, power, norms, deterrence, or other "traditional" security issues and concepts apply "in cyberspace."[195] As with the military's use of similar terms, this is not necessarily a problem, but using other language may add new analogies, comparisons, and policy recommendations.[196] Or it could be helpful to avoid conceptualizing the internet and its effects as a singular "thing," by any name, and instead discuss it for what it is: a collection of actors, technologies, systems, institutions, problems, policies, effects, and so on.[197] Finally, one could use multiple terminologies simultaneously, and thus draw on diverse underlying metaphors.[198] While the "imperfections" of any particular metaphor are a possible constraint, they can also be "a source of creativity and innovation,"[199] especially when disparate metaphors are put in conversation with one another.

Consolidated foundational metaphors like those embedded in "cyberspace domain" may "work as self-fulfilling prophecies in which the phenomena so described gets progressively remade to fit its dominant metaphor."[200] This is particularly the case with technological systems that are created gradually over time or that involve ongoing maintenance and adjustment—features of almost any large complex system and certainly of global computer networks.[201] How technologies are represented shapes how they are politically constructed, refashioned, and deployed. Such representations demonstrate a complex mix of instrumentalist and deterministic processes: labels are deployed for specific purposes but often have unintended effects in terms of supporting some arguments and foreclosing others.

The specific case of linguistic representations in cybersecurity also suggests several broad points about the politics of language. First, it shows that examining implicit meanings and metaphors, not just explicitly made arguments, can be useful for understanding rhetorical processes and effects. Second, in addition to the customary focus on open contestation—arguments and analogies deployed instrumentally—we can look at what elements of language are *not* contested and what underlying ideas are then supported or precluded. In order to identify how language becomes consolidated, it is useful to trace it back to the point at which it was still unsettled—when terminology remained an open rather than closed controversy.[202] Third, the example of how the label "cyberspace" became so consequential suggests a novel pathway by which traditionally "nonpolitical" factors like popular culture come to have political effects.[203] Here, Gibson's novels may not have been globally popular, but they were read by a specific community of people central to the early development of the internet. The term "cyberspace" and its connotations then migrated out into broader discussions. This suggests that cultural elements can have effects even if their origins are not widely known, following a different path from, say, the use of the label "Star Wars" for the 1980s Strategic Defense Initiative.[204]

While language is extremely important to the political processes around the internet, as this chapter has argued, there are other representations that may play important roles as well. Relevant visual representations, for example, could be in the diverse attempts to map the internet (sometimes even discussed as an effort to "map cyberspace")[205] or in the use of visual representations in media and popular culture of particular cybersecurity actors or events.[206]

While those representations are important, given the challenge of visualizing the complexity of the internet and related technologies, language is unlikely to be displaced as the key representational mechanism. The labels and implicit metaphors used by militaries, analysts, and even scholars can reshape the technological environment, redefine the "terrains" of conflict, and determine what is and is not a "domain of warfare." One important mechanism—evident in the preceding chapter on digital mapping and central to the next chapter on remote warfare by drone—operates through affect, or how particular labels, tools, or arguments *feel* right or wrong. After all, as William Gibson himself described it, cyberspace is "not a place . . . it only feels like it is."[207]

5

Drone Warfare

Representing Remote Operations

WHILE MUCH OF THE DISCUSSION of remotely piloted aircraft or drones has focused on their material impact on conflict, there is far more to this technology and its effects. As Michael Boyle argues: "Perhaps the greatest consequence of the emergence of drones for war and peace is their impact on our thinking."[1] What kinds of ideational effects, then, have emerged from these technologies and their uses? The answer is complex: new ideas are neither the inevitable consequences of technological capabilities, nor entirely divorced from those material factors. In other words, drone warfare and its politics are certainly shaped by the technical features of current and possible future systems, but they are not deterministically structured by them. In the specific case of drone use in US counterterrorism and counterinsurgency operations,[2] representational processes play a central but underappreciated role in changing ideas about the utility, ethics, and consequences of remote or autonomous warfare. Representations are deeply implicated in what exactly is a drone, what those drones do, how they are used in specific contexts, and how future possibilities are imagined for drones to be autonomous, rather than remotely operated.

Virtual Territories. Jordan Branch, Oxford University Press. © Oxford University Press (2025).
DOI: 10.1093/9780190063658.003.0005

In fact, this evolving form of warfare is utterly dependent on representations and representational logics. The entire system of US drone operations is focused on specific representations *made possible by* drone systems—particularly visual imagery and the identification of targets—and how to obtain, improve, and deploy those representations. This system has then been criticized, defended, and restructured through representations *of* drone warfare: debates about the legality and ethics of remote warfare, targeted killing, and weapon autonomy are all filtered through an array of representational imagery, language, and narrative, all of which carry rhetorical power beyond any objective description of actual drone capabilities or actions. The intersection of these two representational dynamics—representations through drones of the world and representations of drones in debates—is revealed by the framework in this book, providing new insights into how this form of warfare has evolved and may transform in the future.

This complex interplay of representations is apparent in one of the most-discussed incidents from US drone operations over the past two decades. In February 2010, a convoy of civilian vehicles travelling in a remote part of Afghanistan was misidentified as carrying enemy military forces and was attacked by a US drone strike, killing up to two dozen civilians.[3] This incident—which is an exceptionally tragic example of the civilian costs of US drone strikes and indicative of problems in many other known incidents—has become a core narrative in discussions of drone warfare, US operations in Afghanistan, and especially their dangers to civilians.[4]

Visual representations—and ideas and expectations about those images—were fundamental both to the incident itself and to how it was later understood. In the hours leading up to the strike, drone operators saw through drone video feeds what they considered clear indications that the individuals in the vehicles were militants, hypothesized to be in the area because US special forces had recently been deployed nearby. After the strike, as it became apparent that those killed and injured were not combatants—and many, in fact, were women and children—members of the drone operations team quickly shifted from their earlier confidence in their identification to professing instead that there was simply "no way to tell from here" exactly who had been in the vehicles.[5]

The purportedly detailed and accurate imagery provided by drone surveillance is what gives operators and commanders the *idea* that they can identify who is and is not a combatant and a threat to US forces. As one Air Force general put it (albeit only after the incident became public), the high-tech cameras and sensors can provide "a false sense of security that you can see everything, that you can hear everything, that you know everything."[6] Of course, his statement that it is a *false* sense of security is itself a representation, post facto, of tools that in nearly all other official discussions are represented as providing accurate, precise, and useful information for targeting decisions.

Finally, narratives of this incident have come to represent US drone operations in general—for critics, but also for proponents. Among those critical of the US drone program for its legitimation of assassination, high civilian cost, and possible violations of the laws of war, the disregard of contrary evidence by the drone operators before the strike and the resulting casualties suggest that these systems are not nearly as discriminating, proportionate, and ethical as the military claims. But for proponents of the drone program, this incident also serves an important representational purpose. Because it was (eventually) exposed and discussed, and the US military apologized to the Afghan government and "promised 'a thorough investigation to prevent this from happening again,'"[7] for proponents this incident stands in as the exception that proves the rule: poor training, communication failures, and a few mistakes that led to a tragic but unforeseeable outcome. It serves then to reinforce the legitimacy of the *idealized* drone strike: based on *correct* interpretations of *highly accurate* visual imagery and other intelligence, with a vast decision-making process oriented around minimizing civilian harm while accomplishing military goals. Of course, the fuzzy images from drone cameras in this incident were anything but exceptional, as the visual representations that drones provide in practice, rather than in theory, are often far from perfect.[8]

The generation, rhetorical and political deployment, and downstream consequences of these interwoven representations—representations provided by drone systems and representations of drones and drone strikes—are an important and overlooked element in tracing the consequences of drones and their use. In fact, "drone warfare" itself—an assemblage of technologies, institutions, practices, rhetoric, and ideas—is produced by these complex representations. While the word "drone"[9] evokes an image of an aircraft without a pilot on board (or often the bulbous-headed Predator specifically), the institutional and material systems of drone warfare extend far beyond the aircraft itself. The relevant systems include a vast array of military bases and sites where, estimates hold, between ninety and two hundred personnel are involved in the operation of a single Predator.[10] Moreover, focusing on remote aircraft as a "shiny" new technology may have distracted from more consequential developments, beginning with the policy of targeted killing.[11]

Thus we should "[move] away from a hardware-centric idea of an isolated object and . . . examine the infrastructures and surrounding networks that create, sustain, and authorize drone operations."[12] Broadening our scope to include the larger networks and systems in which material technologies, actors, and policies are entwined builds on the suggestion from Latour (and others within science and technology studies) to examine the interweaving of material artifacts with human actors, motivations, and institutions.[13] Then we will "not view the drone in isolation, but rather see it as intimately connected to other military and security practices," including in the US case the larger "lethal surveillance" system of counterterrorism operations.[14] Those operations constitute a vast assemblage of humans and machines,[15] in which the position of humans in the use of military force has been transformed by the large-scale deployment of aircraft without a pilot on board, capable of both surveillance and attack.[16] (The absence of an on-board pilot is foundational both to the technological systems and to the types of policies that these systems have been used for.) The entire assemblage—including the ideas and policies that are enabled, constituted, and sometimes demanded by the availability of these artifacts and networks—should be the object of analysis.[17] Representations, as this chapter will demonstrate, are core to constructing that assemblage and to its effects.

Most existing studies have focused on the various *capabilities* made possible by drones and their use: debating the relative cost of aircraft without pilots, the application of force without any risk to personnel, persistent surveillance of individual targets, and so on. Those capabilities have important consequences for conflict, for international law and norms, and for state transformation—consequences examined in the existing literature.[18] Yet many of those consequences do not emerge solely out of the capabilities themselves but instead from how those devices, systems, operations, and practices have been represented, in language, visual images, legal concepts, and political rhetoric. Some representations have been subject to intense and explicit contestation, and others have emerged unintentionally. All have changed how the practice and effects of using drones have been evaluated and planned. Representations, in short, are fundamental to how this new form of warfare functions in international politics—and even to what separates drones from other forms of "remote killing."

In order to explore this essential but underexamined aspect of drones and their effects, this chapter demonstrates just how central representations are to the use of drones by the United States: in debates about drones and their uses, in drone technology itself, and in planning for the prospect of weapons that are fully autonomous, rather than remotely piloted.[19] The representational politics of drones illustrate the complex mix of instrumental and deterministic logics at work around technological systems: drones and their representations not only provide useful tools—rhetorical, ideational, and material—they also drive new policies and impose constraints on action.

Debating (Representations of) Drone Use

The past two decades have seen an explosion of research on drones and their use in many settings, focusing predominantly on the military use of drones by the United States.[20] One of the first works that brought wide attention to the issue was Peter Singer's *Wired for War*, which examined military robotics in general but focused on the rapidly growing use of technologies like the Predator or Reaper: aircraft operated remotely and capable of both surveillance and attack.[21] Much of the early debate among scholars and journalists was shaped by two of Singer's core assumptions: first, that drones and other military robotic systems are fundamentally novel and, second, that they will inexorably continue to develop and come to be widely adopted.[22] As the discussion has broadened, however, a wider variety of approaches and analyses have emerged, including from scholars in political geography,[23] science and technology studies,[24] and philosophy,[25] as well as from activists.[26] Debates continue over the status of US drone strikes in international law,[27] the possible future development of weapons that are autonomous rather than remotely operated,[28] the ethics of remote killing without risk to the operator,[29] the level of civilian casualties that have resulted,[30] the effectiveness of drone strikes as a counterterrorism strategy,[31] and the consequences of drone technology for conflict escalation, deterrence, and interstate war.[32]

Many of these questions involve legal or ethical evaluations of drone technologies and their uses, evaluations that have been shaped—albeit in many cases implicitly—by how drone operations are represented. While the next section examines the representations created by drone systems, here I want to highlight the underappreciated way in which the choice of who or what represents drone warfare—visually or narratively—has shaped important debates about the entire system. In particular, evaluations are foundational to the choice of a comparison or reference: that is, what are drones better or worse than, in terms of legality or ethics?

For example, many arguments supporting drone strikes as precise, discriminating, or civilian-protecting have relied on a comparison to historical or contemporary piloted bombing. One early editorial in the *Wall Street Journal* justified the "more moral" status of drones by arguing that "never before in the history of air warfare have we been able to distinguish as well between combatants and civilians as we can with drones."[33] But why is the history of air warfare specifically relevant to a campaign whose goals are so different from those of previous air warfare campaigns? The widely discussed defense of drone strikes by Bradley Strawser also relies on the idea of using drones "in place of inhabited aerial vehicles," rather than comparing them to other tools.[34]

These arguments gain rhetorical power from the way that specific, widely used representations have made the comparison to piloted aircraft appear commonsensical. In particular, the use of particular elements to represent the overall enterprise of drone operations has been essential. Although drone operations are constituted by an enormous network of actors, institutions, hardware, infrastructure, policies, and actions, existing discussions tend to rely on two visual and conceptual shorthands: either the pilotless aircraft itself, or the pilot (and, occasionally, also the sensor operator) at a military site far from the drone's operating area. Holding either of these as representative of drone operations as a whole elides an enormous network of widely dispersed elements: maintenance and launch infrastructure, command and decision-making around target selection, and the technological networks that make that extensive chain possible. Leaving these elements out obscures where decisions are made and how particular targets are selected or created.[35] Yet it also makes it far easier to compare drone strikes to, for example, piloted bombing, with clear consequences for how those strikes are evaluated.

Visually, representing the vast complex of drone warfare in a single image would be challenging; much simpler is the commonly used image of a single drone such as a Predator. Emphasizing this key artifact— a remotely piloted *aircraft*—supports comparisons with other aircraft or closely related weapons systems and platforms. This representational bias has played an essential role in enabling the "confusion between the *form* of the weapon and its *function*," identified by Grégoire Chamayou.[36] Evaluations of legality, ethics, or cost are then implicitly shifted toward comparisons with the use of tools similar in form rather than options that have very different forms but are "currently available for the same tactical function."[37] Thus drone strikes are compared to the use of piloted bombers, rather than to the deployment of special operations teams on the ground or other covert means of achieving the same goal of targeting individual militants. The visual images of aircraft so commonly deployed in reporting on drone operations provide implicit—but essential—support for the overemphasis on similarity in form.

In addition to representing drone operations with the aircraft itself, another common means of representing drone warfare—particularly in narratives about these systems—is through discussions of the remote pilots who do most of the flying and fire the weapons. Although these systems are actually "operated by a whole team of humans . . . [including] multiple technical operators, military officers, and legal advisors,"[38] the pilots have been put front-and-center by both critics and defenders of drone operations.

This symbolic representation has supported specific arguments. Critics have emphasized certain aspects of the pilot's experience, especially the way that flying and firing on targets remotely is similar to a video game, leading to a "playstation mentality" that undervalues the lives of civilians. The US military, for its part, has responded with reports of significant psychological stress among pilots, including reports of them exhibiting a form of post-traumatic stress disorder (PTSD).[39] In both cases, narrowing the focus to pilots implicitly supports those specific arguments and undermines possible responses.

For critics, the callousness of a "video-game-playing" pilot is used to represent the entire targeted killing program.[40] Yet that program actually relies on a vast apparatus of "lethal surveillance," which certainly makes use of drones and remote pilots but is by no means limited to those specific aircraft and operators.[41] The overall system of infrastructure, intelligence, and analysis and its use in targeted killing need to be critically examined, and the entire effort is not as easily subject to the critique that it reduces violence to a video game. If your concern is with the decision to kill individual targets at a vast remove, why focus only on the individual who pushes the button, when so many others are involved in putting that drone in place and in choosing the target? Exclusively using pilots to represent remote operations, however, enables and empowers this particularly evocative critique.

For defenders of drone strikes, on the other hand, focusing on pilots as the key representative of drone strikes has helped to normalize these operations, painting them as convincingly similar to traditional military actions.[42] If drone pilots have PTSD and thus are injured by carrying out their duties, emphasizing the role of the pilot obscures the fundamental asymmetry in physical danger that is inherent to the entire system. Some defenders have even argued that, given this risk of PTSD and psychological harm, drone pilots are displaying military courage.[43] The peculiarity of focusing so closely on the experiences of drone pilots—for both sides of the debate—becomes clear when considering how other military personnel are often discussed, even those who are similarly "pulling the trigger" on powerful weapons: "The drone pilot gathers a level of attention that is not afforded the gunner of the AC-130 or the Apache helicopter."[44]

In addition to the choice of a particular object (a single drone) or specific individual (the pilot) to represent drone operations as a whole, other important narrative representations are constituted by the histories or lineages of drones and their military use. Any narrative of the history of drones is itself a representation, with consequences for how systems are used, for how those uses are evaluated or judged, and for future technological developments.

The most common version of the history of drones and their use focuses on what I will call, for lack of a better term, "no-pilot-on-board aircraft," an awkward but accurate phrase. (As militaries are constantly pointing out—correctly—these vehicles are not currently *un*-piloted, they are *remotely* piloted, and *unmanned* is an unnecessarily gendered phrasing.[45]) The term "drone" itself has been contested, even as it has gained nearly universal use.[46] For military officials and personnel in particular, the term "drone" has pejorative connotations, implying drudgery or suggesting "mindless action."[47] The US Air Force has specifically promoted "remotely piloted vehicles/aircraft," with the clear intention of emphasizing the *piloted* aspect of operations, and thereby tying these systems to the service's long history of pilot skill.[48]

Histories of remotely piloted aircraft are often deployed—intentionally or not—in ways that support comparing contemporary drones to piloted aircraft. This is the "lineage . . . most often assigned by historians or journalists who focus on the aerial hardware."[49] The various historical aircraft considered include remotely controlled target-practice aircraft (appearing from very early in the air age), World War II experiments with un-piloted bombing (e.g., Allied bombers whose crews bailed out after takeoff or German V-1 flying bombs), Cold War surveillance aircraft like the Lighting Bugs used by the United States during the Vietnam War, and finally the gradual emergence in the 1980s and 1990s of the recognizable immediate predecessors to the Predator (particularly in the 1991 Gulf War and in the Balkan conflicts). This story culminates in the test-firing of a missile from a Predator drone—previously unarmed—in early 2001, and then the deployment and use of these systems after 9/11.[50]

Most of these narratives avoid presenting a teleological story of progress, and many emphasize the enormous political contestation around the development and deployment of these devices and the contingency of what eventually emerged.[51] Moreover, what is included in these narratives is factually accurate: aircraft without pilots on board were developed and used in multiple contexts throughout the twentieth century, and some aspects of contemporary drone use can be traced to specific earlier examples.

Nonetheless, overemphasizing this lineage can be misleading. It is only in retrospect that those links appear so obvious or commonsensical—during World War II, for example, even "the possibilities of aerial bombing in war more generally" were still being worked out,[52] so moving from piloted to unpiloted bombing was far from inevitable.[53]

Focusing on the aircraft itself has led to specific debates, especially between those arguing that drones and their uses are new and "disruptive" and others contending that drones simply represent a continuation of various long-term developments.[54] There are political implications of which side one takes on this debate,[55] but more generally I would argue that the entire argument presupposes a narrow focus on the aircraft. When we widen the scope beyond the mere absence of a human pilot, and focus instead on the entire system of artifacts, institutions, and policies, other histories of the drone come to light.[56] Today's drone operations emerge as much out of these other histories as from the developments in remote aircraft technologies.

For one, there are important elements of contemporary drone practice that emerged out of various technological innovations and applications during the Cold War and after, only indirectly related to removing the pilot from the aircraft. During the Vietnam War the United States sought to build an "electronic battlefield," in which US forces would gain total knowledge of the war through networks of sensors and computational analysis.[57] Un-piloted Lighting Bug surveillance drones were a part of this, but it involved far more systems, including networks of sensors meant to track movements along the Ho Chi Minh Trail, an analysis center in Thailand to collate data, and then targeting instructions sent to piloted aircraft on where to bomb. The efforts in subsequent decades to pursue a Revolution in Military Affairs (RMA) laid other foundations for drone operations.[58] The three core features of the RMA—stealth, precision, and information—have little to do with removing pilots from the cockpit.

Other lineages include the history of policies that drones have been put toward, especially targeted killing—assassinating individuals outside of traditional conflict zones.[59] That policy may currently rely on remotely piloted aircraft, but it did not depend, historically or logically, on this specific technological system. Another broad lineage that contemporary drone operations have drawn on is the ability to use force from ever-increasing distances: "remote killing" as a broader concept, in other words.[60] In fact, drone operations have come to involve a particular type of action at a distance: "remote-split" operations. This refers to the way in which the control functions for the system are split across different personnel in diverse spatial locations, all of them remote from immediate danger.[61]

Finally, the *asymmetry* of contemporary drone operations points toward a different lineage, one that highlights the importance of political context alongside technological features in evaluating these systems. Drone technology is not inherently asymmetrical (both sides to an interstate conflict could use drones), but its deployment by US counterterrorism operations has been enormously asymmetrical. Emphasizing this allows us to better situate drone use historically as a particular form of remote violence. Beginning in the late nineteenth century, artillery and other weapons have allowed for firing on targets far beyond visual range, and since then various tools have, as noted above, increased the distance at which violence is exerted. But when we analyze such tools and their legal or ethical implications, it is one thing to think of their use by both sides to a conflict and a very different thing to consider their use in a context where they are only available to one side. Long-distance artillery deployed in wars between state militaries has one set of implications for reciprocity, discrimination between combatants and civilians, and proportionality. Weapons used only by one side—and used in contexts where that one-sidedness is an essential condition for their use—suggest a different set of ethical implications.

Predator-type drones, for example, have long had the potential to be deployed by both sides to a conflict, and they have begun appearing in interstate wars.[62] But those situations are very different from the asymmetrical deployments of US counterterrorism operations since 2001. Many drones are highly vulnerable to standard air defenses, or at least to drone-specific defenses achievable for a state military, especially a military capable of deploying its own drone systems. If possible future developments of drone systems make them less vulnerable, the strategic considerations around their use will start to resemble the piloted aircraft that they may functionally replace. For now, however, how drones have been used, especially in US counterterrorism campaigns, *relies* on the asymmetry afforded by the US military having access to these tools and the other side—networks of non-state actors—having no equivalent or countervailing capabilities. The lack of reciprocity extends to both surveillance and attack: only one side can view or kill the other. This lack of reciprocity is the foundation for the appeal of drones to US officials, for how their effects are evaluated, and for what their future development might be.

That asymmetry suggests a lineage to colonial warfare rather than to traditional interstate conflict, as a number of authors have suggested.[63] Hugh Gusterson has made the case most clearly: "Drone warfare is continuous with a long tradition of colonial war-fighting technologies."[64] As it is currently practiced, drone warfare resembles colonial deployments of force from a distance, which included advanced firearms but also ship-to-shore artillery and bombing civilian populations lacking aircraft or air defenses. It does not resemble the "duel-like" conception of great-power warfare of the colonial era, whether eighteenth-century battles involving maneuver or the trenches of World War I.[65] Like the US use of drones today, colonial warfare was in part built on technological asymmetries: machine guns, for example, were an extraordinary tool of European domination when they were deployed against indigenous forces without such weapons, yielding military domination by one side, the ability to overcome vast disparities in manpower, rapid termination of conflicts, and so on. When those same weapons were used by *both* sides to conflict in World War I, on the other hand, they contributed toward the resulting stalemate and attrition. The lineage to colonial violence can be traced through the twentieth century, including in the electronic battlefield and un-piloted aircraft used by the United States in the Vietnam War—itself an asymmetrical conflict that succeeded France's colonial war.

This lineage to colonial asymmetrical uses of force informs what the various features and policies mean and how they have come together. The defining features of drone warfare today—piloting aircraft remotely, splitting control over vast distances, killing from afar, and targeting individuals—are fundamentally shaped by the context of "radical asymmetry."[66] Asymmetry is foundational to the purported benefits as much as to critiques, and focusing on the representational politics of drones helps to highlight that lineage of asymmetrical context and use rather than the conventional focus on the technological hardware.

Representations Produced by Drones

As well as being represented in particular, consequential ways, drones have also produced an enormous body of representations, most obviously with the novel forms of visual imagery provided by a persistent surveillance platform. Yet the relevant representations extend beyond the actual capabilities of drones. First, in many cases drones' *idealized* capabilities have been more important than their actual capabilities in practice, particularly in terms of the claimed detail, accuracy, and coverage of drone video feeds and the role that those claims have played in discourses about drone use. In other words, the representation *of* drones as providing detailed, complete, and vivid visual information often reflects rhetoric more than reality, and that rhetoric itself has been consequential for drone justifications, critiques, uses, and further technological developments. A second representational process beyond visual imagery involves how the tools, and again the rhetoric around these tools, has allowed for the identification of particular individuals as targets—not just by "seeing" them, but also by producing the very idea that it is possible to identify an individual as a target based on this type of observation. In other words, the legal representation of specific individuals as "combatants" or "legitimate targets" has emerged out of the multiple types of visual and rhetorical representation around drones.

The way in which drones have become a medium for a particular type of vision, by generating specific types of visual representations, has been an important line of study. As Roger Stahl puts it, drones have served as "a *medium* for managing the visual relationship between Western centres of power and the rest of the world."[67] Derek Gregory's discussion of the "scopic regime" constituted by drones and their use highlights the specific "mode of visual apprehension" that drones have made possible.[68] The type of vision afforded by drones is central both to critics—the resemblance to video-game interfaces, for example—and to supporters—vision enabling the claims of precision that justify drone use. In either case, visual representations are essential to the way that "killing is now conducted over an even greater distance and is not only projected onto but also executed *through* a screen."[69]

For supporters, that action through a screen has significant benefits. The drone's ability to loiter and its telescopic view from above provide a level of detail and long-term surveillance that allows for careful targeting decisions that can be more discriminating and civilian-protecting. The sense of "proximity" to the battlefield and possible "intimacy" with those in view is claimed to increase the ability and motivation to distinguish combatants from civilians and to use force in ways that fit better with the laws of war.[70]

For critics, the vision provided by drones has a number of shortcomings that undermine those purported benefits, shortcomings that may be inherent to the technology rather than exceptions.[71] The images provided by drones are often grainy, due to the limits of the cameras and bandwidth or conditions like weather.[72] While the level of detail is impressive, it is usually insufficient for detecting the specific factors essential for identifying individuals or their combatant status, including distinguishing among faces and differentiating between weapons and other objects.[73] The close viewing enabled by drones is, by design, only one-way; targeted individuals are not seeing operators in return, nor can they communicate in any way. Moreover, the video has no audio, yielding silent, "ghostly" images.[74] All of these shortcomings undermine the implicit argument that visual detail, sense of proximity, and a clear overview will give operators more tools and incentives to choose targets carefully and discriminate between combatants and noncombatants successfully.

There are several effects that emerge from the representations created by drones, and how those representations are themselves portrayed. First, even if the visual images provided by drones are extremely detailed (which, again, may often not be the case with the actual technical limitations and specific conditions), that level of detail may have deleterious effects. As Boyle points out, "the provision of vivid imagery from drones may not always be a net positive for decisionmaking."[75] Vivid imagery can lead to false confidence in the information being drawn from it, it can lead decision-makers to place more stock in visual information than in other sources, and it can promote other cognitive or psychological biases.[76] As with the digitization of mapping discussed in Chapter 3, more vivid imagery does not necessarily lead to better outcomes. Second, Gusterson points out that the extended video observation made possible by drones' loitering capabilities can lead to "remote narrativization,"[77] whereby drone operators create stories about the individuals they observe. While it is conceivable that this "construction of narrative . . . makes possible an empathic response" and thus reduces the "moral distance" potentially created by remote operation,[78] it is equally conceivable that those narratives are based on preconceived ideas about the targets' identities, actions, or motivations. Those narrative representations are shaped by the particular characteristics of drones as surveillance tools.

Third, and most consequential, are the effects of how political actors describe and portray the images created by drones—in other words, linguistic representations *of* drone vision. Principal among these are the constant references to drone vision as "precise," with drones portrayed as able to read details as small as license plates. The use of this rhetoric of precise and accurate vision is essential to many arguments in favor of drone use and gives implicit support to assertions that drones are inherently better able to distinguish and protect civilians. So, when Gusterson points out that "the claims of low civilian casualties made by US leaders have intuitive force and plausibility in the context of a drone's technological capabilities,"[79] it would be more accurate to highlight the *rhetoric* around drone capabilities rather than the capabilities themselves, since that rhetoric is often far from the reality. In fact, these "visual technologies are not omnipotent or omniscient, but highly fallible because of the limitations of humans and technology, and within the human-technology relationship."[80] Yet discussions of drones, sometimes even by critics, have taken for granted the technological capability to conduct detailed surveillance by video. A report from Human Rights Watch, for example, emphasizes how drones fail to be sufficiently discriminating or proportionate *in spite of* the "surgical precision" of these systems' technology.[81] The technological precision, in short, goes uncontested.

Discourses emphasizing drones' precision in targeted attacks—that is, the purported ability to hit the specific intended target—thus rely on the implicit assumption that the vision provided by drones is also precise. Yet others have noted that drones' technical capabilities and limitations are essential to understanding whether drones respect the laws of war: "The visual component of drone warfare, and the political context within which it operates, simply cannot deliver the accuracy needed to distinguish between legitimate and illegitimate targets."[82] As the 2010 incident discussed at the top of this chapter revealed clearly, in practice "the images were fuzzy and small objects were difficult to identify."[83] This limitation, however, is only highlighted in these purportedly exceptional cases of mistaken identification, while the general expectation remains that drones provide accurate and detailed imagery.

This representation of drone vision as precise is what has shaped, and maybe even inspired, the contemporary debate about civilian harm: once tools became available that were at least represented as being capable of achieving an extraordinary degree of distinction, then it becomes possible to expect this precision, and thus to argue that drones in practice are not precise or civilian-protecting enough. Similar to many of the political consequences of the telegraph discussed in Chapter 2, beliefs about capabilities may be as consequential as actual capabilities.

One of the most important consequences of this broad acceptance that drones have at least the potential for detailed and accurate vision is the rhetorical support it provides for targeting individuals as "militants" or "combatants."[84] As multiple investigative reports have documented, US counterterrorism operations have pursued two tracks of targeting individuals: "personality" strikes on individuals identified by name and "signature" strikes based on an individual's pattern of life (or signature) revealed by persistent surveillance and signals intelligence.[85] The claim that those patterns are meaningfully observable depends on the purported capabilities of drones in terms of detailed and persistent observation of individuals.[86] In other words, the very category of a militant who can be identified by remote observation alone is *produced* by drone surveillance—or, more accurately, by the rhetoric of drone

surveillance and its technical capabilities.[87] Those rhetorical representations are what have made possible the use of this type of label to justify
individual targeting.

Representing the Future: Autonomous Drones

Focusing on representational processes also has implications for the expected next step in drones: fully autonomous systems. Because truly
autonomous weapons—those that make independent decisions to carry
out attacks—are still largely hypothetical, the discussion takes place at
the level of representations.[88] There are few actual autonomous capabilities, only representations of what those capabilities might one day
be. This makes the debates entirely about assumptions: assumed capabilities, assumed technological development trajectories, and assumed
consequences for conflict, civilian protection, and so on.

The first common assumption is that autonomous systems are inevitable, and once developed, they will inevitably proliferate, at least
among technologically advanced states. One US Department of Defense (DoD) publication, for example, lists a number of inherent
benefits to autonomy that will support its adoption: "AI [artificial intelligence] and ML [machine learning] will allow the development of
systems that are capable of learning and making high-quality decisions
autonomously. This ability to learn will directly result in the development of unmanned systems with greater levels of autonomy, which will
impart expanded and improved functionality."[89] Similar language is
used by scientists working on elements of autonomous systems, drawing on the (sometimes implicit) assumption that autonomous weapons
will simply be better at waging war: "The trend is clear: warfare will
continue and autonomous robots will ultimately be deployed in its
conduct."[90] These kinds of "autonomy will happen" statements appear throughout official and analyst discussions of the issue,[91] but
also in studies critical of future autonomy—critics similarly assume
autonomy to be inevitable, even as they express concerns about its
consequences.[92]

As some critics have pointed out, however, the presentation of autonomy as inevitable serves to normalize one path of technological development, erasing questions of whether it is possible or whether it should be pursued at all.[93] Instead, the debates skip to next-order questions including how to make autonomous systems comport with the laws of war. Proposals for programming an "ethical governor" into autonomous weapons build on this logic: autonomy is inevitable, it needs to be made to fit with the laws of war, so a technological solution to that problem should be the goal.[94] Yet critiques of an algorithmic solution to targeting issues note the possibly insurmountable challenge of coding software to follow the laws of war, given "the incompatible nature of combining absolutist [don't use weapon X] and consequentialist [don't do Y if it leads to Z] frameworks."[95] This, again, serves to naturalize the pursuit of such capabilities. "Whether that goal [a successful ethical governor] can ever be achieved (which is unlikely) is far less important than its rhetorical role in making the case for developing autonomous systems."[96] In other words, the representation of autonomous systems as inevitable is what is doing the work, in terms of supporting research and planning for those systems, normalizing their possible use, and then reducing the debate to questions of whether (or how) such systems can be made to fit with the existing international legal frameworks.[97] The "discursive construction of future weapons systems as truly autonomous agents" is a representational process central to the entire pursuit.[98]

Even defining what constitutes autonomy is challenging and involves a host of assumptions and possibly arbitrary decisions about where to place the threshold for full autonomy. Most studies define autonomy as existing along a spectrum, from a decision completely under human control; to automatic systems, which perform a clearly understood action once set to do so; to (hypothetical) autonomous systems, in which "the weapon system, not a person, selects and engages targets."[99] Yet this spectrum may oversimplify how human-machine interaction already works, and what it would be like with "more autonomous" systems. For example, some DoD publications emphasize the "collaboration between the computer and its operator/supervisor" as the actual goal. Similarly, analysts drawing on STS have highlighted the way that supposedly autonomous systems will be part of "a complex assemblage involving human and technical organizers,"[100] just as human operators currently exist within an assemblage of other humans and machines. Moreover, the notion of a clear threshold—a line distinguishing between, on the one hand, automatic systems that behave deterministically and thus predictably and, on the other, autonomous systems that behave nondeterministically and thus unpredictably—belies the complexity and sometimes impenetrability of the systems that already exist, and the likely persistence of deterministic programming at the foundation of even highly complex future systems.[101]

Regardless of the definitional challenge of drawing a clear threshold for autonomy, the decision-making processes of weapon systems may eventually be complex enough to be "effectively autonomous," to be perceived as making their own decisions rather than following clear-cut and predictable rules. This shift—even if it is in part at the level of representations rather than true autonomy—will change the nature of the separation or distancing between the use of lethal force and the human(s) most closely involved with the targeting and firing decision. Existing remotely operated drone systems already create an enormous geographic distance between operators and targets, thereby increasing the moral or ethical distance for the operator. This may allow targets to be seen as less human or make it more likely that civilians are interpreted to be combatants.[102] Autonomy of the type envisioned by proponents, however, would yield further distancing, in two ways.

First is the increased separation in time between some of the key decisions by humans and lethal actions by autonomous systems. Current drone operations have a temporal separation, but it is limited to the lag produced by the communication link—several seconds at most. With systems programmed to "make their own decisions," someone has programmed them, with complex rules about how to follow specific directives, choose targets, engage them, and so on.[103] The human doing that programming works at a significant separation in time: months or years could pass between when the code is written and the autonomous system carries out those if-then decisions resulting in engagement with a target. Even the operator who gives the autonomous system an order for engagement will be separated by a significant amount of time from the targeting and firing decision.

Second, the complexity of the programming, and the difficulty of following exactly *how* the system has made its decision, yields another novel form of distancing with hypothesized autonomous systems: an enormous cognitive separation created by *unintelligibility*. With effectively autonomous weapons, the decision process may be unintelligible to the operator, or in the case of a system without an operator directly monitoring it, unintelligible to the commander who gives the system its orders. If those individuals do not understand how the system takes the input (direct orders or general instructions) and yields a particular output (i.e., decides on a target or engagement), that increases the distance between the closest human and the use of lethal force.

In the case of machine learning (one of the likely routes toward autonomous systems), the decision-making process may be unintelligible even to the system's programmers. "Machine-learning systems, particularly those that run on deep neural networks, could be said to operate like 'black box' systems: the input and output of the system are observable but the process leading from input to output is unknown or difficult to understand."[104] Or, as a report from a DoD science advisory group states the problem: "the sheer magnitude, millions or billions of parameters (i.e., weights, biases, and so on), which are learned as part of the training of the net . . . makes it impossible to really understand exactly how the network does what it does. Thus the response of the network to all possible inputs is unknowable."[105] This makes the system fundamentally unintelligible to the humans operating it, or even to those who designed it.

These two additional forms of distancing that autonomy would yield have implications for how future systems are compared to existing remotely operated drones. Proponents of drone autonomy have argued that it is the geographic distance between pilot and target enabled by remote operation that is ethically problematic, implying that when the decision-maker is the weapon itself this geographic distance will have disappeared—along with the ethical challenge.[106] Yet the novel forms of distancing revealed here—separation in time and in comprehensibility—may be even more dangerous. They would create a further "moral buffer" by providing "a sense of remoteness . . . allow[ing] humans to act through a device to reach a particular goal instead of having to act on a sentient being to achieve this same goal."[107] At least remote operation presents the possibility—however unlikely, and often undermined by operator biases and prior beliefs—of some kind of "empathic bridging" through persistent surveillance.[108] Autonomous systems, in short, would displace and perhaps amplify this problem.

Moreover, the unintelligibility of autonomous systems—particularly those based on machine learning—logically precludes any meaningful human control. Both militaries and activists emphasize the importance of some form of potential human control, often put in terms of features like predictability, reliability, transparency, and accountability.[109] The DoD has also emphasized the need to always have "appropriate levels of human judgment over the use of force," by being "understandable" and providing "traceable feedback."[110] Yet an inevitable paradox emerges. Consider a 2017 DoD report, which states as a tactical benefit that "elevated levels of autonomy will increase the decision speeds of unmanned systems and allow them to perform tasks that require decision cycles faster than human reaction time." It also argues that "autonomous systems must exhibit run-time transparency, and be capable of explaining decisions and actions, as well as communicating goals and plans in a concise and usable format to human operators."[111] "Run-time transparency" is meaningless, however, if the decision cycle is faster than humans can follow, and "explaining decisions" is often impossible for machine learning systems. Any effectively autonomous system—any system that can be represented as "making its own decisions" in spite of its code having been written by someone—will likely fail to meet the criteria for meaningful control.

So the real challenge is the separation between the use of lethal force and the human decisions that lead to that use of force—separation through time and unintelligibility, in the case of the supposedly inevitable autonomous systems. But separation, in space, in empathy, and so on, has always been a key challenge in making war ethical or lawful. Given the "automation bias" already evident with existing automatic systems (i.e., those clearly falling short of autonomy), many of the challenges of losing meaningful control are already here.[112] We should stop trying to draw a firm line between some imagined future of autonomous weapons as problematic in a novel way and instead recognize that, as they actually would be developed, those weapons would exacerbate the existing ethical dilemmas of distancing.

Unaccountable Weapons for "Ungoverned" Territories

Focusing on a clearly delineated future shift to autonomous systems obscures how force is already being used in ways that, except for the technological element, exhibit many of the features and dangers of hypothetical autonomy. For example, many of the US military agencies responsible for covert operations are subject to complex forms of oversight, potentially obscuring their internal workings regardless of the military tools used.[113] This yields organizational rather than technological black boxes where inputs (broad direction in terms of counterterrorism or counterinsurgency) are translated, in ways sometimes not well understood by higher levels of command, into outputs (operations against specific targets). Or there is the "algorithmic" nature of the broader security and targeting complex, in which there is often no single human decision that is directly responsible for the use of force, but instead a complex and largely unintelligible process.[114] Those concerned about the loss of meaningful control in future autonomous technologies should also worry about existing forms of fundamentally nontransparent, unaccountable uses of force, all of which increase the distance—in multiple forms—between a political or military decision-maker and the end result.

All of these distancing technologies, organizations, and processes connect to one of the key drone genealogies discussed above: a lineage to colonial forms of violence. Both then and now, the essential context has been asymmetry, both material and social: the technological capabilities of the weapons and their application in specific settings. In nineteenth-century imperialism, it was colonial spaces where opposing forces had no access to industrial weaponry; today the setting is "ungoverned" territories where denial by air power or anti-aircraft weapons is limited and slow-moving drones can be flown with relative impunity.

Yet the ungoverned nature of those territories is not merely observed and represented through drone surveillance; drone strikes have helped to make or keep those spaces ungovernable.[115] Targeted killing as a practice has significantly undermined the legitimacy of governments in targeted areas like parts of Yemen and Pakistan: "The appearance of powerlessness in the face of drones is corrosive to the appearance of competence and legitimacy,"[116] and governments that allow drone strikes within their territory can be "delegitimized" by that action.[117] In other words, everything about drones and their use is shaped by the fact that they are deployed in ungoverned spaces, from the ability to fly undefended low-speed drones to the inability for outsiders to easily gather information on civilian causalities. And a major impact of drone use is to reinforce those characteristics, thus making drones continue to be the only ready option for applying state power to these spaces. In short, "ungovernable spaces are produced"[118] by drones and their representations—drone vision, representations of drones, and drones as a symbol.

A further parallel with imperial uses of technologies is in the way that drones have been used to represent broader concepts or normative commitments, primarily the idea of a "civilized" form of warfare. As Chapter 2 demonstrated, in the nineteenth century both weapons and nonmilitary technologies were held up as symbols of European superiority, a representation that served to justify their use in colonial contexts.[119] Today, drones fulfill a similar symbolic function, serving as a "sign of American strength."[120] Not just strength, however, but because of their purportedly more discriminating and proportionate uses, drones are also held up as symbols of a specifically *ethical* form of warfare.[121] This supports a narrative of a modern, civilized military confronting uncivilized opponents.[122]

Representations, thus, are essential to understanding the concept of the drone, drone warfare, and broader drone uses today. As with digital mapping and cybersecurity, descriptions, images, labels, and other representations have changed the consequences of the information technology revolution in dramatic ways. These lessons extend beyond the specific three fields discussed here, as is explored in the next, concluding chapter.

6

Conclusion

Representing the State

ACROSS THE CASES DISCUSSED IN this book, from diverse periods and involving various forms of information technology, representational processes have been central to reshaping political contestation, institutions, and identity. This concluding chapter begins by reviewing the three representational dynamics that run throughout the book—representations produced by technologies, representations of technologies, and technologies themselves as a representation of something else—and by expanding on the consistent role of affect in how those representations work. These dynamics allow us to rethink the technology–politics intersection overall and the nature of international relations theories themselves. I then explore how representations suggest a redefinition of the concept of the state itself, and I conclude by considering what the book suggests about the nature and trajectory of contemporary international conflicts.

Virtual Territories. Jordan Branch, Oxford University Press. © Oxford University Press (2025).
DOI: 10.1093/9780190063658.003.0006

Technological Representations, Affect, and Their Effects

Information technologies have produced numerous forms of representation, from visual to textual. Many of these have reshaped interests, interactions, ethical debates, and the evaluation of outcomes, driving institutional and behavioral change. In the nineteenth century, censuses served as a novel form of representation of the state's entire population, and cartographic techniques produced new visual images of national identities, reinforcing state centralization. In imperial spaces, statistics and maps created important representational tools of administration from afar. In the digital era, mapping has created new virtualized territories, reshaping the negotiating processes involved in drawing boundaries. Drones have provided a particular form of "vision" essential to the persistent and targeted surveillance of individuals. The purported accuracy of these images has been highlighted by proponents as a fundamental improvement in the ability to distinguish between civilians and combatants, while critics have emphasized the limits of such imagery in practice.

Representations of these same technologies have similarly played key roles across the cases in this book. The impact of the telegraph in the nineteenth century was not only practical but also ideational, as the representation of the telegraph as instantaneous and connecting supported arguments for national cohesion and imperial centralization. Digital mapping's impact was also in part driven by how these systems have been perceived and understood: the expectation of immediacy and precision has driven negotiators to fixate on the smallest calculations of territory, and the sense of realism in virtual terrain systems has provided much of their rhetorical power. The politics of cybersecurity have been even more fundamentally shaped by representations of the internet and related systems, as the metaphors implicit in the very terms used have provided rhetorical tools for particular interests. The term "cyberspace," in fact, preceded the modern internet it came to describe, emerging out of fiction but later shaping real-world policy discussions and, more recently, military doctrine and planning. Finally, discussions of drones are entirely about representations: representations of a singular pilot or remote aircraft, of a video-game mentality, of imagery as precise or grainy, and of a possibly autonomous future.

Finally, technological systems themselves have often been deployed, intentionally or not, as representations of broader concepts or identities. Nineteenth-century Europeans held up their technological achievements as a measure of civilization and superiority, justifying global imperial domination. Censuses and maps were powerful symbols of state consolidation and authority. At Dayton, high-tech US mapping technology was a potent symbol of US capabilities, given that the most evocative systems had literally been used to plan bombing missions. Cybersecurity doctrine—and the very recognition of this as an important domain for military competition—has become a demonstration of a government's technological sophistication, seen in global imitation of US institutions. And similarly to nineteenth-century technological discourses, drones work symbolically as signs of sophistication and superiority—with the additional layer of claiming to be more humane, more ethical in terms of protecting noncombatants.

Across these diverse representational dynamics, the role of affective or emotional processes repeatedly appears, suggesting a novel perspective on the study of emotion in international politics. A growing body of IR research has demonstrated that emotions and affect reshape information processing, calculations of risk and cost, the use of analogies, and receptivity to particular arguments.[1] Although these processes often operate "below conscious awareness,"[2] they can be manipulated strategically by political actors: displaying affect for others to observe, shaping others' affective responses, and so on.[3] While this IR scholarship has rarely connected affect with the politics of technological change,[4] emotional and affective processes are integral to technological development. At the individual level, "every tool is known through the body. We develop a feel for it."[5] That "feel" of a technology can shape decisions involving that system, altering both technological innovation and the processes of political interaction through or around technology.

In all the cases examined in this book, the affective "feel" inspired by or tied to particular technologies has played an essential role. The importance of the telegraph in the nineteenth century relied not only on the actual ability to communicate rapidly at great distances— revolutionary even if often limited in practice—but also on the *feeling* of control that this gave officials in centralizing states and imperial centers. At Dayton in 1995, the positive affective valence attached to the "fun" experience of using novel digital mapping systems was a core part of those technologies' appeal, and it was essential to the negotiators being convinced by the information presented. The use of drones for targeted killing is likewise shaped by how the technologies provide a feeling of detailed and accurate observation, precise targeting, and thus an ethical means of remote killing—practical limitations and repeated mistakes notwithstanding.

Moreover, terminology and its effects are structured by affective elements. The very choice of "cyberspace" as the label for global information networks reflects an affective appeal that this term and its implicit spatial metaphors have for government and military officials, and the rhetorical power of that term likewise has drawn on the positive affect inspired by the notion of a virtual space within which actions take place. Similarly, when the US Air Force discusses a prospective autonomous aircraft as a "wingman," assisting and subordinate to a human pilot, this suggests something more familiar and comforting than a fully independent autonomous system.[6]

As such examples illustrate, affective and linguistic processes are often closely linked. Because many primary metaphors for complex concepts are "derived from bodily experience"[7]—and emotion and affect are somatic, or embodied[8]—the structuring effect of language and metaphor often relies on emotion.[9] Methodologically, linguistic elements like discourses may be one of the most readily available ways to study affect and to observe its role in political processes.[10] For example, the discussion of cyberspace in Chapter 4 suggests how to move beyond the simple contention that emotions matter in IR to understand one particular route for how and why they matter.

With the digital technologies discussed in this book, the affective or emotional impact often relies on *virtualization*: the creation of artificial replicas of real-world spaces, processes, or interactions. Virtualization is far from new—simulations and representations have long been applied with mapping, mathematical modeling, and other forms[11]—but the evocative and realistic nature of digitally enabled virtualizations marks a significant departure. Digitization has in some cases blurred the line between simulation and real-world phenomena, particularly in the feel of systems such as remotely operated weapons.[12] The affective reactions to territories, groups, or individuals shift with realistic virtual depictions rather than abstract representations. While virtualizations, especially in the military context, have always been promoted as technical tools that enable the more efficient pursuit of existing objectives,[13] in fact the effects are more complex and often involve the symbolic or emotional power of virtualization more than any practical benefits.[14]

Focusing on representations, in short, reveals factors (such as affect) that are often overlooked in conventional IR studies of these technologies and their effects. How state actors negotiate over territory is deeply shaped by representations, not just by the various types of value—intrinsic or symbolic—that particular territories might have in a bargaining model of negotiation. The "revolutionary" nature of cybersecurity for international politics is structured by the terminological representations brought to bear as much as by the technical features of global networks themselves. And the numerous debates about the ethics and legality of drone strikes are shaped by the representations of drones and the expectations that those create—only a weapon represented as exceedingly precise could be expected to achieve the exacting standard of civilian protection to which drones are sometimes held.

In addition, this book's core contention—that representations are everywhere in international politics, and increasingly so—also has implications for the theoretical tools we use in the academic discipline of IR. In other words, just as Bially Mattern argues that "emotions may shape not just world politics but also our knowledge of it," so too do representations shape our theories and arguments.[15] Nearly all theories emphasize some form of complexity—from realism's complex calculations of power, to liberalism's intricate trade and information networks, to constructivism's recursive transformation of political identity. Like complex technological systems, these conceptual frameworks require representation to be comprehensible. Sometimes this takes the form of visual images such as diagrams and flow charts, with their obvious simplifications, but representation also operates when metaphors are consistently applied—the billiard-ball model of the state, for example. Representations are necessary and are not inherently problematic, but we should recognize the work that they do in building and rhetorically supporting competing arguments.

Representations and the State

Focusing directly on representation and its interaction with techno-logical systems can thus bring new perspective to core IR theories and concepts, well beyond the specific cases in this book. The following ex-plores one such possibility: rethinking the concept of the state, as well as other political institutions.[16] Specifically, we can reconceptualize states as the combination of three elements: *rules* about organization, author-ity, and action; material *infrastructures* of control and communication; and *representations* in visual, linguistic, and other forms. In other words, a political institution is not just the "rules of the game" for interaction; it also involves the material tools of interaction and the methods of representing those interactions.[17]

Defining states as the combination of diverse elements draws on existing arguments positing that organizations or institutions are con-stituted by disparate components.[18] Thus I emphasize the interplay of material and ideational factors, shifting away from the traditional priv-ileging of rules and ideas as what the state *is* and material tools and representational practices as what a state *does*. In other words, most studies of the state that incorporate infrastructural and representational technologies present those elements either as *tools* of state power; as *causes* of state formation, persistence, or failure; as *signs* or observ-able measures of the state's existence or features; or as the *effect* of the state and its actions. Instead, I argue that the state *is all three*: rules, infrastructures, and representations.[19]

The first element is the *rules* about organization, authority, and in-teraction that states embody, or are expected to embody. Much of the existing discussion in political science has focused here, emphasizing the history of sovereignty as a concept, how society and state are under-stood to be distinct, and the shift over time to a purely spatial-territorial concept of how political claims are separated.[20]

Those rules are then put into practice by *infrastructures*, technologi-cal systems that do more than provide material conditions for statehood or state action. Instead, certain infrastructures can themselves be con-sidered a component of statehood, just as much as the rules defining sovereignty, legitimacy, or territory.[21] For example, Mann's history of political organization distinguishes between the "despotic power" to command across a range of actions and "infrastructural power" comprising "the capacity of the state . . . to implement logistically political decisions throughout the realm,"[22] dependent on the "routinized media through which information and commands are transmitted."[23] Similarly, Mukerji's concept of "logistical power" emphasizes large-scale infrastructural projects,[24] and Guldi's study of the British "infrastructure state" explores how "political activity is engendered by changes in infrastructure" like road networks.[25]

Political organization has always been constituted by infrastructures of control, and modern states are particularly infrastructural (as is modernity writ large), relying on information, communication, transportation, and bordering technologies.[26] Taxation requires recordkeeping, dependent on some form of material information storage and retrieval. The Weberian state's *successful* claim of a monopoly on the legitimate use of force requires the ability to support such a claim at a distance, through road networks, ship technology, and later railroads and further mechanized transportation systems.[27] Modern state infrastructures are especially focused on implementing the ideal of linear borders. Although territorial ideas developed earlier, it was only when those borders were materially instantiated that statehood took on its contemporary spatial form.[28]

The third element of statehood is composed of the *representations* that embody the state and that allow actors to make sense of what the state is or should be. The state as rules is unobservable, and the material infrastructures of the state are vast and difficult to grasp in their entirety. Instead, when actors think about, discuss, and enact the state they deploy a host of representations—from visual imagery in mapping, to linguistic terminology, to written legal descriptions.[29] While existing research on the emergence of the state has incorporated representations such as cartography,[30] here I push this connection further, moving beyond the argument that "mapping made the state," so to speak, to argue that mapping *is* (part of) the state. Thongchai's work on national identity in Siam/Thailand can be read through this lens: the country's "geobody" existed less in demarcated boundaries on the ground than in a variety of map representations, from careful surveys to "logo maps" of the country's outline. Or consider Mitchell's study of late nineteenth- and twentieth-century Egypt.[31] As land was mapped in increasing detail for taxation, the site of governance moved from the land itself to the "map room," where the representational artifacts (i.e., maps) were stored, examined, and measured.

While mapping is central to the territorial nature of statehood, other representations also constitute the state, including the nineteenth-century developments in statistics and censuses discussed in Chapter 2. Furthermore, at the level of international law, representations in legal conventions and concepts define a part of what makes a modern state. The 1933 *Montevideo Convention* posits that "the State as a person of international law should possess the following qualifications: (a) a permanent population; (b) a defined territory; (c) government; and (d) capacity to enter into relations with the other States."[32] For the international dimensions of sovereignty and statehood, this legal representation is essential—what is and is not recognized as a state is part of what constitutes statehood.

Existing arguments often focus on the *effects* of these infrastructural and representational technologies on state-building. Again, here I suggest shifting our perspective to how these systems themselves are part of the state. Especially when we think about something like borders, it is hard to conceptualize the territorial nature of the state without including infrastructures and representations. The *rule* of clearly delineated territories alone is not what shapes international politics. What matters is the combination of the hegemonic status of that rule (states are supposed to be defined by boundaries) with the ways in which the rule is instantiated and represented materially.

This three-part concept of statehood helps reframe questions in several areas: the emergence or origins of statehood; the persistence of most—though not all—states in spite of numerous contemporary challenges; and the nature of historical, existing, or hypothetical alternatives to the state.

Looking for single origin of "the state" is impossible, even if we were to maintain the conventional focus on rules.[33] Including infrastructures and representations further highlights the diverse histories of the state's components, allowing us to trace when and how each emerged and came to be embedded in the state. Then we can parse out the relationships among the components of statehood within the evolution of this institution over time, seeing each take on its modern form by different logics. In other words—and admittedly contrary to how my earlier work framed this question[34]—we could move away from asking if certain representations or infrastructures were drivers of state formation and instead ask how, when, and why they have constituted part of state formation itself.

This concept can also shed new light on the challenges to statehood posed by contemporary globalization—or at least bring a fresh perspective to the discussion. Much of this debate has started by identifying particular features of contemporary politics, society, or economics that undermine or threaten the state, framed largely in terms of *rules* of statehood such as the claim to exclusive control within boundaries. Thus boundary-crossing or boundary-erasing threats undermine a state's claim to control its territory, or changes in the logic of collective action due to the increasing scale of market activity undermine the effectiveness of the state as a political means to manage those activities.[35]

Yet the state, mysteriously, persists. This becomes less mysterious when we think about the state as composed of more than rules. While challenges may undermine the idea of exclusive, centralized authority, a more complex picture emerges when we include infrastructures and representations. Certain infrastructures of statehood are threatened by globalization, but others are strengthened by those same forces. For example, global networks have eroded the ability of some states to control information within their borders, but they have also given strong states new opportunities to exercise informational surveillance and control.[36] An even greater disconnect exists between representational aspects of statehood and the weakening ideas of the state. Supposedly state-undermining globalization processes have not created or supported new representations that are able to challenge the territorial state in maps, language, or international law. There are few if any representations of alternatives to the state that are as evocative and convincing as the mapped territory.[37] Thus the state survives, as its representational element remains strong, perhaps even hegemonic, as a means of depicting and thus understanding the political world.

Even the states that have "failed" in recent decades can be understood through this lens. Such states have fallen short of "full" statehood in different ways: some no longer exert authority successfully over the entirety of "their" territory, while others face no competitors within their boundaries but do not have the expected type of state capacity.[38] This is often framed in terms of a failure to live up to the expected ideal of statehood. For example, studies of areas of "limited statehood" examine deficits in legitimacy, defined as "the population's sense of obligation or willingness to obey the authority."[39] While this captures part of the nature of state failure or weakness, it misses other, essential elements. As Peer Schouten provocatively argues, state failure may be as much about *material* shortfalls as it is about the failure of a social contract between ruler and ruled.[40] Thus state failure involves both a weakened social contract *and* the absence, removal, or destruction of material infrastructures.

Finally, this concept helps explain the absence of significant alternatives to territorial statehood—that is, organizational forms that could directly replace the state. For one, it is difficult to imagine an alternative that would operate as successfully across all three elements. How could we represent new possibilities for political organization in a more convincing fashion, in a world socialized to accept the nation-state map? Part of why the existing way of mapping became so closely integrated with the state was because it was taken up for a variety of purposes, motivated by commercial, scientific, and artistic as well as political goals.[41] New representations thus need to be more than a novel way to depict a nonstate form of organization; they also need to be convincing and appealing enough to be incorporated into how an organization is identified, and how it identifies itself.

The absence of readily identifiable alternatives to the state, viable across all three dimensions, does not mean that the state is immutable. Tensions and contradictions between the three elements may eventually yield significant institutional change. Thus, while today the dominance of the mapped image of the state supports its persistence, over time the tension between that representation and weakening ideas of territorial sovereignty and national identity, as well as the increasingly complex digital infrastructures of governance, could be sources of transformation.

This concept could be extended to other large-scale institutions, beyond the state. How do those institutions function in terms of rules, infrastructures, and representations? The United Nations, for example, is both a collection of rules (goals of cooperation and peaceful conflict resolution as well as procedures for membership, voting, and decision-making) and a host of infrastructures and representations. The UN flag, for example, was explicitly designed to embody and reinforce those ideas.[42] Informal institutions or international regimes can also be understood through this lens. Global trade, for example, rests not only on a collection of rules about liberalization, reciprocity, and comparative advantage but also on the material infrastructure of containerized shipping and the linguistic representations of trade as an inevitable feature of modernity. Even when some of the core rules of liberal trade have been threatened or undermined by policy changes (such as the shift toward explicit protectionism by the United States), the physical infrastructures of trade were more likely to be jeopardized by material factors (such as COVID-era supply chain disruptions).

Finally, conceptualizing institutions in this way suggests that closer conversation between STS and IR might provide analytical benefits for STS, not just for IR.[43] If institutions are assemblages of components including material infrastructures and representations, then the relevant technological systems—often the subject of STS—may follow patterns of change and persistence noted by IR studies of institutions. For example, the variety of ways in which institutions transform over time identified by historical institutionalism could apply to large technical systems: layering of old and new, drift from one set of goals and practices to another, and so on.[44]

Virtual Territories

Expanding our definition of the state also takes us back to the core discussion of this book: how technological change interacts with statehood through representations. The longstanding discussion of the driving force of warfare in historical statebuilding—"how war made states, and vice versa," in Charles Tilly's phrase—can be reframed through this book's lens.[45] Representations of war helped to create the state, and the state is itself in part a representational product of warfare. Today, major wars may have declined, but imagining and planning for warfare continues. The ways in which contemporary and future war is represented, then, will have significant impacts on the possible transformation of the state, just as representations have always been central to this dynamic.

In the ongoing conflicts of the moment—Israel-Gaza, Russia-Ukraine, and more—representational systems are more integrated than ever into how these wars are fought, justified, and criticized. The use of precision weapons in massive numbers on civilian centers, the deflection of (some) targeting decision-making onto algorithmic systems, and the ever-increasing volume of images and video in official propaganda and individual social media reporting merely represent some of the most prominent examples. All of this takes place through representations, of digital tools and using them.

Key territories of contestation are becoming virtual—through realistic and evocative representations, through territorializing discourses applied to digital networks, and through the undermining of traditional territorial divisions through remote or even autonomous warfare. To understand the implications of these virtualizations, we need to recognize the importance of representations, both through technology and of technology. Only then does the full array of implications for states and their future trajectory emerge.

Notes

Chapter 1

1. The following discussion draws on media reports on these systems, particularly Abraham (2024); McKernan and Davies (2024); and Davies et al. (2023).
2. Abraham (2024).
3. Abraham (2024).
4. McKernan and Davis (2024).
5. Abraham (2024).
6. Abraham (2024).
7. Davies et al. (2023).
8. Davies et al. (2023).
9. Abraham (2024).
10. McKernan and Davies (2024).
11. Davies et al. (2023).
12. Naksashima and Ryan (2016).
13. Clinton (2015).
14. Nakasone (2019b, 12).
15. Holbrooke (1998, 283).
16. PSU (2010, episode 3, chapter 1, 3:15).
17. To clarify: there is an enormous difference between viewing a video of an actual aerial fly-over of particular terrain (which is of course subject to choices of routing, visual filters, zoom, etc.) and viewing terrain on a virtual system like these. Both are representations, but one is a visual representation of the world using (possibly manipulated) imagery and the other is *entirely constructed* through implicit and explicit choices about coding, data sources, user interface, etc.
18. This suggests that there are two counterfactual scenarios for negotiating such a specific boundary, both of which would have significantly different

effects from the use of this representational system. The principals could have negotiated over traditional paper maps, at an excruciating level of detail, but that would have left Milosevic without that convincing feeling that the existing offer was impractical. Alternatively—in theory if not actually possible in this case—the principals could have been flown in a helicopter over the actual territory being discussed. Even then, however, the outcome could have been different. Only with the use of a constructed and manipulable digital representation can the feeling of actual terrain be so *strategically* deployed, as the US mediators did, to achieve an agreement.

19. Hutchison (2016, esp. ch. 3) offers an excellent summary of the discussion of representation and its application to international politics. See also the discussions among historians of representation and cultural practices (e.g., Hansen 2015, 3–9).

20. Among the many constructivist approaches that emphasize language, discourse, and rhetoric, I have found especially useful Onuf (1989), Kratochwil (1989), Milliken (1999), Risse (2000), and Krebs and Jackson (2007).

21. Enloe (2014); Daggett (2019); Onuf (1989; 2013).

22. Bousquet (2009).

23. Allen (2018).

24. Useful reviews are provided by Herrera (2006), Fritsch (2011), Mayer et al. (2014), McCarthy (2017).

25. With some exceptions, of course, even very early ones. For example, Robert Gilpin's early work examined the role of science and technology policy in national competitiveness broadly (e.g., Gilpin 1975). See also Skolnikoff (1992), which considers twentieth-century technological changes and their possible effects on international politics. See below for more recent work that reverses this trend.

26. For thorough reviews of how the major theories of IR differ in their (often implicit) approaches to technology, see in particular Fritsch (2011, 35–39); Herrera (2006, ch. 2); McCarthy (2015, ch. 2); Carr (2016, ch. 2); Mayer et al. (2014, 15–18); Hoijtink and Leese (2019, 5–8). For an IR-inflected appraisal of determinism, see Dafoe (2015). The following paragraphs draw on these accounts. Note that this dichotomy may seem dated as an analytical framework from the perspective of other fields such as science and technology studies, many of which have moved on productively to other debates about technology and society. Yet it does reflect the framework brought to IR (albeit often implicitly), and it thus continues to shape how technology is understood in this particular field.

27. As discussed in McCarthy (2015, 22–23).

28. As Herrera (2006, 28–29) argues about how neorealism understands nuclear weapons and McCarthy (2015, 29) notes with regards to globalization theory.

29. A huge body of literature across academic disciplines has considered the significant transformations in information technologies in recent decades, often emphasizing the importance of digital computing. Manuel Castells, for example, emphasizes "electronics based technologies, microelectronics, computers, and telecommunications" and the "networking logic" that has made those technologies pervasive (Castells 1996, 41, 61). See also, from international relations, Deibert (1997, ch. 5); and, from a security-studies perspective, Weidmann (2015, 264).

30. There is also an instrumentalist interpretation that emphasizes how new technologies empower non–state actors, rather than states. In terms of the implications for states, however, this reads as a somewhat deterministic argument: states are being undermined by technological change. Many of these arguments instead temper their predictions of state decline with a recognition of the ways in which state capacity is also sometimes increased by new technologies.

31. Most prominently in Waltz (1979).

32. E.g., Schweller (2014, 25–26). Note, however, that Schweller combines this view with some discussion of how non-state actors are also empowered by new technologies. Both points, however, are implicitly instrumentalist.

33. Reviewed by McCarthy (2015, 29). To be fair, much of this discussion does not take an explicitly deterministic approach to technology. Yet it builds on an implicit set of ideas about technological change and other aspects of globalization having effects on states that are largely exogenous to the political processes of institutional change. See Farrell and Newman (2019) for a useful critique of this broad approach, not in terms of technological change but instead in terms of globalization's institutional transformation more generally.

34. Mayer (2017, 124ff) highlights this, labeling it as the problem of "externalism." See also McCarthy (2015); Fritsch (2011).

35. On bringing STS and IR together, see Herrera (2006); Fritsch (2011); Mayer et al. (2014); Mayer and Acuto (2015); Mayer (2017); McCarthy (2017); Nexon and Pouliot (2013). For a useful illustration in one field (cybersecurity), see Balzacq and Dunn Cavelty (2016).

36. For a helpful overview of STS for nonspecialists, see Sismondo (2010). Work that I found particularly useful includes Winner (1977; 1980); Feenberg (2002); Jasanoff (2004); Bijker et al. (2012); and Smith and Marx (1994). While different approaches within STS do view the relationship between technology and politics in different ways, here I am simply building on a series of core insights shared across much of the STS literature. Those core insights are sometimes framed in different ways by different STS traditions, and there are true disagreements about the relative importance of, say, social or material factors. In terms of suggesting adjustments to how IR approaches technology, however, the commonalities within STS are helpful to highlight.

37. Winner (1977, 323).
38. Mayer (2019, 87), italics in original.
39. Singh (2019, 3). See also Evans et al. (2017).
40. As Adler-Nissen and Drieschova (2019, 9), define them, affordances are "possibilities for action—i.e., how an object or technology both enables and constrains the tasks that users can possibly perform with it." Their article is especially helpful on applying this concept to international politics.
41. E.g., as Lindsay (2020a) does with regards to military organizations' use of information technology.
42. Lynch and Woolgar (1990) is a key text in how the field of STS has approached representation. (See also Coopmans et al. 2014 for a later reevaluation.)
43. Lynch and Woolgar (1990, 13).
44. Lynch and Woolgar (1990, 5).
45. Lynch and Woolgar (1990, 1).
46. Hutchison (2016, 113, 114).
47. Bleiker (2018). The well-documented role of the map image in constituting state sovereignty and national identity is merely the most obvious example (e.g., Thongchai 1994).
48. Bleiker (2018, 3). That edited volume covers an enormous range of types of visual politics.
49. Scott (1998) does not make this connection to representation explicitly, but any number of representational devices and practices are central to his argument about how states see what they seek to control. See Adler-Nissen and Drieschova (2019) for an extension of this argument, building directly on Latour's concept of *inscriptions*: "the technologies through which actors seek to translate the messiness of the world—in the laboratory, the battlefield or the market—into tangible knowledge that is concrete and visible enough for governing purposes" (Adler-Nissen and Drieschova 2019). See also Latour (1986). Chapter 2 of this book illustrates these concepts in more detail in the context of their role in nineteenth-century imperialism and state-building.
50. Hutchison (2016, 117ff). In fact, these forms of representation are so prevalent that their importance often goes unnoticed.
51. Laffey and Weldes (1997, 210). For a discussion of the problematic nature of "representing" sovereignty and the state in IR theory, see Weber (1995).
52. A position from the history of political thought argued by Quentin Skinner (1978, xiii).
53. On representation and affect, see Hutchison (2016).
54. Onuf (2013, 208). See Chapter 2 for more discussion of this from a historical perspective.
55. Nye (2006, 4); see also Drieschova (2017, 20). For overviews of the discussion of emotion in international relations, see, among others,

Crawford (2000); McDermott (2004, ch. 6); Mercer (2010); Sasley (2010; 2011); Hutchison (2016); and the 2014 forum in *International Theory* 6(3).

56. Particularly relevant here is the work of Bruno Latour (1986; 1987; 2005), discussed in more detail in Chapter 2. Political contestation is shaped both by who is arguing what and by the various "allies" that are brought to bear, including representational artifacts that Latour calls *inscriptions*. These inscriptions are made more powerful when they are more *mobile*—able to be brought from one setting to another—and increasingly *immutable*—repositories for "harder facts" (i.e., settled and no longer debated). See also Mitchell (2002). The notion that nonhuman things can be "allies" in arguments is one of the more contested parts of Latour's actor-network theory. Interpreted broadly, however, this simply emphasizes the role of tools—including representational tools—in what is otherwise seen as a matter entirely of ideas or rhetoric.

57. As the case studies in Lynch and Woolgar (1990) demonstrate.

58. As Nye (2006, 3) puts it, "the meaning of a tool is inseparable from the stories that surround it."

59. Mosco (2004, 29).

60. Rogers and Hill (2014, 6), drawing on Marshall McLuhan's model of a probe.

61. The book generally follows the logic of *abduction*, which suggests that the researcher take theoretical arguments and concepts that are logically convincing and apply them to a new area or set of phenomena. See Friedrichs and Kratochwil (2009) for a thorough discussion of abduction, and Lindsay (2020a) for a suggestive application. The goal of this method is to discover "patterns of similarity and difference within a complex field," with an emphasis on identifying the conditions of possibility for particular outcomes rather than isolating causal effects (Friedrichs and Kratochwil 2009, 719; for earlier foundations see Hacking 1975).

62. Farrell (2012, 36), discussing how to study the internet in political science.

63. On the challenge of defining technology, see among many others Carr (2016, 19); Nye (2006, 15); Bimber (1994, 87–88).

64. E.g., technologies as "specific objects intended for a function, such as machines, devices, and tools" (Dafoe 2015, 5).

65. For example, "the practical application of knowledge especially in a particular area," https://www.merriam-webster.com/dictionary/technology (accessed January 9, 2017).

66. As Winner (1977, 11–12) puts it, the "whole body of technical activities."

67. Fritsch (2011, 28).

68. Software, for example, is not exactly a material artifact (though it is instantiated in physical storage or computing media), nor does it fit in the *completely* nonmaterial category of ideas and practices. Yet it is increasingly

consequential in the same ways that tangible artifacts are (Kitchin and Dodge 2011).

69. Note that the three contemporary case studies are largely US-focused. The United States has been a first-mover in many technological areas, particularly in the deployment of technologies for state purposes. For all three contemporary issues—remote warfare with drones, geospatial intelligence, cybersecurity—the United States has played an outsized role in how new technologies have been used and their interaction with politics. These cases nonetheless illustrate mechanisms around representation that can be identified in other intersections of technological and political change.

Chapter 2

1. While today we commonly designate this category as information and communication technologies (or ICTs), an unintended anachronism in this term is itself revealing: "Until the mid-nineteenth century, 'communication' referred equally to the movements of information and of physical goods" (Otis 2001, 1). The word "information," on the other hand, has seen its modern usage from at least the fourteenth century (OED Online). As discussed below, it was the telegraph that first allowed a significant amount of information to be sent by means other than transporting—or *communicating*—physical media.

2. In other words, the goal of this chapter is not to provide a novel historical interpretation of the broad sweep of nineteenth-century international politics. Instead, I draw on a synthesis of secondary work across academic disciplines in order to highlight the role of representations of and through technologies.

3. What Mann (1984) calls "infrastructural power."

4. See Osiander (2007) for one convincing argument *against* the effort to find a singular moment of state emergence. This is also explored more in Chapter 6.

5. As emphasized by Abernethy (2000).

6. Sharman (2019), Conclusion.

7. Although this is contested. For example, Wallerstein (1974) argues that the key features of the modern world system emerged in the sixteenth century, and have only changed in less fundamental ways since then.

8. Standage (1998) is the classic study along these lines, but numerous others have made similar points (e.g., Deibert 1997, ch. 5). Note that the accuracy of this comparison has also been contested (Müller 2016).

9. Mosco (2004).

10. Deibert (1997, 117).

11. Buzan and Lawson (2015).

12. Deibert (1997, ch. 5); Blum (2012).

13. Vitalis (2015).
14. E.g., Macdonald (2014); Sharman (2019); Phillips and Sharman (2015).
15. Buzan and Lawson (2015, 255).
16. Deibert (1997, 2) even notes the correlation between significant changes in the prehistoric archeological record and "physiological changes in the vocal tract that permitted the spoken word"—a biological information technology.
17. Scott (2017, 144).
18. Jasanoff (2004).
19. Mann (1986); Ferguson and Mansbach (1996).
20. See Abernethy (2000) for an overview of the waves of European colonial expansion and contraction. See Burbank and Cooper (2010) for a sense of the global nature of early modern imperialism.
21. Crosby (1997), 227.
22. Biggs (1999); Branch (2014); Stransbjerg (2008). See also Deibert (1997).
23. While this book does not use Latour's terminology, it is useful to situate my argument in the context of his work and that of other science and technology scholars who have highlighted the complex integration of ideational and material factors in creating and circulating representations. (See especially Latour 1986; 1987; 2005.) Political contestation is shaped both by who is arguing what and by the various "allies" that are brought to bear, including representational artifacts that Latour calls *inscriptions*. These inscriptions are made more powerful when they are more mobile—able to be brought from one setting to another—and increasingly immutable—repositories for "harder facts" (i.e., settled and no longer debated). Their power operates in *centers of calculation*: locations of contestation, planning, and governance where inscriptions can be used to argue about, understand, and attempt to control phenomena from afar. Politics in the modern era involves exercising rule through the use of various such centers of calculation—from an official's desk, to a council chamber, to a government agency. Given that decision-making beyond the immediately local level inherently relies on representations of subject territories, resources, or people, those representational inscriptions are essential to governance.
24. Mitchell (2002, 115).
25. Hostetler (2001).
26. Turnbull (1996, 7).
27. As seen in particular with the *relaciones geográficas* of the late sixteenth century (Mundy 1996).
28. As Benton (2009, 30) notes: "both law and geography produced ways of structuring understandings of empires as configurations of corridors and enclaves, objects of a disaggregated and uneven sovereignty." Representations shaped understandings—and practices—of colonial rule.
29. Sharman (2019).

30. Cosgrove (2001). As Brotton (1997, 19) argues, maps during this period were "valued for their ability to operate within a whole range of intellectual, political and economic situations, and to give shape and meaning to such situations."
31. Brotton (1997, 57).
32. Zandvliet (2007, 1445, 1446).
33. Abernethy (2000).
34. Sharman (2019).
35. Phillips and Sharman (2015, ch. 5).
36. See Headrick (1981) for the classic study of technology and nineteenth-century empire. Maier (2016) offers a useful overview of this argument applied to state-building.
37. This argument, again, does not deny the importance of various technological capabilities in military force, communication, and so on. Instead, it draws on the broader argument that changing ideas of imperial or state-building legitimacy were *also* integral (Sharman 2019). As the following demonstrates, many of those legitimating ideas relied on representations of and through technologies.
38. Maier (2016, 11).
39. Bayly (2016, 2).
40. Bayly (2016, 39).
41. Deibert (1997, ch. 1).
42. This point draws largely on Adas (1989) and Adas (2006).
43. Adas (1989, 3).
44. For example, Adas (1989, 153) argues that racial theories of empire were made to fit with this technological comparison, rather than the former driving the latter. Relatedly, Bell (2021) demonstrates that racial and technological justifications for empire were closely interwoven.
45. Adas (1989, 144).
46. Adas (1989, 9).
47. Adas (2006, 1–5).
48. E.g., Maier (2016, 11); Headrick (1991, 11).
49. As Bayly (2016, 3) demonstrates with regard to British representations of Afghanistan.
50. See, among many others, McNeill (1982); Headrick (1981); Maier (2016); Sharman (2019).
51. See Herrera (2006) on the international politics of nineteenth-century railroads.
52. Maier (2016, 187).
53. As Adas (1989) makes clear.
54. New weapons had a complex relationship with imperialist ideology: see, e.g., Mize (2018) for the "conspicuous absence" of these tools from British colonial military painting of the era.
55. McNeill (1982, 163).

56. See McNeill (1982, 217ff).
57. Hansen (2015, 68).
58. Of course, any number of other technologies, at various scales, could also be analyzed in this way. For example, Barder (2016) demonstrates the importance of barbed wire as both a tool and a symbol of imperialism and conquest, and the resulting lineage from late-nineteenth-century practices to the present day.
59. On the history of statistics, see among many others Hacking (1990), Haggerty (2002), Desrosières (1998).
60. Consider, for a famous example, the eleventh-century *Domesday Book*, which catalogued, manor-by-manor, William the Conqueror's new realm in England.
61. Hacking (1990, 18, 2).
62. Hacking (1990, 29).
63. Anderson (1991, 168).
64. Curtis (2001, 18); see also Hacking (1990, 34).
65. Maier (2016, 191).
66. Haggerty (2002, 99).
67. Latour (1986, 28).
68. Desrosières (1998, 117).
69. Anderson (1991).
70. Curtis (2001, 36).
71. Shirk (2019); see also Haggerty (2002, 99).
72. Hacking (1990), 18. See also Desrosières (1998), ch. 6.
73. Agar (2003, 119).
74. Curtis (2001, 32).
75. As Kalpagam (2014) demonstrates in the case of British India.
76. Patriarca (1996, 4–5).
77. Patriarca (1996, 3).
78. Patriarca (1996, 125).
79. Patriarca (1996, 177, 208).
80. Patriarca (1996, 4).
81. Bayly (1993, 33).
82. Bayly (1993, 26).
83. Bayly (1993, 34).
84. Allen (2018, 117ff).
85. Allen (2018, 134).
86. Anderson (1991, 174). See also Thongchai (1994).
87. Branch (2014).
88. Benton (2009).
89. See Mitchell (2002) for an example of this from early twentieth-century Egypt, as mapping moved the "practical activity" of land measurement out of the field and into the map room.

90. This draws on Hansen (2015).
91. Hansen (2015, 53).
92. Hansen (2015, 3).
93. Hansen (2015, 14).
94. Hansen (2015, 10, 14).
95. This case relies on Edney (1997); for some related points see also Bayly (1993, 34).
96. Edney (1997, 15).
97. Edney (1997, 32), italics original.
98. Edney (1997, 17).
99. The parallels are highlighted most prominently by Standage (1998), but Wenzlhuemer (2013, 5–7) documents a wide range of arguments along these lines. As the latter points out, however, there are a number of important differences: the nature of the informational content that was possible, who had access to the new communication system, the different roles played by human mediators within each system, and the more prominent way in which physical distance continued to matter far more in telegraphy. On the "dematerialization" of information, see Wenzlhuemer (2013, 9).
100. On the political and social history of the telegraph, see among many others Wenzlhuemer (2013); Headrick (1991). Müller (2016) provides a survey of recent literature.
101. Headrick (1991, 12).
102. Headrick (1991, 24).
103. Wenzlhuemer (2013, 76).
104. Bayly (2004); Buzan and Lawson (2015, 69); Wenzlhuemer (2013, 9).
105. As Yang (2010, 23) notes with regard to post–Meiji Japan.
106. Winseck and Pike (2007, 338).
107. Winseck and Pike (2007, 338).
108. Bayly (1993, 5, 14).
109. Bayly (2016, 20–21).
110. Innis (1950).
111. Carey (2009, 163ff); Wenzlhuemer (2013, 78); see also Headrick (1981).
112. Headrick (1991, 68).
113. Winseck and Pike (2007), arguing against this interpretation.
114. Numerous works have problematized the traditional narrative, including Winseck and Pike (2007); Wenzlhuemer (2013); Hayles (2012); Ogle (2015).
115. Carey (2009, 165).
116. E.g., the descriptions quoted in Headrick (1991, 3) and Bell (2005, 554–556).
117. Hayles (2012, 124).
118. Ogle (2015, 204). An interesting sign of nineteenth-century Europeans' "obsession with long-range communication" was in how they perceived

others' capabilities, such as the reported practice among Africans of using "talking drums" to communicate. "Europeans inflated this phenomenon into a great myth, that Africans could speak to one another across their continent by the throbbing of tom-toms in the night" (Headrick 1981, 207).

119. Wenzlhuemer (2013, 214).
120. On the optical telegraph, see especially Field (1994).
121. Field (1994, 323); Wenzlhuemer (2013, 64–65).
122. For a detailed discussion of the French optical system, see (Field 1994).
123. Field (1994, 321); Wenzlhuemer (2013, 63).
124. Headrick (1991, 11).
125. Field (1994, 320).
126. Carey (2009).
127. Field (1994, 341).
128. Field (1994, 341).
129. Headrick (1991, 11).
130. On the telegraph and diplomacy, see among others Headrick (1991); Nickles (2003).
131. Headrick (1991, 75).
132. Nickles (2003) demonstrates this across a number of issues.
133. Illustrated most directly by US diplomacy with Europe before and after the working transatlantic cable was laid in 1866 (Nickles 2003, 72ff).
134. Nickles (2003, 34).
135. Nickles (2003, 47ff).
136. Headrick (1991).
137. Nickles (2003, 93).
138. Headrick (1991, 139–140).
139. Wille (2016, 166).
140. Wille (2016, 170); comparing how the United States dealt with diplomatic recognition of new French governments in 1848 versus in 1870.
141. For example, in 1931 a Belgian diplomat grew alarmed at US president Hoover's use of a radiotelephone, fearing that diplomats would no longer be needed when heads of state "can discuss matters almost face to face" (Nickles 2003, 10). There are interesting parallels here to the concerns some diplomats have expressed regarding the replacement of face-to-face diplomacy with remote interactions through the internet. As Chapter 3 explores in the context of digital mapping and boundary negotiations, however, new tools have often been most consequential by *reshaping* face-to-face meetings, not by replacing them.
142. Headrick (1991, 105).
143. Yang (2010).
144. Siefert (2020).
145. On this metaphor see especially Otis (2001) and Bell (2005).
146. Carey (2009, 166).

147. Otis (2001, 1).
148. Otis (2001, 13, 22).
149. Otis (2001, 12, 19).
150. Otis (2001, 120).
151. Otis (2001, 121).
152. Lakoff and Johnson (1980); Agar (2003).
153. Yang (2010, 15, 22).
154. Bell (2005, 553).
155. Otis (2001, 49).
156. Headrick (1991, 52). But see Winseck and Pike (2007) for an interpretation that emphasizes commercial motivations and actors even in imperial telegraphy.
157. Adas (1989; 2006).
158. Yang (2010, 5, 8).
159. Yang (2010, 11).
160. Yang (2010, 406).
161. My discussion here draws extensively on Bell (2005).
162. Bell (2005). Note that this had followed a reimaging of the meaning of distance *within* Great Britain during the expansion of railroads earlier in the nineteenth century (Bell 2021).
163. Bell (2005, 526).
164. Bell (2005, 539).
165. Bell (2005, 560).
166. Bell (2005, 528).
167. Bell (2005, 528).
168. Bell (2021).
169. Bell (2005, 528).
170. E.g., Buzan and Lawson (2015).
171. Mosco (2004).

Chapter 3

1. An extensive body of research has examined dispute origin, persistence, and termination, including the possibility of negotiated resolutions. E.g., Goertz and Diehl (1992); Lustick (1993); Huth (1996); Goertz et al. (2016).
2. Wood (2000, 78, 76).
3. Clinton Digital Library (1996, 13).
4. This definition is from the *History of Cartography* project (Harley and Woodward 1987, xvi). It is usefully expansive and includes the high-tech (Geographic Information Systems, Google Earth, etc.) as well as the low-tech (such as hand-drawn sketches). While I discuss technologies that are themselves not strictly representational or graphical, such as GPS devices, I do so in the context of how they have become embedded in digital mapping. For example, the GPS system on its own is concerned

with coordinate location and position finding, not graphical representation, but it is employed extensively to create and use cartographic representations. (See Rankin 2016 for a thorough discussion of GPS itself as a "nonrepresentational" technology.)

5. Negotiations over other issues—resources, trade policies, legal jurisdictions, and so on—also sometimes rely on maps, but those uses remain outside the scope of this chapter. However, some of the potential interactions between the cartographic tools used and the processes and outcomes of negotiation explored below might also appear in this broader category of all negotiations that use maps.

6. E.g., Harley (2001); Crampton (2010); Pickles (2004); Wood (2010).

7. The idea of "maps as communication devices" was promoted in the mid-twentieth century by scholars such as Arthur Robinson, who hoped to make the study of mapmaking "scientific" (Crampton 2001, 235). This view has been largely abandoned in the academic study of mapping. Note, however, that mapping techniques today do rely on computing and other "information and communication technologies" (ICTs).

8. Crampton (2001, 246–249); Kitchin et al. (2012, 494–495).

9. See Branch (2014, ch. 6).

10. Ross and Stillinger (1991, 391).

11. Hopmann (1996, 28–30). The literature on international negotiation is vast; particularly useful works include Hopmann (1995; 2002); Iklé (1964); Kremenyuk (1991). See O'Neill (2018) for a review.

12. Hopmann (2002, 69).

13. Hopmann (1995, 25–26).

14. E.g., Fearon (1995, 390–395); Powell (2002, 23–26).

15. Iklé (1964, 59–60).

16. Iklé (1964, 167–172).

17. On prospect theory in international relations, see Levy (1997); Boettcher (2004); McDermott (2004); and Mercer (2005), among many others.

18. McDermott (2004, 140).

19. Mercer (2010, 2); Holmes and Yarhi-Milo (2016); Holmes (2013).

20. Sasley (2010, 689, 690, italics in original).

21. McDermott (2004, 64); see also Mercer (2010, 8–10).

22. Walter (2003); Shelef (2016).

23. E.g., Barston (2013, ch. 4).

24. E.g., Bjola and Holmes (2015).

25. E.g., Purdy et al. (2000). One of the few exceptions is Adler-Nissen and Drieschova (2019), which looks specifically at the effects on diplomatic practices of digital writing and text-editing tools.

26. Holmes (2015, 13).

27. E.g., Pigman (2010, 109–120).

28. Cohen and Meerts (2008, 153).

29. Some focusing explicitly on this issue (e.g., Wood 2000) and others discussing it more incidentally.

30. My point here is not to caricature a position that might be easily dismantled—the arguments presented in these studies are carefully considered and offer an accurate description of some of the potential effects of digital mapping. Yet they leave out a significant portion of the possibility space of what digital mapping can do to disputes and negotiations over territory. Those other possibilities are what this chapter explores in detail.

31. Blake (1995, 48). This distinction between "propaganda" and "properly surveyed" maps builds on a progress-focused understanding of the history of cartography, which has been critiqued extensively (e.g., Crampton 2001; Harley 2001; Wood 2010). In short, all maps have inherent distortions, emphasizing certain things and eliding others.

32. Corson and Minghi (1996).

33. This short essay (Wood 2000), quoted also at the top of this chapter, is one of the few studies to directly examine the issue of digital mapping and territorial negotiation. It bears close reading because it lacks a complete picture of the context-sensitive and potentially ambiguous effect of digital cartography's new capabilities. The Geographer's office is tasked with providing mapping support to US diplomats and also with determining official US positions regarding international boundaries.

34. Wood (2000, 72).

35. Wood (2000, 78, 76).

36. Wood (2000, 77).

37. Claussen (2009, 258).

38. While many government mapping systems are classified and thus cannot be easily examined, commercial technologies suggest how government technologies are used, and state actors sometimes use publicly available tools or systems closely emulating them.

39. Miller (2006, 191–193); Crampton (2010, ch. 3).

40. Individuals judge outcomes based in part on how easily information regarding those outcomes can be recalled (McDermott 2004, 63).

41. Ross and Stillinger (1991, 398).

42. Iklé (1964, 213).

43. Schelling (1960, 54–58).

44. Schelling (1960, 58).

45. Hassner (2006/2007, 125).

46. Pinfari (2013, 5).

47. On the history and politics of GPS, see Rankin (2015; 2016).

48. "An equal exchange does not feel equal to either side; each side would only feel comfortable with an unequal exchange that benefitted itself" (McDermott 2004, 139).

49. Dalton (2013, 265). On the international security implications of remote sensing in general, see (Avtar et al. 2021).

50. Leslie (2016, 173).

51. Lindsay (2010, 647).
52. See Kuhn (2008) on the metaphors built into many digital mapping systems.
53. Shim (2018).
54. Hegarty et al. (2009, 182).
55. Sheppard and Cizek (2009, 2104, 2107); Perkins and Dodge (2009, 557–558).
56. As, for example, in the use of satellite imagery by NATO to argue that Russia was behaving aggressively in Ukraine in 2014 (Shim 2018).
57. On the link between emotions and the visual, see Bleiker (2018, 9–11).
58. Sheppard et al. (2008, 4).
59. E.g., Goodchild (2007); Haklay (2013). This democratization is of course limited, especially in terms of the availability of enormously useful tools like satellite imagery. Although NGOs and other non-state actors have used remote sensing, only the most well-resourced can afford extensive and up-to-date imagery. See Rothe and Shim (2018).
60. Rankin (2016).
61. Leszczynski (2012, 80–83).
62. Livingston (2015, 5); see also Olbrich and Witjes (2015); Rothe and Shim (2018).
63. Livingston (2015, 25).
64. See, for example, the literature on "digital diplomacy": Dizard (2001); Bjola and Holmes (2015).
65. Kaye (n.d., 8–9).
66. Goddard (2010, ch. 2).
67. Kumar (2010, 159–165).
68. Perkins and Dodge (2009, 556); Quiquivix (2014).
69. Leszczynski (2012, 79, 82); Dalton (2013, 265); Rankin (2015).
70. Wood (2000, 78).
71. Leslie (2016, 183).
72. An idea proposed by, among others, Claussen (2009, 276–277).
73. Kaye (n.d., 1).
74. Johnson (1999, 1).
75. On these challenges, see Hopmann (2002); Matz (2004); and Holmes and Yarhi-Milo (2016).
76. The available information on mapping at the Dayton negotiations comes from general sources on the negotiations and from a few brief reports specifically on mapping. The latter include Johnson (1999), Hasik (2008, ch. 6), and Corson and Minghi (1996). One of the main general sources is Richard Holbrooke's (1998) book on Dayton, which is of course problematic because it is the memoir by one individual with a particular point of view and interests (Hopmann 2002, 76). There is also a declassified internal report from the US State Department (US Department of State 1997), as well as a collection of internal State

Department documents (available at the Clinton Digital Library: https://clinton.presidentiallibraries.us/collections/show/37). Information on mapping is sprinkled throughout these general sources. Although this represents a significant body of material (especially when compared to other cases of digital mapping in negotiation), it still generates an array of challenges. First, nearly all the material is very US-centric in terms of authors, focus, and so on. Very little is reported directly from the three Balkan delegations on their use of, or reaction to, the new digital mapping systems. In addition, the American sources rely on an overlapping set of materials: Holbrooke's memoir was written in conjunction with the State Department internal report (with very similar structures and impressions), and most of the declassified primary documents served as sources for those two secondary works. Second, it is difficult to get a clear cross-time picture of a single issue or discussion. Ideally we would have information on how negotiations over a particular issue proceeded before and after the introduction of a digital mapping tool (since these systems, while present in Dayton from the beginning, were sometimes brought to bear only at a particular point). Unfortunately, the level of detail in existing reports is inadequate for this task. Finally, the challenge of parsing out what commentators *expected* to see in terms of the effects of digital mapping from what may have actually been the impact is difficult, given that some of the core sources were written by individuals who were at Dayton specifically to provide technical mapping support (e.g., Johnson 1999). Thus, when a US mapping expert at Dayton writes that "digital mapping became a core tool, used wisely, that contributed significantly to the success of negotiations at Dayton" (Johnson 1999, 2), this is not necessarily false, but it is exactly what we would expect his analysis to conclude. The more general sources on Dayton do not share the explicit goal of highlighting technical novelty, but it could be that the apparently "shocking" and impressive nature of new mapping tools has increased the emphasis placed on them post facto.

77. Formed in 1972, the military DMA was merged in 1996 with other mapping and imaging agencies to form the National Imagery and Mapping Agency, renamed the National Geospatial-Intelligence Agency (NGA) in 2003.
78. Johnson (1999, 2).
79. Holbrooke (1998, 280–281); US Department of State (1997, 229–230).
80. Johnson (1999, 2).
81. Hasik (2008, 100).
82. Johnson (1999, 3–4).
83. Corson and Minghi (1996, 34–37); Hasik (2008, ch. 6); Johnson (1999, 2).

84. Holbrooke's next-day memo to Secretary of State Warren Christopher mentions "the substantial amount of scotch consumed by many of the group" (Clinton Digital Library 1995d).

85. Watters (1996).

86. US Department of State (1997, 232); see also Holbrooke (1998, 283).

87. Johnson (1999, 1).

88. Johnson (1999, 2). Only in some of the lower-level negotiations that followed Dayton is there evidence of direct, hands-on use of digital tools, unmediated by printouts and pencils.

89. Crampton (1996, 359).

90. Holbrooke (1998, 291–293).

91. Spatial calculations were performed by technical aides, for whom GIS "delivered an incredible relief from drudgery" (Johnson 1999, 4).

92. A body made up of representatives from the United States, the United Kingdom, France, Germany, and Russia.

93. Clinton Digital Library (1995a).

94. Clinton Digital Library (1996, 13). Note that this first-hand account (from Chris Hoh of the State Department) does not match some other narratives (such as Holbrooke 1998, 294), which instead cite a poster highlighting Federation gains (and containing the 55–45 figure) as what alerted Milosevic to the shift in percentages. In either case, the calculation was done by the DMA mapping team, using GIS tools.

95. Crampton (1996, 358).

96. Johnson (1999, 5).

97. What does not appear at Dayton is the *focal point* issue noted earlier—more likely in a negotiation over a boundary through less well-known and emotionally charged territories, in which finding a common focus would be helpful.

98. US Department of State (1997, 196).

99. Clinton Digital Library (1995b; 1995c). See also US Department of State (1997, 216, 219).

100. Holbrooke (1998, 101).

101. US Department of State (1997, 206). US delegation memos report the same, "shouts, anger, highlight talks" over maps (Clinton Digital Library 1995b).

102. As is explored most effectively by Thongchai (1994). See also Krishna (1994); Batuman (2010); Kumar (2010).

103. Holbrooke (1998, 283).

104. Watters (1996).

105. Clinton Digital Library (1995d).

106. Clinton Digital Library (1996, 13).

107. Mercer (2014, 524).

108. For example, Libicki (1997, 56) describes the Serbians as being "visibly shaken" by the display.
109. Clinton Digital Library (1995d).
110. Mapping agencies have found that principals sometimes request that official maps contain specific features that they have used on Google products. Yet the tendency remains for technicians to operate the more complex systems and for principals to observe (UN GIS interview, August 23, 2017).
111. In 2016 the company launched versions of Google Earth for several virtual reality platforms.
112. "Ethiopian Foreign Minister Reaffirms Desire for Normalization Talks with Eritrea," April 7, 2006, http://wikileaks.org/plusd/cables/06ADDISABABA941_a.html (accessed December 16, 2016).
113. Abbink (2003, 223).
114. Péninou (1998, 48).
115. Guazzini (2009, 128). See Ciampi (2001) on the difficulties in delineating this border based on historical sources.
116. See http://dehai.org/demarcation-watch/ (accessed May 19, 2025).
117. EEBC (2006, para. 19).
118. EEBC (2006, para. 20).
119. UNSC (2008, Annex II, para. 11).
120. EEBC (2006, para. 20, 23–26).
121. E.g., Kaikobad (2009, 218).
122. UNSC (2008, para. 23).
123. E.g., Kaikobad (2009, 220–221). For a more positive analysis, see Claussen (2009, 275–277); see Rankin (2016, 197) for a different interpretation.
124. Kaikobad (2009, 221).
125. Claussen (2009, 277).
126. Kaikobad (2009, 221).
127. Indeed, this is why Rankin (2016, 285) argues that the EEBC's decision is far from novel or particularly transformative—many consequential boundaries or spatial markers in today's world are not physically instantiated. As he effectively points out, the coordinate grid of GPS may not be visible without a device, but neither is it an abstract representation like a map. Instead, "GPS has created a parallel reality: an intangible knowledge space of electronic points that shares space with the physical world but does not refer to it. In many cases it can even take precedence" (Rankin 2016, 280).
128. "Vea la foto satelital de Google y ahí se ve la frontera" (Look at the satellite photo from Google and there one sees the border); Jacobs (2012).
129. Jacobs (2012). See also Merel (2016).
130. Mackey (2010).
131. Geens (2010).
132. Jacobs (2012).

133. Jacobs (2012).

134. Kaye (n.d., 3).

135. Gravois (2010); Merel (2016).

136. *The Economist*, September 4, 2014.

137. Merel (2016).

138. Rankin (2016; 2015); Quiquivix (2014).

139. E.g., Goddard (2010); Hassner (2009); Toft (2003).

140. E.g., the rapid expansion of the US National Geospatial-Intelligence Agency (Ambinder 2011).

141. Crampton et al. (2014); Crampton (2015).

142. Crampton (2015, 3).

143. Nakashima and Warrick (2013). On the geospatial implications, see Crampton (2015).

144. Dalton (2013, 268).

Chapter 4

1. Benedikt (1991, 1), © Massachusetts Institute of Technology, by permission of The MIT Press.

2. DoD (2011, 5).

3. Joint Chiefs (2018, xii).

4. Nakashima (2019); Sanger and Perlroth (2019).

5. On the history of cybersecurity as a policy area, see, among many others, Healey (2013); Warner (2012).

6. E.g., Buchanan (2016); Choucri (2012); Demchak and Dombrowski (2011); Gartzke (2013); Kello (2017); Lindsay (2013); Rid (2013); Valeriano and Maness (2015). A wider array of approaches has also emerged, relating cybersecurity to internet governance (DeNardis 2014; Raymond and DeNardis 2015), securitization (Hansen and Nissenbaum 2009), STS (Dunn Cavelty 2018), norm development (Finnemore and Hollis 2016), history (Healey 2013; Warner 2012), territoriality (Herrera 2007; Lambach 2019; Sheniak 2014), and language (Dunn Cavelty 2013; Lawson 2020; Lupovici 2016).

7. Following Raymond (2019, 36), I combine constitutive and causal claims, addressing first how it has been possible to construct cybersecurity threats in specific ways and then why certain institutional and policy responses have followed.

8. Lakoff and Johnson (1980, 5).

9. Lakoff (1992, 205).

10. Gibbs (2008); Lakoff and Johnson (1980); Lakoff (1992); Semino (2008).

11. Khong (1992); also Bousquet (2009); Drulák (2006); Lawson (2014); Onuf (2013), ch. 3.

12. Semino (2008, 5). On conceptual metaphor theory: Lakoff and Johnson (1980).

13. Larsson (2017, 7–8).

14. Semino (2008, 33).
15. Many metaphors are "not noticed as being metaphorical" (Lakoff and Johnson 1980, 27).
16. Determining how consistently and by whom is difficult. A foundational metaphor *exists* when a speaker uses a term with metaphorical implications, observable in surrounding text. That metaphor is *consequential* when it is used widely in a community (see below for more).
17. Focusing on rhetoric sidesteps the contested argument that metaphors directly shape thought. Semino, e.g., argues that, while we are not "completely blinkered and straitjacketed by the metaphors we conventionally use ... in some cases we may be," supporting a "weak version of the Sapir-Whorf hypothesis" (2008, 33).
18. Crawford (2002, 13).
19. Sandholz (2008, 103).
20. Krebs and Jackson (2007, 42, 45).
21. Khong (1992).
22. The effects of foundational metaphors can be distinguished from other linguistic processes by two elements. First, here *metaphors* implicitly connect otherwise distinct concepts, defining a narrower scope of meaning-making than narratives, norms, or rules. Second, the importance of *implicit* meanings differentiates this from securitization (Buzan et al. 1998) or instrumentally using a label—e.g., *combatant*—with explicit legal or normative consequences (Kinsella 2005). Yet foundational metaphors often work alongside other processes: narratives or stories, for example, help define policy problems, but "the framing of problems often depends upon metaphors underlying the stories" (Schön 1993, 138). Among the diverse ways in which social facts shape contestation, foundational metaphors are distinguished by being metaphors implicit in shared terminology.
23. Lustick (1993, 55) discusses this with reference to political contestation in general.
24. Krebs (2015, 5).
25. It is difficult to set a threshold on *how widely* a term must be accepted. Nonetheless, when multiple sides to an ongoing debate use the same terminology—implying the same metaphorical correspondences—that community's language has at least provisionally been settled. While never permanent, language often remains stable for identifiable periods.
26. E.g., studies suggesting "cyber analogies": Goldman and Arquilla (2014); Greathouse (2014); Karas et al. (2008); Manjikian (2015; 2016); Nye (2011); Perkovich and Levite (2017). For analysis: Betz and Stevens (2013); Dunn Cavelty (2013); Graham (2013); Lapointe (2011); Lawson (2012); Libicki (2012); Stevens (2016).
27. For critical discussions of this analogy, see Gartzke (2013); Goldman and Arquilla (2014); Lawson (2020); Stevens (2016); Schneider (2021).

28. Dunn Cavelty (2013) is closest to my approach, examining language both "setting the linguistic rules of the game and . . . used instrumentally" (118). I focus on metaphors implied by terminology *used* by decision-makers, rather than the *creation* of available "threat representations."
29. Kamis and Thiel (2015, 4).
30. Karas et al. (2008); Lapointe (2011). Betz and Stevens (2013, 149) note that "cyberspace" may represent cybersecurity's "ur-metaphor."
31. Semino (2008, 6).
32. Larsson (2017, 28). The next section demonstrates this in the US case with *cyberspace* and *domain*.
33. Rid (2016, 209ff); McCaffery (n.d.). Although he later acknowledged that the source for the "cyber" part of the term was the word "cybernetics," Gibson admits he had little knowledge of cybernetics and its ideas (see below for more on connections to cybernetics).
34. Gibson (1991, 27).
35. Mueller (2017a, 418).
36. Gibson (1984, 69).
37. Gibson (1984, 69). For discussion, see Edwards (1996, 308) and Stone (1991, 104).
38. I.e., systems by which a user, often wearing a headset monitor and possibly other gear, "moves within" a virtual space. See Rid (2016, 219–220).
39. Rid (2016, 195–196), which notes the importance of these two publications, draws a clearer line around the conceptual change, arguing that 1991 marked a significant transformation. I think the two texts actually show more of a gradual evolution, albeit with a strong hint of what is to come.
40. Benedikt (1991).
41. Benedikt (1991, 122).
42. The transitional character of this publication is illustrated by the fact that most of the articles in the issue do not use cyberspace terminology, and some instead discuss networks in nonspatial terms.
43. Edwards (1996, 19–20); Rid (2016, 219–220).
44. Barlow (1996).
45. Silverman (2015).
46. E.g., Goldsmith (1998); Johnson and Post (1996); Lessig (1999). Commentary: Blavin and Cohen (2002); Cohen (2007); Hunter (2003); Lemley (2003); Yen (2002).
47. Lessig (1996, 1403).
48. Lakoff and Johnson (1980, 17).
49. Maglio and Matlock (1998); Matlock et al. (2014). See also Cohen (2007, 212); Hunter (2003; 444); Larsson (2017, 29ff).
50. Contingent origins do not preclude path-dependent effects: e.g., the QWERTY keyboard (David 1985).
51. Rid (2016).

52. Hunter (2003, 473).
53. Vinge (1981); Vinge (2001, 20); Rid (2016, 206ff).
54. The Google Books Ngram Viewer shows a post-2000 decline (Wagner 2019, 61). See also Graham (2013, 178); Betz and Stevens (2013, 150).
55. Graham (2013, 178); see also, e.g., Betz and Stevens (2013, 150); Thomas (2013, 9).
56. For how many definitions combine tangible networking hardware and intangible information, see Rajnovic (2012). For definitions more focused on the experiential aspects, see Dodge (2008, 15); Thomas (2013, 7).
57. Healey (2013, 280); but see Futter (2018) and Lupovici (2016).
58. Arquilla and Ronfeldt (1993, 57); Lindsay (2017, 494); Rid (2016, 3).
59. Arquilla and Ronfeldt (1993).
60. Rid (2012).
61. Stevens (2016, 22).
62. Dunn Cavelty and Egloff (2019, 44).
63. Diverse approaches study ideas through documents (e.g., Builder 1989; Raymond 2019; Semino 2008). For this type of project, contemporary documents are more useful than later interviews, given the tendency to project current vocabulary backward. Although accessing *all* relevant documents is impossible (especially with classification), I reviewed an extensive sample covering all *types* of US military documents, classified and unclassified: memos, vision documents, strategies, doctrines, etc. The quoted documents are representative of overall trends.
64. White House (1984).
65. Warner (2015).
66. US Air Force (1995).
67. Joint Chiefs (1996).
68. NSA (1995).
69. Black (1997).
70. Joint Chiefs (2000, 72).
71. E.g., Air Force (1995, 8).
72. Joint Chiefs (2004, 18).
73. Joint Chiefs (2006, ix).
74. Specifically, cyberspace is "a global domain within the information environment consisting of the interdependent network of information technology infrastructures, including the Internet, telecommunications networks, computer systems, and embedded processors and controllers" (US Strategic Command 2009, 8).
75. Joint Chiefs (2000, 72).
76. Joint Chiefs (2000, 61).
77. Alexander (2007, 60).
78. See Heftye (2017) and Nakayama (2019).

79. Joint Chiefs (2021). In other words, while "domain" began to appear in this publication as part of terms like "air domain" or "cyberspace domain," there is no entry defining "domain" itself. See also Allen and Gilbert (2009, 2).
80. Betz and Stevens (2013); Lapointe (2011); Manjikian (2010).
81. US Strategic Command (2009, 8); Dunn Cavelty (2013, 108).
82. Dunn Cavelty (2013, 107).
83. Joint Chiefs (2006, 13).
84. US Strategic Command (2009); Cartwright (2010).
85. DoD (2011).
86. See this chapter's epigraph.
87. US Army (2010); US Air Force (2011); US Navy (2012); US Coast Guard (2015).
88. DoD (2011); DoD (2015); DoD (2018).
89. QDR (1997–2014).
90. DoD (2010a, 1).
91. DoD (2013).
92. White House (2012).
93. US Cyber Command (2016).
94. Bertoli and Raio (2018).
95. Cartwright (2010, 1); US Army (2010, i).
96. In author interviews, officials repeatedly mentioned new terminology being motivated by the desire to make one's mark in a new position.
97. E.g., DoD (2018); Joint Chiefs (2018).
98. E.g., Nakasone and Sulmeyer (2020).
99. DoD (2023).
100. It is impossible to tell purely from the documents themselves how authors use terms like this: willingly, grudgingly, or even ironically. Yet the impact on debate and contestation, discussed next, occurs regardless of the original authorial intent or attitude.
101. Sanger (2018).
102. On state–society contestation, see Coles-Kemp et al. (2018); Dunn Cavelty (2013); Dunn Cavelty and Egloff (2019); Hansen and Nissenbaum (2009); McCarthy (2018). On language: Kamis and Thiel (2015); Stevens (2016, 184).
103. As noted regarding cybersecurity by former Defense Secretary Carter (2019, 340).
104. Brooks (2016).
105. Although cyberspace terminology and metaphors have been *rhetorically effective*—making certain policies easier to promote—the resulting policies are not necessarily *objectively effective*.
106. Dunn Cavelty (2013, 113); Manjikian (2015, 3).

107. Lynn (2010, 101–102). See also Alexander (2007).
108. Hayden (2016, 130).
109. E.g., Lute and McConnell (2011).
110. Hayden (2011, 4); see also Libicki (2012). Hayden's memoir (2016) makes similar points.
111. Lambach (2019); Stevens (2016, 74). This suggests studying *positive affect* in cybersecurity, adding to research on negative emotions like fear (Betz and Stevens 2013, 149; Dunn Cavelty 2012, 116; Lawson 2020).
112. Healey (2013, 55); Libicki (2012, 332).
113. Brooks (2019, 387).
114. Brooks (2019, 386).
115. Clarke and Knake (2019, 94).
116. Healey (2013); Warner (2012). While DoD certainly had a hand in the creation of the internet, the importance of that is contested (Townes 2012) and for decades other interests dominated internet structure and governance.
117. This chapter focuses on *institutional* interests and arguments; on the role of specific individuals see Kaplan (2016) and Nakayama (2019).
118. US Air Force (1995, 8); Hayden (2016, 127).
119. Healey (2013, 35); Nakayama (2019).
120. Kass (2006, 9).
121. Capaccio (2017).
122. This language may even prove useful for promoting cyber operations to its own service branch, as a "Cyber Force" (e.g., Stavridis and Weinstein 2014).
123. Healey (2013, 73–75). Cyber Command was operational in 2010 and elevated to a unified combatant command in 2018.
124. Hollis and Ohlin (2018, 441).
125. A point made by, among others, Betz and Stevens (2013); Dunn Cavelty (2012, 119); Heftye (2017); Lapointe (2011, 16); Lawson and Middleton (2019, 14–15); Libicki (2012); Stevens (2016).
126. E.g., Builder (1989).
127. Hayden (2016, 143).
128. Kaplan (2016, 219–220); White House (2012).
129. NSA (1995); Black (1997).
130. Kaplan (2016, 211) argues that, once Cyber Command was operational, offensive operations "emerged as a consuming, even dominant, activity at Fort Meade."
131. Sulmeyer (2017).
132. Going forward, some connection between Cyber Command and NSA will almost certainly persist. While discarding the dual-hat has long been discussed (Kaplan 2016, 257; Sulmeyer 2017), the arrangement represents a "sticky" institutional design—who wants to be the first *non*–dual-hatted NSA director or CYBERCOM commander?

133. Secretary of Defense (2009).
134. Lynn (2010, 101–102).
135. DoD (2010b).
136. E.g., Alexander (2011); Alexander (2013).
137. US Cyber Command (2018); Smeets and Lin (2018); Schneider (2019).
138. Nakasone (2019a, 7).
139. Though Kreps and Schneider (2019) suggest that escalation fears may be misplaced.
140. Nakasone (2019b, 12).
141. Rhetoric also used by Hayden (2016, 132). Interestingly, the contention that the US military "defends forward" in "the physical domains" elides the fact that, even within this metaphorical framework, the analogy only applies to oceans and, to a lesser degree, to airspace. Placing land forces on the territory of an adversary is an explicitly hostile action, and treated universally as an act of war. Thus the specific examples come from non–land domains.
142. For example, *New York Times* reporter David Sanger put it this way: "Cybercom couldn't be going to the White House every time it wanted to do [a cyber operation], just the way the Navy doesn't go to the White House every time it wants to go run a group of destroyers down through the South China Sea or go do patrolling along the DMZ in South Korea." *The Daily*, June 18, 2019.
143. Rid and Buchanan (2018, 7).
144. E.g., the report from the "Cyberspace Solarium Commission," led by elected officials and including multiple federal agencies, closely tracks DoD language (King and Gallagher 2020).
145. For example, Libicki (2012) argues that "cyberspace is not a warfighting domain," but leaves largely unquestioned the *cyberspace* label itself. Yet the consequences these critics have attributed exclusively to the *domain* label actually only follow from how *domain* and *cyberspace* have together formed a single, cohesive concept, with a set of implied territorial metaphors that would not have emerged with either term on its own.
146. NDAA (2019, section 1642). Clarke and Knake (2019); Sanger and Perlroth (2019); Chesney (2019).
147. E.g., Barlow (1996).
148. The DoD case was prominently argued in *Foreign Affairs* by Lynn (2010), with a response in *Wired* by Lute and McConnell (2011).
149. Lakoff and Johnson (1980, 17) note the prevalence of spatial metaphors across complex issues.
150. Recalling that "internet" originally referred only to "internetworking" projects like ARPANET.
151. E.g., "internet governance" literature largely avoids spatial language and metaphors, focusing instead on network-type characteristics like "control points" (DeNardis 2014; Raymond and DeNardis 2015).

152. Lambach (2019, 7–8). E.g., this suggests historical analogies to communication networks like the telegraph, with distinct implications for security (Gartzke and Lindsay 2015) or legality (Goldsmith 1998).
153. See Biersteker (2002) on the contrast between territorial control and "control of networks" in general.
154. On biological metaphors in general, see Betz and Stevens (2013); Dunn Cavelty (2013, 110ff); Lapointe (2011). *Ecosystem* has been suggested by analysts (Osenga 2013, 49–51) and policymakers (Lute and McConnell 2011).
155. E.g., "information superhighway" was used to argue for federal investment in the early internet (Blavin and Cohen 2002, 269–270).
156. White House (1997). The document makes one reference to "activities extending over vast reaches of physical and virtual space" (White House 1997, A-8). See also Braman (2014, 49); Collier and Lakoff (2008); Warner (2012).
157. See especially Collier and Lakoff (2008).
158. Carr (2016).
159. Warner (2012, 795).
160. White House (1998).
161. DHS (2011). See also DHS (2003) for similar language. See also Futter (2018).
162. US Strategic Command (2009, 8); DHS (2011, D-2).
163. E.g., DHS (2016); DHS (2018).
164. DHS (2018). While Clarke and Knake (2019, 171) argue that it was "just a reorganization of things that were already in DHS," that reorganization seems to have been effective at preventing a repeat in 2020 of some of the 2016 interference (CISA 2020).
165. E.g., Carter (2019, 341).
166. Sanger (2018).
167. As to *why* it does not, see the discussion above on the close fit that spatial terminology provided with military concepts and staffing.
168. DoD (2020).
169. Buchanan (2016).
170. But see Kreps and Schneider (2019).
171. See https://www.dhs.gov/mission (accessed May 20, 2025).
172. Manjikian (2016).
173. The following explores, briefly, linguistic processes and cybersecurity elsewhere, particularly international reactions to US terminology. Of course, comparing terms and metaphors across languages has inherent challenges, including the mistranslation of words or divergent connotations (Giles and Hagestad 2013; Kamis and Thiel 2015; Zeng, Stevens, and Chen 2017).
174. E.g., U.K. Cabinet Office (2009). Emulation of US policy includes the very idea of releasing a cybersecurity strategy (Kerttunen and Tikk 2019, 10).

175. NATO (2014, para. 72–73).

176. E.g., a 2015 Chinese strategy mentions "threats from such new security domains as outer space and cyber space" (PRC 2015; see also Zeng, Stevens, and Chen 2017). This suggests the possibility that a single terminology could eventually serve as a focal point for international cybersecurity contestation (Farrell and Glaser 2017, 13).

177. Some other communities have thus been instrumentally motivated to adopt the cyberspace-domain framework, regardless of whether it provided the same institutional and intuitive fit that explains its uptake in the US military.

178. On cybersecurity language and international law: Boer (2017); Sauter (2015).

179. Schmitt (2013); Schmitt (2017). Although states do not see these manuals as binding and some analysts consider them irrelevant (e.g., Lucas 2016, 17), they serve as the first point of discussion and frame subsequent debate (Corn 2017; Raymond 2019, 206). Legal discourses are often shaped by "conceptual path dependence" (Larsson 2017, 50).

180. Schmitt (2013, 3, 258). They have also drawn implicitly on language used by US officials (e.g., State Department lawyer Harold Koh [2012] on international law "in cyberspace"), itself reflecting earlier legal scholarship (discussed above).

181. Schmitt (2013, 16); Schmitt (2017, 11). E.g., the second edition begins by affirming: "The principle of State sovereignty applies in cyberspace" (Schmitt 2017, 11). International legal debates often define "cyberspace with reference to territory" (Manjikian 2015, 4). See also Mueller (2020).

182. Finnemore and Hollis (2016, 460).

183. DeNardis (2014); Lambach (2019, 13–14).

184. Schmitt (2017, 17–27).

185. I.e., are cyber weapons munitions or information? (Schmitt 2017, 553–562).

186. Hollis and Ohlin (2018).

187. Post-*Tallinn* discussions have continued to debate how law applies "in cyberspace" (e.g., Ginsburg 2017).

188. UNGA (2013); UNGA (2015).

189. In 2017 the GGE failed to yield a consensus report. See Henriksen (2019); Maurer (2019); Raymond (2020); Tikk and Kerttunen (2018).

190. Giles and Hagestad (2013); Tikk and Kerttunen (2018); Creemers (2023). *Information security* includes controlling internet content alongside blocking malware or preventing network intrusions. While authoritarian governments' deployment of this concept is explained well by instrumental motivations, this chapter's framework suggests additional questions: What metaphors are implied by these terms? How do those metaphors fit with different interests? How might contestation around cybersecurity then be reshaped in countries where these terms predominate?

191. OEWG (2021).
192. Zeng et al. (2017, 449).
193. Mueller (2017b, 35). See also Mueller (2020).
194. Sauter (2015, 66).
195. E.g., Borghard and Lonergan (2017); Finnemore and Hollis (2016); Gartzke (2013); Kello (2017).
196. E.g., Gartzke and Lindsay (2015) on deception in communication networks, Demchak and Dombrowski (2011, 35) on the internet as a "substrate," or Lindsay (2020b) on cyber conflict as "a large-scale intelligence problem" not a military issue.
197. I.e., "bundle of mechanisms" (Farrell 2012, 36).
198. For related suggestions: Lawson and Middleton (2019, 16); Manjikian (2016).
199. Lawson (2020, 197).
200. Dodge (2008, 118); drawing on Sawhney (1996).
201. Sauter (2015, 64) notes that communication policy—shaped by metaphors—can be particularly consequential for the further development of related technologies.
202. Latour (1987).
203. Carpenter (2016) suggests looking for the actual impact of pop culture on politics.
204. Stimmer (2019).
205. E.g., Dodge (2008).
206. Shires (2019); Dunn Cavelty (2019).
207. Gibson (1988, 180).

Chapter 5

1. Boyle (2020, 278).
2. This chapter focuses on this specific set of uses, leaving aside the longstanding use of remote platforms for pure surveillance and the increasing deployment of remote aircraft in interstate war.
3. The initial reporting on this incident was in Cloud (2011); many later analyses of drone warfare have explored its causes and implications. See, among many others, Gregory (2011a); Gusterson (2016); Suchman (2015).
4. Wilcox (2017, 12) notes how central this one incident has become to discussions of drone operations.
5. Quoted in Cloud (2011) and numerous analyses (e.g., Gregory 2011a, 202).
6. Quoted in Cloud (2011).
7. Gen. McChrystal, quoted in Cloud (2011).
8. Suchman (2015). See below for more analysis of the importance of visual representations, and discursive representations of them.

9. I discuss the issues around nomenclature and labeling below, since "drone," "unmanned aerial vehicle," and another labels constitute important representations of these devices and their use.

10. Elish (2017, 1104). See also Shaw (2013).

11. Carvin (2015, 132).

12. Elish (2017, 1103).

13. At least in how I have read Latour's suggestion, it strikes me as a reasonable proposition to value *both* material and social factors in our analysis, even though his effort to push against the predominant focus on social drivers and outcomes is often read as an exclusive emphasis on the material.

14. Kindervater (2016, 224, 229).

15. Williams (2011); Crampton (2016).

16. There is an enormous range of "uninhabited" flying objects that have sometimes been considered together, under a single umbrella concept of "drone." From prototype aircraft that could functionally replace high-tech manned fighter planes, to the well-known Predators and Reapers, to the backpack-sized infantry (or hobbyist) quad-copters: all are sometimes lumped into this single category of analysis. (For discussion, see, e.g., Rogers and Hill 2014; Dunn 2013.) I am not convinced that this broadest scope is the most productive approach, and so I am focusing on the systems that involve aircraft without an on-board pilot that deploy both surveillance and attack capabilities, with at least some personnel at a significant spatial remove from the aircraft itself (i.e., excluding small aircraft that are piloted entirely by line-of-sight control).

17. In other words, it misses as much to focus solely on policy choices alone as it does to focus exclusively on the novel aircraft. While it may be strictly true that, for example, "proportionality depends on the attack—the *way* drones are being used, *not* the weapon itself" (Carvin 2015, 133; italics original), how the systems are used is an emergent effect of the entire network, not a policy choice independent of material systems and resources.

18. See the following section for a brief overview of existing studies.

19. While the analysis in this chapter speaks to the broad role of those representations in the origins, effects, and future of drone warfare, it focuses on the US case, in particular the use of drones in counterterrorism and counterinsurgency operations. (Representational processes are also embedded into the use of remote aircraft in other settings, such as interstate wars like the Ukraine-Russia conflict, but those representations follow somewhat divergent logics. Nonetheless, the discussion of future autonomy, below, does engage with the broader context.) As the predominant global military power over the last two decades—the period when drones have gone from a hypothetical weapon to an everyday reality—the United States has, as with cybersecurity, largely set the terms of the debate about drones. For two decades, the United States used these

tools in open and covert military operations more than any other state, and has most actively pushed the boundaries of how force is used through the deployment of these systems. Note that while most of the influential analyses of the US drone program were written during the Obama presidency (especially in the first half of the 2010s), little has changed in terms of the overall features and effects discussed in this chapter. For example, the first Trump administration only increased the reliance on secrecy, limited oversight, and remote operation that its predecessor had used (Swan 2019). This suggests that many aspects of these uses of drone systems are here to stay.

20. Among the many books on the topic, those particularly relevant to this chapter's focus include Singer (2009); Cavallaro et al. (2012); Benjamin (2013); Rogers and Hill (2014); Kaag and Kreps (2014); Gusterson (2016); and Boyle (2020).

21. Singer (2009).

22. Critics have also highlighted the disconnect between Singer's professed alarm about the destabilizing political effects of military robotics and his implicit celebration of those same novel technologies (e.g., Suchman 2015, 11–13).

23. Shaw (2013); Gregory (2014; 2011a; 2011b).

24. Rogers and Hill (2014).

25. Chamayou (2015).

26. Cavallaro et al. (2012); Benjamin (2013).

27. E.g., Kaag and Kreps (2014, ch. 4).

28. See the discussion later in this chapter on autonomy.

29. Summarized effectively by Gusterson (2016, ch. 4) and Kaag and Kreps (2014, ch. 5).

30. Especially in Cavallaro et al. (2012).

31. Early interventions noted the difficulty of measuring the effectiveness of drone strikes (esp. Carvin 2012; Boyle 2013), while more recent work has attempted to address that challenge (e.g., Mir and Moore 2019; Mir 2018; Shah 2018).

32. Boyle (2020) provides a thorough overview of the current debate in IR and security studies scholarship about drones.

33. Quoted in Gregory (2011a, 199–200).

34. Strawser (2010, 346).

35. As pointed out by Elish (2017), among others.

36. Chamayou (2015, 140), italics original.

37. Chamayou (2015, 141).

38. Leese (2019, 54).

39. On this debate, see among others Gusterson (2016, 79ff); Holmqvist (2013); Rogers and Hill (2014, ch. 4); Chamayou (2015, 106ff); Boyle (2020).

40. It is not just external critics of the drone program that use this language. Macdonald and Schneider (2019) found that ground soldiers specifically differentiated traditional pilots and drone operators, with the latter considered "video game player[s]." In their interviews with ground soldiers, "not one survey response referred to the UAV pilot as a 'pilot'" (243).
41. Kindervater (2016).
42. This may have been an intentional effort to shift the narrative away from the "video game mentality" accusations. See Stahl (2013, 670ff); Chamayou (2015, 109). See also Hasian et al. (2015) for a thorough analysis of the circulation of the narrative of drone pilot stress and PTSD.
43. Kirkpatrick (2015).
44. Stahl (2013, 664).
45. Yielding alternatives such as Strawser's (2010, 343) suggestion of "uninhabited aerial vehicles," perhaps chosen to maintain the acronym UAV.
46. From critics like the American Civil Liberties Union (ACLU)—"we should use the term that people would most clearly and directly understand. That word is 'drones.'" (Stanley 2013)—to defenders of the policy like President Obama in a 2013 speech—"remotely piloted aircraft commonly referred to as drones" (Obama 2013). Outside the United States, a similar pattern of habitual usage has emerged: "In Switzerland, France and Germany, 'drone' is also the most widely used term both in civil society and amongst public and private drone users" (Klauser and Pedrozo 2015, 286). For a careful history of the use of "drone" in this context, see Benchoff (2016).
47. Boyle (2020, ch. 1); Lindsay (2020a, ch. 6); Kaag and Kreps (2014, 21); Chamayou (2015, 26ff); Gusterson (2016); Hasian et al. (2015, 174). Gregory (2011a, 207). One officer of a drone unit "fines his subordinates $5 every time they use the word *drone*," concerned with how it demeans their skills and hands-on role (Gusterson 2016, 52).
48. Hasian et al. (2015, 174); Gustersen (2016, 52).
49. Elish (2017, 1106).
50. For various versions of this history—from diverse perspectives and with varying degrees of recognition that the lineage worth tracing may extend well beyond these specific aircraft—see among many others: Hall and Coyne (2014); Benchoff (2016); Kaag and Kreps (2014, ch. 1); Boyle (2020, ch. 2); Gregory (2011a); Chamayou (2015, ch. 2); Lindsay (2020a, ch. 6); and Kindervater (2016).
51. See especially Lindsay (2020a, ch. 6); Boyle (2020, ch. 2). Macdonald and Schneider (2025) makes a similar point regarding the broader history of remote operations in land and sea as well as air.
52. Kindervater (2016, 225).

53. Similarly, the application of the term "drone" to these historical un-piloted aircraft only occurred retrospectively, once modern drone systems were developed (Benchoff 2016).

54. On the former, see, e.g., Dunn (2013); on the latter, see Sullivan (2006) for an early statement ("Rather than being a new and revolutionary idea, pilotless aircraft are a tried and true branch of military research and development" [44]). Drones can even be seen as part of the modern "qualitative arms race" of military hardware that began in the nineteenth century (Buzan and Lawson 2015, 245ff).

55. As Chamayou (2015, 93ff) notes, representing drones as "nothing new" is a powerful justification for their use.

56. The combination of diverse lineages and developments in current drone use has been noted by others, including Chamayou (2015, ch. 2) and Gregory, who argues that we should examine the wider "matrix of military violence that these remote platforms help to activate" (2014, 7).

57. See Edwards (1996, ch. 4); Shaw (2016); Feuer (2020); among others.

58. Grayson (2016, 329).

59. See especially Carvin (2012; 2015). Shaw (2016, 539) traces this to the US Cold-War "history of targeted killings and counterinsurgencies, especially in Latin America and Vietnam."

60. Carvin (2015) emphasizes this.

61. See Elish (2017) on "remote-split" operations; see also Gregory (2014) on the spatial distribution of drone operations. Note that the "self-selected professional lineage" described by many drone pilots includes Vietnam-era remote sensor and bombing systems, as much as flying aircraft in the cockpit (Elish 2017, 1106).

62. For example, they were used effectively by Azerbaijan in the 2020 Nagorno-Karabakh War (Hecht 2022), as well as in the Russian invasion of Ukraine that began in 2022.

63. See, e.g., Adas (2006); Chamayou (2015, 93); Shaw (2013); Williams (2007; 2015).

64. Gusterson (2016, 56).

65. Williams (2015).

66. Williams (2015, 93); see also Rogers and Hill (2014, 12).

67. Stahl (2013, 659).

68. Gregory (2011a, 190); Gregory (2014). See Der Derian (2009) for a discussion of the broader digital transformation of visual imaging and warfare, and Bousquet (2018) on "scopic regimes" across various technologies of warfare.

69. Gregory (2014, 9).

70. E.g., Strawser (2010, 351) argues that "there is good reason to think . . . that UAV technology actually *increases* a pilot's ability to discriminate."

71. Gregory (2011a; 2014); Chamayou (2015); Kindervater (2017); Grayson and Mawdsley (2019).

72. Edney-Browne (2019, 95).
73. Edney-Browne (2019, 96).
74. Kindervater (2017, 31).
75. Boyle (2017/2018, 179).
76. Boyle (2020).
77. Gusterson (2016, 65ff).
78. Coeckelbergh (2013, 89).
79. Gusterson (2016, 86).
80. Edney-Browne (2019, 89).
81. HRW (2010).
82. Wilcox (2018, 114).
83. Cloud (2011); see also Suchman (2015); Wilcox (2017).
84. This is distinct from more foundational effort to define "combatant" as a status to begin with. See Kinsella (2005).
85. Especially Cavallaro et al. (2012). See also Shaw (2013). Note that "personality" strikes on known and named individuals are also enabled by drone vision and the real-time representations provided to analysts and operators. Carrying out assassination in an entirely remote fashion is a novel capability.
86. Chamayou (2015, 46ff).
87. See Gregory (2014). Of course, war has always involved killing individuals who looked and acted like an enemy—based on uniform, position, activity, etc. But the combination of individualized targeting, nonconventional warzones, and remote operation is new, and requires the ability to claim that a specific individual fits a profile that does not match the standard military target but is still legitimate.
88. As of 2024, the examples of actual use of "fully" autonomous weapons remain contested. See, e.g., the possible use of an autonomous drone in Libya (Cramer 2021).
89. DoD (2017, 18).
90. Arkin (2010, 332).
91. E.g., Work and Brimley (2014); Mayer (2015).
92. E.g., Future of Life Institute (2015).
93. See, among others, Chamayou (2015, 212–213).
94. The work of Arkin (2010) is the key example of this logic and effort.
95. Roff (2014, 213–214). See also Suchman (2015, 14–15).
96. Rogers and Hill (2014, 119).
97. A similar dynamic is traced by Farocki back to the initial publicity around "smart bombs" in the first Gulf War: a label and concept that actual capabilities at the time rarely lived up to, but that nonetheless served "to make the idea of a seeing bomb so popular and common that, thereafter, they would have to be ordered, developed, and paid for" (Farocki 2004, 21).
98. Leese (2019, 49).

99. Horowitz (2016, 26). See Leese (2019) and Boulanin and Verbruggen (2017) for discussions of the concept of a spectrum of autonomy.
100. Hayles (2017, 136). See also Leese (2019, 46ff).
101. On the question of deterministic versus nondeterministic programming here, see Cummings (2017) and Boulanin and Verbruggen (2017).
102. On the distancing created by remote operations and its complex effects, see Coeckelbergh (2013); Williams (2015); Shaw (2013); Kindervater (2017); Gregory (2011b).
103. Or, even in the case of machine learning systems which have been trained on data rather than directly programmed with explicit decision rules, humans have written the training code.
104. Boulanin and Verbruggen (2017, 17).
105. JASON (2017, 28–29).
106. Arkin (2010, 336) argues that "When killing at a maximum range, one can pretend they are not killing human beings, and thus experience no regret." If the weapon is not operating at maximum range since it is itself choosing targets, this issue disappears. It remains unexplained, however, what the autonomous-system analogue to human regret would be.
107. Cummings (2004, 30).
108. See Coeckelbergh (2013) on the simultaneous bridging and distancing effects of remote operations.
109. This list draws on Roff and Moyes (2016).
110. DoD (2012, 2–3).
111. DoD (2017, 20–21).
112. Leese (2019, 43).
113. See Niva (2013, 198).
114. See Amoore (2009).
115. Williams (2015).
116. Boyle (2013, 15). See also Boyle (2020, ch. 3).
117. Kaag and Kreps (2014, 47).
118. Agius (2017, 374).
119. Adas (2006).
120. Gusterson (2016, 25).
121. Agius (2017).
122. Adas (2006).

Chapter 6

1. On emotion in international relations, see, among others, Crawford (2000); McDermott (2004, ch. 6); Mercer (2010); Sasley (2010; 2011); Hutchison and Bleiker (2014); Kertzer and Tingley (2018); and the 2014 forum in *International Theory* 6(3). A number of scholars have argued for a

focus on affect rather than the more general category of emotion: e.g., Hutchison and Bleiker (2014, 496); Bially Mattern (2014, 593–594).

2. Hall and Ross (2015, 853).

3. Hall and Ross (2015, 860–861).

4. With some exceptions, such as research on the psychological effects of cyberattacks: Shandler et al. (2023).

5. Nye (2006, 4).

6. See Lipton (2023).

7. Gibbs (2008, 9). See also Hayles (1999) on the deeply "embodied" nature of information.

8. McDermott (2014); Holmes (2013; 2014).

9. Onuf (2013, 42); Khong (1992, 225).

10. Koschut et al. (2017) suggests such a move.

11. Indeed, the systems used by states to make legible and thus "see" their territories have always been forms of virtualization (Scott 1998; Mitchell 2002).

12. E.g., the purported video-game mentality felt by drone operators (Chamayou 2015, 107). See also Lindsay (2010); Shaw (2013).

13. Represented most clearly by the dream of an electronic or automated battlefield pursued by the US military since the 1960s (Edwards 1996, 144; Bousquet 2009, 126).

14. As Edwards (1996, 29) notes, computing can have "subtle, profound, and *material* effects *solely through its function within a system of ideas*" (italics in original).

15. Bially Mattern (2014, 589).

16. This is explored in more detail in Branch (2024).

17. Scholars at the intersection of STS and IR have pointed toward a connection between technological systems and political institutions in several ways: technological systems *function like* institutions (McCarthy 2015, 4; Herrera 2006, 7), there are some explicitly "technological institutions" (McCarthy 2013, 472 n10) or "sociotechnical institutions" (Lindsay 2020a), and technological systems *interact with* social and political institutions (Lindsay 2014/15, 42 n108). Here I simply want to push this one step further, arguing that nearly all political institutions have, as one core definitional component, representational and infrastructural technologies.

18. Prominent among these are the concepts of *assemblages* and *actor-networks*, both of which emphasize particular ways in which diverse elements function as a whole. There are enormous bodies of literature—somewhat overlapping—on these two theories. My goal here is to draw on the overall argument about diverse elements combining without relying on the more complex or controversial claims. See, e.g., Passoth and Rowland (2010); Mitchell (1991).

19. For a related approach, see Carroll (2006, 3, 17), whose study of how the modern state was "materially engineered" defines the state as a combination of ideas and discourses, practices and organizations, and territory, infrastructure, and population.

20. This is apparent in the oft-cited definition of the state from Max Weber: the state is "that human community which (successfully) lays claim to the monopoly of legitimate physical violence within a certain territory" (Weber [1919] 1994, 310–311, italics removed). Although physical violence is prominently mentioned, the key elements differentiating states from other organizations are ideational: the claimed legitimacy of the use of force, the monopoly of those claims (i.e., sovereignty as final authority), and the territorial limits of those claims.

21. This draws on a broad reading of arguments from STS, as well as applications of STS in political science that highlight how technological systems are *similar to* political institutions: both are created by agents but later shape the context for action (see, among others, McCarthy 2015; Lindsay 2017). Here, I am arguing something different, that institutions *are* in part technological, or infrastructural. In other words, if Winner's much debated position is that some technologies have a politics (Winner 1977, 1980; see also Joerges 1999; Woolgar and Cooper 1999; Rowland and Passoth 2015), I simply want to invert that basic insight: if technologies are political, then perhaps *politics is also technological.*

22. Mann (1984, 188–189).

23. Mann (2008, 358). See Soifer and Vom Hau (2008) for more discussion.

24. Mukerji (2010).

25. Guldi (2012, 3). Rowland and Passoth (2015, 140) note that Guldi leaves ambiguous whether the state *has* infrastructure or *is* itself infrastructural.

26. E.g., Easterling (2014); Edwards (2003); Larkin (2013).

27. See Maier (2016) for a broad historical perspective.

28. The infrastructures of borders and bordering are varied: from walls and physical barriers that both mark and enforce a boundary to systems of identity and control such as the modern passport regime (Shirk 2019). The literature on border infrastructure is vast, particularly in political geography (e.g., Newman and Paasi 1998). For political science examples, see Simmons (2017); Hassner and Wittenberg (2015).

29. STS research has examined various representational devices, from material artifacts to models, discourses, and other means (e.g., Lynch and Woolgar 1990; Coopmans et al. 2014).

30. In earlier work, for example, I argued that the specific territoriality of the modern state, with its focus on discrete boundaries and homogenous spatial claims, was shaped and made possible by developments in mapping technology (Branch 2014). This built on work by historians and others on the connection between mapping and national identity (Thongchai 1994), boundary creation (Sahlins 1989), and other processes.

31. Mitchell (2002, ch. 3). This draws on the related work by Latour (1986) on the role of inscriptions.
32. League of Nations (1936).
33. Branch (2017).
34. In Branch (2014), I focused on demonstrating how mapping served as an important condition of possibility for the emergence and consolidation of the modern state—particularly its territorial definition. The concept here suggests a different question, asking how those representations emerged, how they interacted with the ideational and infrastructural elements of statehood, and how the state *as a whole* came to be consolidated in its "modern" form.
35. From international relations, see, e.g., Cerny (1995).
36. E.g., Farrell and Newman (2019) highlight how the structure of global networks has increased, rather than undermined, the power of some states, such as the United States' unique position as a network hub and the capabilities this has provided.
37. Murphy (2013).
38. Ironically, in most cases, these "failed" states exhibit far more capacity and authority than many historical political organizations, before the consolidation of the modern state. See Brooks (2005).
39. As in, e.g., Risse and Stollenwerk (2018).
40. Schouten (2013).
41. Branch (2014).
42. McLaughlin (1995).
43. As others have argued, this conversation should go in both directions (e.g., Mayer et al. 2014).
44. Fioretos (2011).
45. Tilly (1992, 67).

REFERENCES

Abbink, Jon. 2003. "Badme and the Ethio-Eritrean Border: The Challenge of Demarcation in the Post-War Period." *Africa: Journal of the International African Institute* 58 (2): 219–231.

Abernethy, David. B. 2000. *The Dynamics of Global Dominance: European Overseas Empires, 1415–1980.* Yale University Press.

Abraham, Yuval. 2024. "'Lavender': The AI Machine Directing Israel's Bombing Spree in Gaza." *+972,* April 3. https://www.972mag.com/lavender-ai-israeli-army-gaza/.

Adas, Michael. 1989. *Machines as the Measure of Men: Science, Technology, and Ideologies of Western Dominance.* Cornell University Press.

Adas, Michael. 2006. *Dominance by Design: Technological Imperatives and America's Civilizing Mission.* Harvard University Press.

Adler-Nissen, Rebecca, and Alena Drieschova. 2019. "Track-Change Diplomacy: Technology, Affordances and the Practice of International Negotiations." *International Studies Quarterly* 63 (3): 531–545.

Agar, Jon. 2003. *The Government Machine: A Revolutionary History of the Computer.* MIT Press.

Agius, Christine. 2017. "Ordering without Bordering: Drones, the Unbordering of Late Modern Warfare and Ontological Insecurity." *Postcolonial Studies and Ontological Insecurities* 20 (3): 370–386.

Alexander, Keith B. 2007. "Warfighting in Cyberspace." *Joint Forces Quarterly* 46: 58–61.

Alexander, Keith B. 2011. "Building a New Command in Cyberspace." *Strategic Studies Quarterly* 5 (2): 3–12.

Alexander, Keith. 2013. "Commander, United States Cyber Command, Statement before the Senate Committee on Armed Services." March 12. https://nsarchive2.gwu.edu/NSAEBB/NSAEBB424/docs/Cyber-091.pdf.

Allen, Bentley. 2018. *Scientific Cosmology and International Orders*. Cambridge University Press.

Allen, Patrick D., and Dennis P. Gilbert Jr. 2009. "The Information Sphere Domain: Increasing Understanding and Cooperation." In *The Virtual Battlefield: Perspectives on Cyber Warfare*, edited by Christian Czosseck and Kenneth Geers. IOS Press.

Ambinder, Marc. 2011. "The Little-Known Agency that Helped Kill Bin Laden." *The Atlantic*, May 5. http://www.theatlantic.com/politics/archive/2011/05/the-little-known-agency-that-helped-kill-bin-laden/238454/.

Amoore, Louise. 2009. "Algorithmic War: Everyday Geographies of the War on Terror." *Antipode* 41 (1): 49–69.

Anderson, Benedict. [1991] 2016. *Imagined Communities: Reflections on the Origin and Spread of Nationalism*. Revised ed. Verso.

Arkin, Ronald C. 2010. "The Case for Ethical Autonomy in Unmanned Systems." *Journal of Military Ethics* 9 (4): 332–341.

Arquilla, John, and David Ronfeldt. 1993. "Cyberwar is Coming!" *Comparative Strategy* 12 (2): 141–165.

Avtar, Ram, Asma Kouser, Ashwani Kumar, Deepak Singh, Prakhar Misra, Ankita Gupta, Ali P. Yunus, Pankaj Kumar, Brian Alan Johnson, Rajarshi Dasgupta, Netrananda Sahu, and Andi Besse Rimba. 2021. "Remote Sensing for International Peace and Security: Its Role and Implications." *Remote Sensing* 13 (3): 439.

Balzacq, Thierry, and Myriam Dunn Cavelty. 2016. "A Theory of Actor-Network for Cyber-Security." *European Journal of International Security* 1 (2): 176–198.

Barder, Alexander D. 2016. "Barbed Wire." In *Making Things International 2: Catalysts and Reactions*, edited by Mark B. Salter. University of Minnesota Press.

Barlow, John Perry. 1996. A Declaration of the Independence of Cyberspace. https://www.eff.org/cyberspace-independence.

Barston, R. P. 2013. *Modern Diplomacy*. 4th ed. Routledge.

Batuman, Bülent. 2010. "The Shape of the Nation: Visual Production of Nationalism Through Maps in Turkey." *Political Geography* 29 (4): 220–234.

Bayly, C. A. 1993. "Knowing the Country: Empire and Information in India." *Modern Asian Studies* 27 (1): 3–43.

Bayly, C. A. 2004. *The Birth of the Modern World, 1780–1914: Global Connections and Comparison*. Wiley-Blackwell.

Bayly, Martin J. 2016. *Taming the Imperial Imagination: Colonial Knowledge, International Relations, and the Anglo-Afghan Encounter, 1808–1878.* Cambridge University Press.

Bell, Duncan. 2005. "Dissolving Distance: Technology, Space, and Empire in British Political Thought, 1770–1900." *Journal of Modern History* 77 (3): 523–562.

Bell, Duncan. 2021. "Cyborg Imperium, c.1900." In *Coding and Representation from the Nineteenth Century to the Present: Scrambled Messages*, edited by Anne Chapman and Natalie Hume. Routledge.

Benchoff, Brian. 2016. "A Brief History of 'Drone.'" *Hackaday*, September 26. https://hackaday.com/2016/09/26/a-brief-history-of-drone/

Benedikt, Michael L., ed. 1991. *Cyberspace: First Steps.* MIT Press.

Benjamin, Medea. 2013. *Drone Warfare: Killing by Remote Control.* Verso.

Benton, Lauren. 2009. *A Search for Sovereignty: Law and Geography in European Empires 1400–1900.* Cambridge University Press.

Bertoli, Giorgio, and Stephen Raio. 2018. "The Elusive Nature of 'Key Cyber Terrain.'" *Journal of Cyber Security and Information Systems* 6 (2): 40–47.

Betz, David J., and Tim Stevens. 2013. "Analogical Reasoning and Cyber Security." *Security Dialogue* 44 (2): 147–164.

Bially Mattern, Janice. 2014. "On Being Convinced: An Emotional Epistemology of International Relations." *International Theory* 6 (3): 589–594.

Biersteker, Thomas. 2002. "State, Sovereignty, and Territory." In *Handbook of International Relations*, edited by Walter Carlsnaes, Thomas Risse, and Beth A. Simmons. Sage Publishing.

Biggs, Michael. 1999. "Putting the State on the Map: Cartography, Territory, and European State Formation." *Comparative Studies in Society and History* 41 (2): 374–405.

Bijker, Wiebe E., Thomas P. Hughes, and Trevor Pinch, eds. 2012. *The Social Construction of Technological Systems: New Directions in the Sociology and History of Technology.* Anniversary ed. MIT Press.

Bimber, Bruce. 1994. "Three Faces of Technological Determinism." In *Does Technology Drive History? The Dilemma of Technological Determinism*, edited by Merritt Roe Smith and Leo Marx. MIT Press.

Bjola, Corneliu, and Marcus Holmes, eds. 2015. *Digital Diplomacy: Theory and Practice.* Routledge.

Black, William B. 1997. "Thinking Out Loud about Cyberspace." *Cryptolog* XXIII, no. 1 (Spring). https://nsarchive2.gwu.edu/NSAEBB/NSAEBB424/docs/Cyber-011.pdf.

Blake, Gerald. 1995. "The Depiction of International Boundaries on Topographic Maps." *IBRU Boundary and Security Bulletin* (April): 44–50.

Blavin, Jonathan H., and I. Glenn Cohen. 2002. "Gore, Gibson, and Goldsmith: The Evolution of Internet Metaphors in Law and Commentary." *Harvard Journal of Law & Technology* 16 (1): 265–285.

Bleiker, Roland, ed. 2018. *Visual Global Politics*. Routledge.

Blum, Andrew. 2012. *Tubes: A Journey to the Center of the Internet*. Ecco.

Boer, Lianne J. M. 2017. "'Spoofed Presence Does not Suffice': On Territoriality in the Tallinn Manual." In *Netherlands Yearbook of International Law*, edited by M. Kuijer and W. Werner. Springer Publishing.

Boettcher, William A., III. 2004. "The Prospects for Prospect Theory: An Empirical Evaluation of International Relations Applications of Framing and Loss Aversion." *Political Psychology* 25 (3): 331–362.

Borghard, Erica D., and Shawn W. Lonergan. 2017. "The Logic of Coercion in Cyberspace." *Security Studies* 26 (3): 452–481.

Boulanin, Vincent, and Maaike Verbruggen. 2017. "Mapping the Development of Autonomy in Weapons Systems." Stockholm International Peace Research Institute, November.

Bousquet, Antoine. 2009. *The Scientific Way of Warfare: Order and Chaos on the Battlefields of Modernity*. Hurst & Company.

Bousquet, Antoine. 2018. *The Eye of War: Military Perception from the Telescope to the Drone*. University of Minnesota Press.

Boyle, Michael J. 2013. "The Costs and Consequences of Drone Warfare." *International Affairs* 89 (1): 1–29.

Boyle, Michael J. 2020. *The Drone Age: How Drone Technology Will Change War and Peace*. Oxford University Press.

Boyle, Michael J., Matthew Fuhrmann, Michael C. Horowitz, and Sarah E. Kreps. 2017/2018. "Debating Drone Proliferation." *International Security* 42 (3): 178–182.

Braman, Sandra. 2014. "Cyber Security Ethics at the Boundaries: System Maintenance and the Tallinn Manual." In *Proceedings: 1st Workshop on Ethics of Cyber Conflict*, edited by Ludovica Glorioso and Anna-Maria Osula. NATO Cooperative Cyber Defence Center of Excellence.

Branch, Jordan. 2014. *The Cartographic State: Maps, Territory, and the Origins of Sovereignty*. Cambridge University Press.

Branch, Jordan. 2017. "Territory as an Institution: Spatial Ideas, Practices and Technologies." *Territory, Politics, Governance* 5 (2): 131–144.

Branch, Jordan. 2024. "Reconceptualizing the State and Its Alternatives: Ideas, Infrastructures, Representations." In *Territorial Imaginaries: Beyond the Sovereign Map*, edited by Kären Wigen. University of Chicago Press.

Brooks, Risa. 2019. "Integrating the Civil-Military Relations Subfield." *Annual Review of Political Science* 22: 379–398.

Brooks, Rosa. 2005. "Failed States, or the State as Failure?" *University of Chicago Law Review* 72 (4): 1159–1196.

Brooks, Rosa. 2016. *How Everything Became War and the Military Became Everything*. Simon & Schuster.

Brotton, Jerry. 1997. *Trading Territories: Mapping the Early Modern World*. Cornell University Press.

Buchanan, Ben. 2016. *The Cybersecurity Dilemma: Hacking, Trust, and Fear Between Nations*. Oxford University Press.

Builder, Carl H. 1989. *The Masks of War: American Military Styles in Strategy and Analysis*. Johns Hopkins University Press.

Burbank, Jane, and Frederick Cooper. 2010. *Empires in World History: Power and the Politics of Difference*. Princeton University Press.

Buzan, Barry, and George Lawson. 2015. *The Global Transformation: History, Modernity and the Making of International Relations*. Cambridge University Press.

Buzan, Barry, Ole Wæver, and Jaap de Wilde. 1998. *Security: A New Framework for Analysis*. Lynne Rienner Publishers.

Capaccio, Anthony. 2017. "U.S. Air Force Space Chief Sees Final Frontier as Battleground." *Bloomberg*, October 17. https://www.bloomberg.com/news/articles/2017-10-17/u-s-air-force-space-chief-sees-final-frontier-as-battleground.

Carey, James W. 2009. *Communication as Culture: Essays on Media and Society*, Revised ed. Routledge.

Carpenter, Charli. 2016. "Rethinking the Political-/-Science-/Fiction Nexus: Global Policy Making and the Campaign to Stop Killer Robots." *Perspectives on Politics* 14 (1): 53–69.

Carr, Madeline. 2016. *US Power and the Internet in International Relations: The Irony of the Information Age*. Palgrave Macmillan.

Carroll, Patrick. 2006. *Science, Culture, and Modern State Formation*. University of California Press.

Carter, Ash. 2019. *Inside the Five-Sided Box: Lessons from a Lifetime of Leadership in the Pentagon*. Dutton.

Cartwright, James E. 2010. "Memorandum: Joint Terminology for Cyberspace Operations." https://nsarchive2.gwu.edu//dc.html?doc=2692112-Document-10.

Carvin, Stephanie. 2012. "The Trouble with Targeted Killing." *Security Studies* 21 (3): 529–555.

Carvin, Stephanie. 2015. "Getting Drones Wrong." *International Journal of Human Rights* 19 (2): 127–141.

Castells, Manuel. 1996. *The Rise of the Network Society. Vol. I of The Information Age: Economy, Society, and Culture*. Wiley-Blackwell.

Cavallaro, James, Stephan Sonnenberg, and Sarah Knuckey. 2012. "Living Under Drones: Death, Injury and Trauma to Civilians from US Drone Practices in Pakistan." Stanford Law School and NYU School of Law.

Cerny, Philip G. 1995. "Globalization and the Changing Logic of Collective Action." *International Organization* 49 (4): 595–625.

Chamayou, Grégoire. [2013] 2015. *A Theory of the Drone*. Translated by Janet Lloyd. The New Press.

Chesney, Robert. 2019. "CYBERCOM's Out-of-Network Operations." *Lawfare*, May 9. https://www.lawfareblog.com/cybercoms-out-network-operations-what-has-and-has-not-changed-over-past-year.

Choucri, Nazli. 2012. *Cyberpolitics in International Relations*. MIT Press.

Ciampi, Gabriele. 2001. "Cartographic Problems of the Eritreo-Ethiopian Border." *Africa: Rivista trimestrale di studi e documentazione dell'Istituto italiano per l'Africa e l'Oriente* 56 (2): 155–189.

Clarke, Richard A., and Robert K. Knake. 2019. *The Fifth Domain*. Penguin Press.

Claussen, Kathleen. 2009. "Invisible Borders: Mapping out Virtual Law?" *Denver Journal of International Law and Policy* 37 (2): 257–278.

Clinton Digital Library. 1995a. "1995-11-07, Don Kerrick to Tony Lake re Dayton SITREP #3 November 7, 1995, 900am." Clinton Digital Library. http://clinton.presidentiallibraries.us/items/show/12581.

Clinton Digital Library. 1995b. "1995-11-13B, Don Kerrick to Tony Lake re Dayton SITREP #8 November 11–13, 1995, 1030am." Clinton Digital Library, http://clinton.presidentiallibraries.us/items/show/12587.

Clinton Digital Library. 1995c. "1995-11-14E, Don Kerrick to Tony Lake re Dayton SITREP #9 November 14, 1995, 110am." Clinton Digital Library, http://clinton.presidentiallibraries.us/items/show/12592.

Clinton Digital Library. 1995d. "1995-11-17, Don Kerrick to Tony Lake re Dayton SITREP #12 November 17, 1995, 1110am." Clinton Digital Library, http://clinton.presidentiallibraries.us/items/show/12597.

Clinton Digital Library. 1996. "1996-10-30, Dayton History Project Interview with Warren Christopher October 30, 1996." Clinton Digital Library, http://clinton.presidentiallibraries.us/items/show/12628.

Clinton, Hillary. 2015. "Hillary Clinton on National Security and the Islamic State." Hosted by Fareed Zakaria. Council on Foreign Relations (CFR), November 19. https://www.cfr.org/event/hillary-clinton-national-security-and-islamic-state.

Cloud, David S. 2011. "Anatomy of an Afghan War Tragedy." *Los Angeles Times*, April 10. https://www.latimes.com/archives/la-xpm-2011-apr-10-la-fg-afghanistan-drone-20110410-story.html.

Coeckelbergh, Mark. 2013. "Drones, Information Technology, and Distance: Mapping the Moral Epistemology of Remote Fighting." *Ethics and Information Technology* 15 (2): 87–98.

Cohen, Julie E. 2007. "Cyberspace As/And Space." *Columbia Law Review* 107: 210–256.

Cohen, Raymond, and Paul Meerts. 2008. "The Evolution of International Negotiation Processes." *International Negotiation* 13 (2): 149–156.

Coles-Kemp, Lizzie, Debi Ashenden, and Kieron O'Hara. 2018. "Why Should I? Cybersecurity, the Security of the State and the Insecurity of the Citizen." *Politics and Governance* 6 (2): 41–48.

Collier, Stephen J., and Andrew Lakoff. 2008. "The Vulnerability of Vital Systems: How 'Critical Infrastructure' Became a Security Problem." In *Securing "the Homeland": Critical infrastructure, Risk and (In)security*, edited by Myriam Dunn Cavelty and Kristian Søby Kristensen. Routledge.

Coopmans, Catelijne, Janet Vertesi, Michael Lynch, and Steve Woolgar, eds. 2014. *Representation in Scientific Practice Revisited*. MIT Press.

Corn, Gary. 2017. "Tallinn Manual 2.0 – Advancing the Conversation." *Just Security*, February 15. https://www.justsecurity.org/37812/tallinn-manual-2-o-advancing-conversation/.

Corson, Mark W., and Julian V. Minghi. 1996. "*PowerScene*: Application of New Geographic Technology to Revolutionise Boundary Making?" *IBRU Boundary and Security Bulletin Summer 1996. Borderlines* 102: 34–37.

Cosgrove, Denis. 2001. *Apollo's Eye: A Cartographic Genealogy of the Earth in the Western Imagination*. Johns Hopkins University Press.

Cramer, Maria. 2021. "A.I. Drone May Have Acted on Its Own in Attacking Fighters, U.N. Says." *New York Times*, June 4. https://www.nytimes.com/2021/06/03/world/africa/libya-drone.html.

Crampton, Jeremy W. 1996. "Bordering on Bosnia." *GeoJournal* 39 (4): 353–361.

Crampton, Jeremy W. 2001. "Maps as Social Constructions: Power, Communication, and Visualization." *Progress in Human Geography* 25 (2): 235–252.

Crampton, Jeremy W. 2010. *Mapping: A Critical Introduction to Cartography and GIS*. Wiley-Blackwell.

Crampton, Jeremy W. 2015. "Collect It All: National Security, Big Data and Governance." *GeoJournal* 80 (4): 519–531.

Crampton, Jeremy W. 2016. "Assemblage of the Vertical: Commercial Drones and Algorithmic Life." *Geographica Helvetica* 71 (2): 137–146.

Crampton, Jeremy W., Susan M. Roberts, and Ate Poorthuis. 2014. "The New Political Economy of Geographical Intelligence." *Annals of the Association of American Geographers* 104 (1): 196–214.

Crawford, Neta C. 2000. "The Passion of World Politics: Propositions on Emotion and Emotional Relationships." *International Security* 24 (4): 116–156.

Crawford, Neta C. 2002. *Argument and Change in World Politics*. Cambridge University Press.

Creemers, Rogier. 2023. "The Chinese Conception of Cybersecurity: A Conceptual, Institutional and Regulatory Genealogy." *Journal of Contemporary China* 33 (146): 173–188.

Crosby, Alfred W. 1997. *The Measure of Reality: Quantification and Western Society, 1250–1600.* Cambridge University Press.

Cummings, M. L. 2004. "Creating Moral Buffers in Weapon Control Interface Design." *IEEE Technology and Society Magazine* 23 (3): 28–41.

Cummings, M. L. 2017. "Artificial Intelligence and the Future of Warfare." Chatham House.

Curtis, Bruce. 2001. *The Politics of Population: State Formation, Statistics, and the Census of Canada, 1840–1875.* University of Toronto Press.

Cybersecurity and Infrastructure Security Agency (CISA). 2020. "Joint Statement from Elections Infrastructure Government Coordinating Council & the Election Infrastructure Sector Coordinating Executive Committees." https://www.cisa.gov/news-events/news/joint-statement-elections-infrastructure-government-coordinating-council-election.

Dafoe, Allan. 2015. "On Technological Determinism: A Typology, Scope Conditions, and a Mechanism." *Science, Technology, & Human Values* 40 (6): 1047–1076.

Daggett, Cara. 2019. "World-Viewing as World-Making: Feminist Technoscience, International Relations, and the Aesthetics of the Anthropocene." In *Science, Technology, and Art in International Relations,* edited by J. P. Singh, Madeline Carr, and Renée Marlin-Bennett. Routledge.

Dalton, Craig M. 2013. "Sovereigns, Spooks, and Hackers: An Early History of Google Geo Services and Map Mashups." *Cartographica* 48 (4): 261–274.

David, Paul A. 1985. "Clio and the Economics of QWERTY." *American Economic Review* 75 (2): 332–337.

Davies, Harry, Bethan McKernan and Dan Sabbagh. 2023. "'The Gospel': How Israel uses AI to select bombing targets in Gaza." *The Guardian*, December 1. https://www.theguardian.com/world/2023/dec/01/the-gospel-how-israel-uses-ai-to-select-bombing-targets.

Deibert, Ronald J. 1997. *Parchment, Printing, and Hypermedia: Communication in World Order Transformation.* Columbia University Press.

Demchak, Chris C., and Peter J. Dombrowski. 2011. "Rise of a Cybered Westphalian Age." *Strategic Studies Quarterly* 5 (1): 32–61.

DeNardis, Laura. 2014. *The Global War for Internet Governance.* Yale University Press.

Department of Defense. 2010a. "Instruction S-5240.23: Counterintelligence (CI) Activities in Cyberspace." December 13. https://nsarchive2.gwu.edu/NSAEBB/NSAEBB424/docs/Cyber-041.pdf.

Department of Defense. 2010b. "U.S. Cyber Command Fact Sheet." May 25. https://nsarchive2.gwu.edu/NSAEBB/NSAEBB424/docs/Cyber-038.pdf.

Department of Defense. 2011. "Department of Defense Strategy for Operating in Cyberspace." https://nsarchive2.gwu.edu/dc.html?doc=2700131-Document-50.

Department of Defense. 2012. "Department of Defense Directive 3000.09, November 21, 2012: 'Autonomy in Weapons Systems.'" https://www.esd.whs.mil/Portals/54/Documents/DD/issuances/dodd/300009p.pdf

Department of Defense. 2013. "Instruction S-3325.10: Human Intelligence (HUMINT) Activities in Cyberspace." June 6. https://nsarchive2.gwu.edu//dc.html?doc=2692127-Document-19.

Department of Defense. 2015. "The Department of Defense Cyber Strategy." https://nsarchive2.gwu.edu/dc.html?doc=2692133-Document-25.

Department of Defense. 2017. "Unmanned Systems Integrated Roadmap, 2017–2042." https://www.hsdl.org/?abstract&did=826737.

Department of Defense. 2018. "Summary: Department of Defense Cyber Strategy." https://nsarchive2.gwu.edu//dc.html?doc=4936880-Department-of-Defense-Summary-Department-of.

Department of Defense. 2020. "Critical Infrastructure Program Glossary." https://policy.defense.gov/OUSDP-Offices/ASD-for-Homeland-Defense-Global-Security/Defense-Critical-Infrastructure-Program/cip_glossary/.

Department of Defense. 2023. "Summary: 2023 Cyber Strategy." https://media.defense.gov/2023/Sep/12/2003299076/1/1/1/2023_DOD_Cyber_Strategy_Summary.PDF.

Department of Homeland Security. 2003. "Homeland Security Presidential Directive 7: Critical Infrastructure Identification, Prioritization, and Protection." https://www.dhs.gov/homeland-security-presidential-directive-7.

Department of Homeland Security. 2011. "Cybersecurity Strategy for the Homeland Security Enterprise." https://www.dhs.gov/xlibrary/assets/nppd/blueprint-for-a-secure-cyber-future.pdf.

Department of Homeland Security. 2016. "Joint Statement from the Department of Homeland Security and Office of the Director of National Intelligence on Election Security." October 7. https://www.dhs.gov/news/2016/10/07/joint-statement-department-homeland-security-and-office-director-national.

Department of Homeland Security. 2018. "Secretary Kirstjen M. Nielsen Remarks to the National Election Security Summit." September 10. https://www.dhs.gov/news/2018/09/10/secretary-kirstjen-m-nielsen-remarks-national-election-security-summit.

Der Derian, James. 2009. *Virtuous War: Mapping the Military-Industrial-Media-Entertainment Network*. 2nd ed. Routledge.

Desrosières, Alain. 1998. *The Politics of Large Numbers: A History of Statistical Reasoning*. Translated by Camille Naish. Harvard University Press.

Dizard, Wilson Jr. 2001. *Digital Diplomacy: U.S. Foreign Policy in the Information Age*. Praeger Publishers.

Dodge, Martin. 2008. "Understanding Cyberspace Cartographies: A Critical Analysis of Internet Infrastructure Mapping." PhD diss., University College London.

Drieschova, Alena. 2017. "Peirce's Semeiotics: A Methodology for Bridging the Material–Ideational Divide in IR Scholarship." *International Theory* 9 (1): 33–66.

Drulák, Petr. 2006. "Motion, Container and Equilibrium: Metaphors in the Discourse About European Integration." *European Journal of International Relations* 12 (4): 499–531.

Dunn Cavelty, Myriam. 2012. "The Militarisation of Cyber Security as a Source of Global Tension." *Strategic Trends 2012: Key Developments in Global Affairs* 12 (4): 499–531.

Dunn Cavelty, Myriam. 2013. "From Cyber-Bombs to Political Fallout: Threat Representations with an Impact in the Cyber-Security Discourse." *International Studies Review* 15 (1): 105–122.

Dunn Cavelty, Myriam. 2018. "Cybersecurity Research Meets Science and Technology Studies." *Politics and Governance* 6 (2): 22–30.

Dunn Cavelty, Myriam. 2019. "The Materiality of Cyberthreats: Securitization Logics in Popular Visual Culture." *Critical Studies on Security* 7 (2): 138–151.

Dunn Cavelty, Myriam, and Florian J. Egloff. 2019. "The Politics of Cybersecurity: Balancing Different Roles of the State." *St. Antony's International Review* 15 (1): 37–47.

Dunn, David Hastings. 2013. "Drones: Disembodied Aerial Warfare and the Unarticulated Threat." *International Affairs* 89 (5): 1237–1246.

Easterling, Keller. 2014. *Extrastatecraft: The Power of Infrastructure Space*. Verso.

The Economist. "How Google Represents Disputed Borders Between Countries." September 4, 2014.

Edney, Matthew H. 1997. *Mapping an Empire: The Geographical Construction of British India, 1765–1843*. Chicago: University of Chicago Press.

Edney-Browne, Alex. 2019. "Vision, Visuality, and Agency in the US Drone Orogram." In *Technology and Agency in International Relations*, edited by Marijn Hoijtink and Matthias Leese. Routledge.

Edwards, Paul N. 1996. *The Closed World: Computers and the Politics of Discourse in Cold War America*. MIT Press.

Edwards, Paul N. 2003. "Infrastructure and Modernity: Force, Time, and Social Organization in the History of Sociotechnical Systems." In *Modernity and*

Technology, edited by Thomas J. Misa, Philip Brey, and Andrew Feenberg. MIT Press.

Elish, M. C. 2017. "Remote Split: A History of US Drone Operations and the Distributed Labor of War." *Science, Technology, & Human Values* 42 (6): 1100–1131.

Enloe, Cynthia. 2014. *Bananas, Beaches, and Bases: Making Feminist Sense of International Politics*. University of California Press.

Eritrea-Ethiopia Boundary Commission (EEBC). 2006. "Eritrea-Ethiopia Boundary Commission: Statement by the Commission." November 27. https://pcacases.com/web/sendAttach/809.

Evans, Sandra K., Katy E. Pearce, Jessica Vitak, and Jeffrey W. Treem. 2017. "Explicating Affordances: A Conceptual Framework for Understanding Affordances in Communication Research." *Journal of Computer-Mediated Communication* 22 (1): 35–52.

Farocki, Harun. 2004. "Phantom Images." *Public* 29: 12–22.

Farrell, Henry. 2012. "The Consequences of the Internet for Politics." *Annual Review of Political Science* 15: 35–52.

Farrell, Henry, and Charles L. Glaser. 2017. "The Role of Effects, Saliencies and Norms in U.S. Cyberwar Doctrine." *Journal of Cybersecurity* 3 (1): 7–17.

Farrell, Henry, and Abraham L. Newman. 2019. "Weaponized Interdependence: How Global Economic Networks Shape State Coercion." *International Security* 44 (1): 42–79.

Fearon, James D. 1995. "Rationalist Explanations for War." *International Organization* 49 (3): 379–414.

Feenberg, Andrew. 2002. *Transforming Technology: A Critical Theory Revisited*. Oxford University Press.

Ferguson, Yale H., and Richard W. Mansbach. 1996. *Polities: Authority, Identities, and Change*. University of South Carolina Press.

Feuer, Anna. 2020. "The Frictionless Battlefield: Nature and Technology in Counterinsurgency Wars." PhD diss., Yale University.

Field, Alexander J. 1994. "French Optical Telegraphy, 1793–1855: Hardware, Software, Administration." *Technology and Culture* 35 (2): 315–347.

Finnemore, Martha, and Duncan B. Hollis. 2016. "Constructing Norms for Global Cybersecurity." *American Journal of International Law* 110 (3): 425–479.

Fioretos, Orfeo. 2011. "Historical Institutionalism in International Relations." *International Organization* 65 (2): 367–399.

Friedrichs, Jörg, and Friedrich Kratochwil. 2009. "On Acting and Knowing: How Pragmatism Can Advance International Relations Research and Methodology." *International Organization* 63 (4): 701–731.

Fritsch, Stefan. 2011. "Technology and Global Affairs." *International Studies Perspectives* 12 (1): 27–45.

Futter, Andrew. 2018. "'Cyber' Semantics: Why We Should Retire the Latest Buzzword in Security Studies." *Journal of Cyber Policy* 3 (2): 201–216.

Future of Life Institute. 2015. "Autonomous Weapons Open Letter AI & Robotics Researchers." July 28. https://futureoflife.org/open-letter-autonomous-weapons/

Gartzke, Erik. 2013. "The Myth of Cyberwar: Bringing War in Cyberspace Back Down to Earth." *International Security* 38 (2): 41–73.

Gartzke, Erik, and Jon R. Lindsay. 2015. "Weaving Tangled Webs: Offense, Defense, and Deception in Cyberspace." *Security Studies* 24 (2): 316–348.

Geens, Stefan. 2010. "About Costa Rica, Nicaragua, Their Mutual Border, and Google." *Ogle Earth*, November 7. http://ogleearth.com/2010/11/about-costa-rica-nicaragua-their-border-and-google/.

Gibbs Jr., Raymond W., ed. 2008. *The Cambridge Handbook of Metaphor and Thought*. Cambridge University Press.

Gibson, William. 1984. *Neuromancer*. Ace Books.

Gibson, William. 1988. *Mona Lisa Overdrive*. Bantam Spectra.

Gibson, William. 1991. "Academy Leader." In *Cyberspace: First Steps*, edited by Michael Benedikt. MIT Press.

Giles, Keir, and William Hagestad II. 2013. "Divided by a Common Language: Cyber Definitions in Chinese, Russian and English." In *2013 5th International Conference on Cyber Conflict*, edited by Karlis Podins, Jan Stinissen, and Markus Maybaum. NATO CCD COE Publications.

Gilpin, Robert. 1975. *Technology, Economic Growth, and International Competitiveness: A Report Prepared for the Use of the Subcommittee on Economic Growth of the Joint Economic Committee, Congress of the United States*. US Government Printing Office.

Ginsburg, Tom. 2017. "Introduction to Symposium on Sovereignty, Cyberspace, and Tallinn Manual 2.0." *American Journal of International Law Unbound* 111: 205–206.

Goddard, Stacie E. 2010. *Indivisible Territory and the Politics of Legitimacy: Jerusalem and Northern Ireland*. Cambridge University Press.

Goertz, Gary, and Paul F. Diehl. 1992. *Territorial Changes and International Conflict*. Routledge.

Goertz, Gary, Paul F. Diehl, and Alexandru Balas. 2016. *The Puzzle of Peace: The Evolution of Peace in the International System*. Oxford University Press.

Goldman, Emily O., and John Arquilla, eds. 2014. *Cyber Analogies*. Naval Postgraduate School.

Goldsmith, Jack L. 1998. "The Internet and the Abiding Significance of Territorial Sovereignty." *Indiana Journal of Global Legal Studies* 5 (2): 475–491.

Goodchild, Michael F. 2007. "Citizens as Sensors: the World of Volunteered Geography." *GeoJournal* 69 (4): 211–221.

Graham, Mark. 2013. "Geography/Internet: Ethereal Alternate Dimensions of Cyberspace or Grounded Augmented Realities?" *The Geographical Journal* 179 (2): 177–182.

Gravois, John. 2010. "The Agnostic Cartographer: How Google's Open-Ended Maps Are Embroiling the Company in Some of the World's Touchiest Geopolitical Disputes." *Washington Monthly*, August 1. https://longreads.com/2010/07/09/the-agnostic-cartographer/.

Grayson, Kyle. 2016. "Drones." In *Making Things International 2: Catalysts and Reactions*, edited by Mark B. Salter. University of Minnesota Press.

Grayson, Kyle, and Jocelyn Mawdsley. 2019. "Scopic Regimes and the Visual Turn in International Relations: Seeing World Politics Through the Drone." *European Journal of International Relations* 25 (2): 431–457.

Greathouse, Craig B. 2014. "Cyber War and Strategic Thought: Do the Classic Theorists Still Matter?" In *Cyberspace and International Relations: Theory, Prospects and Challenges*, edited by Jan-Frederik Kremer and Benedikt Müller. Springer Publishing.

Gregory, Derek. 2011a. "From a View to a Kill: Drones and Late Modern War." *Theory, Culture & Society* 28 (7–8): 188–215.

Gregory, Derek. 2011b. "The Everywhere War." *The Geographical Journal* 177 (3): 238–250.

Gregory, Derek. 2014. "Drone Geographies." *Radical Philosophy* 183 (3): 7–19.

Guazzini, Federica. 2009. "The Eritrean-Ethiopian Boundary Conflict: The Physical Border and the Human Border." In *The 1998–2000 War between Eritrea and Ethiopia: An International Legal Perspective*, edited by Andrea De Guttry, Harry H. G. Post, and Gabriella Venturini. TMC ASSER Press.

Guldi, Jo. 2012. *Roads to Power: Britain Invents the Infrastructure State*. Harvard University Press

Gusterson, Hugh. 2016. *Drone: Remote Control Warfare*. MIT Press.

Hacking, Ian. 1975. *The Emergence of Probability*. Cambridge University Press.

Hacking, Ian. 1990. *The Taming of Chance*. Cambridge University Press.

Haggerty, Kevin D. 2002. "The Politics of Statistics: Variations on a Theme." *Canadian Journal of Sociology* 27 (1): 89–105.

Haklay, Mordechai. 2013. "Neogeography and the Delusion of Democratisation." *Environment and Planning A: Economy and Space* 45 (1): 55–69.

Hall, Abigail R., and Christopher J. Coyne. 2014. "The Political Economy of Drones." *Defence and Peace Economics* 25 (5): 445–460.

Hall, Todd H., and Andrew A. G. Ross. 2015. "Affective Politics After 9/11." *International Organization* 69 (4): 847–879.

Hansen, Jason D. 2015. *Mapping the Germans: Statistical Science, Cartography, and the Visualization of the German Nation, 1848–1914.* Oxford University Press.

Hansen, Lene, and Helen Nissenbaum. 2009. "Digital Disaster, Cyber Security, and the Copenhagen School." *International Studies Quarterly* 53 (4): 1155–1175.

Harley, J. B. 2001. *The New Nature of Maps: Essays in the History of Cartography.* Edited by Paul Laxton. Johns Hopkins University Press.

Harley, J. B., and David Woodward, eds. 1987. *The History of Cartography, Vol.1: Cartography in Prehistoric, Ancient, and Medieval Europe and the Mediterranean.* University of Chicago Press.

Hasian, Marouf Jr., Sean Lawson, and Megan McFarlane. 2015. *The Rhetorical Invention of America's National Security State.* Lexington Books.

Hasik, James. 2008. *Arms and Innovation: Entrepreneurship and Alliances in the Twenty-First-Century Defense Industry.* University of Chicago Press.

Hassner, Ron. E. 2006/2007. "The Path to Intractability: Time and the Entrenchment of Territorial Disputes." *International Security* 31 (3): 107–138.

Hassner, Ron E. 2009. *War on Sacred Grounds.* Cornell University Press.

Hassner, Ron E., and Jason Wittenberg. 2015. "Barriers to Entry: Who Builds Fortified Boundaries and Why?" *International Security* 40 (1): 157–190.

Hayden, Michael V. 2011. "The Future of Things 'Cyber.'" *Strategic Studies Quarterly* 5 (1): 3–7.

Hayden, Michael V. 2016. *Playing to the Edge: American Intelligence in the Age of Terror.* Penguin Books.

Hayles, N. Katherine. 1999. *How We Became Posthuman: Virtual Bodies in Cybernetics, Literature, and Informatics.* University of Chicago Press.

Hayles, N. Katherine. 2012. *How We Think: Digital Media and Contemporary Technogenesis.* University of Chicago Press.

Hayles, N. Katherine. 2017. *Unthought: The Power of the Cognitive Nonconscious.* University of Chicago Press.

Headrick, Daniel R. 1981. *The Tools of Empire: Technology and European Imperialism in the Nineteenth Century.* Oxford University Press.

Headrick, Daniel R. 1991. *The Invisible Weapon: Telecommunications and International Politics 1851–1945.* Oxford University Press.

Healey, Jason, ed. 2013. *A Fierce Domain: Conflict in Cyberspace, 1986 to 2012.* Cyber Conflict Studies Association.

Hecht, Eado. 2022. "Drones in the Nagorno-Karabakh War: Analyzing the Data," *Military Strategy Magazine* 7 (4): 31–37.

Heftye, Erik. 2017. "Multi-Domain Confusion: All Domains Are Not Created Equal." *The Strategy Bridge*, May 26. https://thestrategybridge.org/the-bridge/2017/5/26/multi-domain-confusion-all-domains-are-not-created-equal/.

Hegarty, Mary, Harvey S. Smallman, Andrew Stull, and Matt S. Canham. 2009. "Naïve Cartography: How Intuitions about Display Configuration Can Hurt Performance." *Cartographica* 44 (3): 171–186.

Henriksen, Anders. 2019. "The End of the Road for the UN GGE Process: The Future Regulation of Cyberspace." *Journal of Cybersecurity* 5: 1–9.

Herrera, Geoffrey L. 2006. *Technology and International Transformation: The Railroad, the Atom Bomb, and the Politics of Technological Change*. SUNY Press.

Herrera, Geoffrey L. 2007. "Cyberspace and Sovereignty: Thoughts on Physical Space and Digital Space." In *Power and Security in the Information Age*, edited by Myriam Dunn Cavelty, Victor Mauer, and Sai Felicia Krishna-Hensel. Ashgate.

Hoijtink, Marijn, and Matthias Leese. 2019. *Technology and Agency in International Relations*. Routledge.

Holbrooke, Richard. 1998. *To End a War*. Modern Library.

Hollis, Duncan B., and Jens David Ohlin. 2018. "What if Cyberspace Were for Fighting?" *Ethics & International Affairs* 32 (4): 441–456.

Holmes, Marcus. 2013. "The Force of Face-to-Face Diplomacy: Mirror Neurons and the Problem of Intentions." *International Organization* 67 (4): 829–861.

Holmes, Marcus. 2014. "International Politics at the Brain's Edge: Social Neuroscience and a New 'Via Media.'" *International Studies Perspectives* 15 (2): 209–228.

Holmes, Marcus. 2015. "Digital Diplomacy and International Change Management." In *Digital Diplomacy: Theory and Practice*, edited by Corneliu Bjola and Marcus Holmes. Routledge.

Holmes, Marcus, and Keren Yarhi-Milo. 2016. "The Psychological Logic of Peace Summits: How Empathy Shapes Outcomes of Diplomatic Negotiations." *International Studies Quarterly* 61 (1): 107–122.

Holmqvist, Caroline. 2013. "Undoing War: War Ontologies and the Materiality of Drone Warfare." *Millennium: Journal of International Studies* 41 (3): 535–552.

Hopmann, P. Terrence. 1995. "Two Paradigms of Negotiation: Bargaining and Problem Solving." *Annals of the American Academy of Political and Social Science* 542 (1): 24–47.

Hopmann, P. Terrence. 1996. *The Negotiation Process and the Resolution of International Conflicts*. University of South Carolina Press.

Hopmann, P. Terrence. 2002. "Negotiating Data: Reflections on the Qualitative and Quantitative Analysis of Negotiation Processes." *International Negotiation* 7: 67–85.

Horowitz, Michael C. 2016. "The Ethics & Morality of Robotic Warfare: Assessing the Debate over Autonomous Weapons." *Daedalus* 145 (4): 25–36.

Hostetler, Laura. 2001. *Qing Colonial Enterprise: Ethnography and Cartography in Early Modern China.* University of Chicago Press.

Human Rights Watch (HRW). 2010. "Letter to Obama on Targeted Killings and Drones." December 7. https://www.hrw.org/news/2010/12/07/letter-obama-targeted-killings-and-drones.

Hunter, Dan. 2003. "Cyberspace as Place and the Tragedy of the Digital Anticommons." *California Law Review* 91 (2): 439–519.

Hutchison, Emma. 2016. *Affective Communities in World Politics: Collective Emotions After Trauma.* Cambridge University Press.

Hutchison, Emma, and Roland Bleiker. 2014. "Theorizing Emotions in World Politics." *International Theory* 6 (3): 491–514.

Huth, Paul K. 1996. *Standing Your Ground: Territorial Disputes and International Conflict.* University of Michigan Press.

Iklé, Fred Charles. 1964. *How Nations Negotiate.* Harper and Row.

Innis, Harold. 1950. *Empire and Communications.* Oxford University Press.

Jacobs, Frank. 2012. "Borderlines: The First Google Maps War." *New York Times*, February 28. http://opinionator.blogs.nytimes.com/2012/02/28/the-first-google-maps-war/.

Jasanoff, Sheila, ed. 2004. *States of Knowledge: The Co-Production of Science and the Social Order.* Routledge.

JASON. 2017. "Perspectives on Research in Artificial Intelligence and Artificial General Intelligence Relevant to DoD." https://apps.dtic.mil/sti/pdfs/AD1024432.pdf.

Joerges, Bernward. 1999. "Do Politics Have Artefacts?" *Social Studies of Science* 29 (3): 411–431.

Johnson, David R., and David Post. 1996. "Law and Borders: The Rise of Law in Cyberspace." *Stanford Law Review* 48 (5): 1367–1402.

Johnson, Richard G. 1999. "Negotiating the Dayton Peace Accords through Digital Maps." *USIP Virtual Diplomacy Report*, February 25.

Joint Chiefs of Staff. 1996. "Joint Vision 2010." On file with the author.

Joint Chiefs of Staff. 2000. "Joint Vision 2020." *Joint Forces Quarterly* (Summer): 57–76.

Joint Chiefs of Staff. 2004. "The National Military Strategy of the United States of America." https://archive.defense.gov/news/Mar2005/d20050318nms.pdf.

Joint Chiefs of Staff. 2006. "The National Military Strategy for Cyberspace Operations." https://nsarchive2.gwu.edu/NSAEBB/NSAEBB424/docs/Cyber-023.pdf.

Joint Chiefs of Staff. 2018. "Joint Publication 3-12: Cyberspace Operations." June 8. https://nsarchive2.gwu.edu/dc.html?doc=4560063-Joint-Chiefs-of-Staff-Joint-Publication-3-12.

Joint Chiefs of Staff. 2021. "Joint Publication 1-02. DOD Dictionary of Military and Associated Terms." November. https://irp.fas.org/doddir/dod/dictionary.pdf.

Kaag, John, and Sarah Kreps. 2014. *Drone Warfare*. Polity Press.

Kaikobad, Kaiyan Homi. 2009. "The Eritrea-Ethiopia Boundary Commission: A Legal Analysis of the Boundary Delimitation Decision of 13th April 2002 and Relevant Subsequent Decisions." In *The 1998–2000 Eritrea-Ethiopia War and Its Aftermath in International Legal Perspective*, edited by Andrea De Guttry, Harry H. G. Post, and Gabriella Venturini. TMC ASSER Press.

Kalpagam, U. 2014. *Rule By Numbers: Governmentality in Colonial India*. Lexington Books.

Kamis, Ben, and Thorsten Thiel. 2015. "The Original Battle Trolls: How States Represent the Internet as a Violent Place." PRIF Working Paper No. 23. Peace Research Institute Frankfurt. https://www.hsfk.de/fileadmin/HSFK/hsfk_downloads/PRIF_WP_23.pdf.

Kaplan, Fred. 2016. *Dark Territory: The Secret History of Cyber War*. Simon & Schuster.

Karas, Thomas H., Judy H. Moore, and Lori K. Parrott. 2008. "Metaphors for Cyber Security." Sandia Report SAND2008-5381.

Kass, Lani. 2006. "A Warfighting Domain." Presentation, AF Cyberspace Task Force, September 26. On file with the author.

Kaye, Thomas G. n.d. "Shaping History: International Boundary Depictions Trigger Geopolitical Fallout." Unpublished paper. On file with the author.

Kello, Lucas. 2017. *The Virtual Weapon and International Order*. Yale University Press.

Kerttunen, Mika, and Eneken Tikk. 2019. "Strategically normative. Norms and principles in national cybersecurity strategies." *Cyber Policy Institute, EU Cyber Direct*. April 13.

Kertzer, Joshua D., and Dustin Tingley. 2018. "Political Psychology in International Relations: Beyond the Paradigms." *Annual Review of Political Science* 21: 319–339.

Khong, Yuen Foong. 1992. *Analogies at War: Korea, Munich, Dien Bien Phu, and the Vietnam Decisions of 1965*. Princeton University Press.

Kindervater, Katharine Hall. 2016. "The Emergence of Lethal Surveillance: Watching and Killing in the History of Drone Technology." *Security Dialogue* 47 (3): 223–238.

Kindervater, Katharine Hall. 2017. "The Technological Rationality of the Drone Strike." *Critical Studies on Security* 5 (1): 28–44.

King, Angus, and Mike Gallagher. 2020. Cyberspace Solarium Commission. https://www.solarium.gov/.

Kinsella, Helen M. 2005. "Discourses of Difference: Civilians, Combatants, and Compliance with the Laws of War." *Review of International Studies* 31: 163–185.

Kirkpatrick, Jesse. 2015. "Drones and the Martial Virtue Courage." *Journal of Military Ethics* 14 (3–4)" 202–219.

Kitchin, Rob, and Martin Dodge. 2011. *Code/Space: Software and Everyday Life*. MIT Press.

Kitchin, Rob, Justin Gleeson, and Martin Dodge. 2012. "Unfolding Mapping Practices: A New Epistemology for Cartography." *Transactions of the Institute of British Geographers* 38 (3): 480–496.

Klauser, F., and S. Pedrozo. 2015. "Power and Space in the Drone Age: A Literature Review and Politico-Geographical Research Agenda." *Geographica Helvetica* 70 (4): 285–293.

Koh, Harold Hongju. 2012. "Remarks: International Law in Cyberspace." September 18. https://2009-2017.state.gov/s/l/releases/remarks/197924. htm.

Koschut, Simon, Todd H. Hall, Reinhard Wolf, Ty Solomon, Emma Hutchison, and Roland Bleiker. 2017. "Discourse and Emotions in International Relations." *International Studies Review* 19 (3)" 481–508.

Kratochwil, Friedrich. 1989. *Rules, Norms, and Decisions*. Cambridge University Press.

Krebs, Ronald R. 2015. "How Dominant Narratives Rise and Fall: Military Conflict, Politics, and the Cold War Consensus." *International Organization* 69 (1): 1–37.

Krebs, Ronald R., and Patrick Thaddeus Jackson. 2007. "Twisting Tongues and Twisting Arms: The Power of Political Rhetoric." *European Journal of International Relations* 13 (1) 35–66.

Kremenyuk, Victor A. 1991. *International Negotiation: Analysis, Approaches, Issues*. Jossey-Bass Publishers.

Kreps, Sarah, and Jacquelyn Schneider. 2019. "Escalation Firebreaks in the Cyber, Conventional, and Nuclear Domains: Moving Beyond Effects-Based Logics." *Journal of Cybersecurity* 5 (1): 1–11.

Krishna, Sankaran. 1994. "Cartographic Anxiety: Mapping the Body Politic in India." *Alternatives: Global, Local, Political* 19 (4): 507–521.

Kuhn, Werner. 2008. "Metaphor, Spatial and Map." In *Encyclopedia of Geographic Information Science*, edited by Karen K. Kemp. Sage Publishing.

Kumar, Sangeet. 2010. "Google Earth and the Nation State: Sovereignty in the Age of New Media." *Global Media and Communication* 6 (2): 154–176.

Laffey, Mark, and Jutta Weldes. 1997. "Beyond Belief: Ideas and Symbolic Technologies in the Study of International Relations." *European Journal of International Relations* 3 (2): 193–237.

Lakoff, George. 1992. "The Contemporary Theory of Metaphor." In *Metaphor and Thought*, 2nd ed., edited by Andrew Ortony. Cambridge University Press.

Lakoff, George, and Mark Johnson. 1980. *Metaphors We Live By*. University of Chicago Press.

Lambach, Daniel. 2019. "The Territorialization of Cyberspace." *International Studies Review* 22 (3): 482–506.

Lapointe, Adriane. 2011. "When Good Metaphors Go Bad: The Metaphoric 'Branding' of Cyberspace." Center for Strategic and International Studies.

Larkin, Brian. 2013. "The Politics and Poetics of Infrastructure." *Annual Review of Anthropology* 42: 327–343.

Larsson, Stefan. 2017. *Conceptions in the Code: How Metaphors Explain Legal Challenges in Digital Times*. Oxford University Press.

Latour, Bruno. 1986. "Visualization and Cognition: Thinking with Eyes and Hands." *Knowledge and Society* 6: 1–40.

Latour, Bruno. 1987. *Science in Action: How to Follow Scientists and Engineers Through Society*. Harvard University Press.

Latour, Bruno. 2005. *Reassembling the Social: An Introduction to Actor-Network-Theory*. Oxford University Press.

Lawson, Sean. 2012. "Putting the 'War' in Cyberwar: Metaphor, Analogy, and Cybersecurity Discourse in the United States." *First Monday* 17 (7). https://doi.org/10.5210/fm.v17i7.3848.

Lawson, Sean. 2014. *Nonlinear Science and Warfare: Chaos, Complexity and the U.S. Military in the Information Age*. Routledge.

Lawson, Sean. 2020. *Cybersecurity Discourse in the United States: Cyber-Doom Rhetoric and Beyond*. Routledge.

Lawson, Sean, and Michael K. Middleton. 2019. "Cyber Pearl Harbor: Analogy, fear, and the framing of cyber security threats in the United States, 1991–2016." *First Monday* 24 (3). http://dx.doi.org/10.5210/fm.v24i3.9623.

League of Nations Treaty Series. 1936. Volume CLXV, No. 3802. https://treaties.un.org/doc/Publication/UNTS/LON/Volume%20165/v165.pdf.

Leese, Matthias. 2019. "Configuring Warfare: Automation, Control, Agency." In *Technology and Agency in International Relations*, edited by Marijn Hoijtink and Matthias Leese. Routledge.

Lemley, Mark A. 2003. "Place and Cyberspace." *California Law Review* 91 (2): 521–542.

Leslie, Camilo Arturo. 2016. "Territoriality, Map-mindedness, and the Politics of Place." *Theory and Society* 45 (2): 169–201.

Lessig, Lawrence. 1996. "The Zones of Cyberspace." *Stanford Law Review* 48 (5): 1403–1411.

Lessig, Lawrence. 1999. *Code and Other Laws of Cyberspace*. Basic Books.

Leszczynski, Agnieszka. 2012. "Situating the Geoweb in Political Economy." *Progress in Human Geography* 36 (1): 72–89.

Levy, Jack S. 1997. "Prospect Theory, Rational Choice, and International Relations." *International Studies Quarterly* 41 (1): 87–112.

Libicki, Martin. 1997. "Defending Cyberspace and Other Metaphors." Center for Advanced Concepts and Technology, National Defense University.

Libicki, Martin C. 2012. "Cyberspace Is Not a Warfighting Domain." *I/S: A Journal of Law and Policy for the Information Society* 8 (2): 325–340.

Lindsay, Jon R. 2010. "'War Upon the Map': User Innovation in American Military Software." *Technology and Culture* 51 (3): 619–651.

Lindsay, Jon R. 2013. "Stuxnet and the Limits of Cyber Warfare." *Security Studies* 22 (3): 365–404.

Lindsay, Jon R. 2014/2015. "The Impact of China on Cybersecurity: Fiction and Friction." *International Security* 39 (3): 7–47.

Lindsay, Jon R. 2017. "Restrained by Design: The Political Economy of Cybersecurity." *Digital Policy, Regulation and Governance* 19 (6): 493–514.

Lindsay, Jon R. 2020a. "Cyber Conflict vs. Cyber Command: Hidden Dangers in the American Military Solution to a Large-Scale Intelligence Problem." *Intelligence and National Security* 36 (2): 260–278.

Lindsay, Jon R. 2020b. *Information Technology and Military Power*. Cornell University Press.

Lipton, Eric. 2023. "A.I. Brings the Robot Wingman to Aerial Combat." *New York Times*, August 27. https://www.nytimes.com/2023/08/27/us/politics/ai-air-force.html.

Livingston, Steven. 2015. "Commercial Remote Sensing Satellites and the Regulation of Violence in Areas of Limited Statehood." Center for Global Communication Studies. https://www.academia.edu/85161080/Commercial_Remote_Sensing_Satellites_and_the_Regulation_of_Violence_in_Areas_of_Limited_Statehood.

Lucas, George R. 2016. "Emerging Norms for Cyberwarfare." In *Binary Bullets: The Ethics of Cyberwarfare*, edited by Fritz Allhoff, Adam Henschke, and Bradley Jay Strawser. Oxford University Press.

Lupovici, Amir. 2016. "The 'Attribution Problem' and the Social Construction of 'Violence': Taking Cyber Deterrence Literature a Step Forward." *International Studies Perspectives* 17 (3): 322–342.

Lustick, Ian S. 1993. *Unsettled States, Disputed Lands: Britain and Ireland, France and Algeria, Israel and the West Bank-Gaza*. Cornell University Press.

Lute, Jane Holl, and Bruce McConnell. 2011. "Op-Ed: A Civil Perspective on Cybersecurity." *Wired*, February 14. https://www.wired.com/2011/02/dhs-op-ed/

Lynch, Michael, and Steve Woolgar, eds. 1990. *Representation in Scientific Practice*. MIT Press.

Lynn, William J., III. 2010. "Defending a New Domain: The Pentagon's Cyberstrategy." *Foreign Affairs* 89 (5): 97–108.

Macdonald, Julia, and Jacquelyn Schneider. 2019. "Battlefield Responses to New Technologies: Views from the Ground on Unmanned Aircraft." *Security Studies* 28 (2): 216–249.

Macdonald, Julia, and Jacquelyn Schneider. 2025. *The Hand Behind Unmanned: Origins of the US Autonomous Military Arsenal*. Oxford University Press.

MacDonald, Paul K. 2014. *Networks of Domination: The Social Foundations of Peripheral Conquest in International Politics*. Oxford University Press.

Mackey, Robert. 2010. "The Google Maps War That Wasn't." *New York Times*, November 19. http://thelede.blogs.nytimes.com/2010/11/19/the-google-maps-war-that-wasnt/.

Maglio, Paul P., and Teenie Matlock. 1998. "Metaphors We Surf the Web By." In *Proceedings of Workshop on Personalized and Social Navigation in Information Space*. Swedish Institute of Computer Science.

Maier, Charles S. 2016. *Once Within Borders: Territories of Power, Wealth, and Belonging since 1500*. Harvard University Press.

Manjikian, Mary. 2010. "From Global Village to Virtual Battlespace: The Colonizing of the Internet and the Extension of Realpolitik." *International Studies Quarterly* 54 (2): 381–401.

Manjikian, Mary. 2015. "Confidence-Building in Cyberspace: A Comparison of Territorial and Weapons-Based Regimes." Strategic Studies Institute and US Army War College Press.

Manjikian, Mary. 2016. "Deterring Cybertrespass and Securing Cyberspace: Lessons from United States Border Control Strategies." Strategic Studies Institute and US Army War College Press.

Mann, Michael. 1984. "The Autonomous Power of the State: Its Origins, Mechanisms and Results." *European Journal of Sociology* 25 (2): 185–213.

Mann, Michael. 1986. *The Sources of Social Power: Volume 1, A History of Power from the Beginning to AD 1760*. Cambridge University Press.

Mann, Michael. 2008. "Infrastructural Power Revisited." *Studies in Comparative International Development* 43 (3–4): 355–365.

Matlock, Teenie, Spencer C. Castro, Morgan Fleming, Timothy M. Gann, and Paul P. Maglio. 2014. "Spatial Metaphors of Web Use." *Spatial Cognition & Computation* 14 (4): 306–320.

Matz, David. 2004. "How Much Do We Know About Real Negotiations? Problems in Constructing Case Studies." *International Negotiation* 9: 359–374.

Maurer, Tim. 2019. "A Dose of Realism: The Contestation and Politics of Cyber Norms." *Hague Journal on the Rule of Law* 12: 283–305.

Mayer, Maximilian. 2017. "The Unbearable Lightness of International Relations: Technological Innovations, Creative Destruction and Assemblages." PhD diss., University of Bonn.

Mayer, Maximilian. 2019. "IR'S Constitutive Absence and the Promise of Stair." In *Science, Technology, and Art in International Relations*, edited by J. P. Singh, Madeline Carr, and Renee Marlin-Bennett. Routledge.

Mayer, Maximilian, and Michele Acuto. 2015. "The Global Governance of Large Technical Systems." *Millennium: Journal of International Studies* 43 (2): 660–683.

Mayer, Maximilian, Mariana Carpes, and Ruth Knoblich, eds. 2014. *The Global Politics of Science and Technology*. 2 vols. Springer Publishing.

Mayer, Michael. 2015. "The New Killer Drones: Understanding the Strategic Implications of Next-Generation Unmanned Combat Aerial Vehicles." *International Affairs* 91 (4): 765–780.

McCaffery, Larry. n.d. "An Interview with William Gibson." http://project.cyberpunk.ru/idb/gibson_interview.html.

McCarthy, Daniel R. 2013. "Technology and 'the International' or: How I Learned to Stop Worrying and Love Determinism." *Millennium: Journal of International Studies* 41 (3): 470–490.

McCarthy, Daniel R. 2015. *Power, Information Technology, and International Relations Theory: The Power and Politics of US Foreign Policy and Internet*. Palgrave Macmillan.

McCarthy, Daniel R., ed. 2017. *Technology and World Politics: An Introduction*. Routledge.

McCarthy, Daniel R. 2018. "Privatizing Political Authority: Cybersecurity, Public-Private Partnerships, and the Reproduction of Liberal Political Order." *Politics and Governance* 6 (2): 5–12.

McDermott, Rose. 2004. *Political Psychology in International Relations*. University of Michigan Press.

McDermott, Rose. 2014. "The Body Doesn't Lie: A Somatic Approach to the Study of Emotions in World Politics." *International Theory* 6 (3): 557–562.

McKernan, Bethan, and Harry Davies. 2024. "'The machine Did It Coldly': Israel Used AI to Identify 37,000 Hamas Targets." *The Guardian*, April 3. https://www.theguardian.com/world/2024/apr/03/israel-gaza-ai-database-hamas-airstrikes.

McLaughlin, Donal. 1995. *Origin of the Emblem, and other recollections of the 1945 U.N. Conference*, edited by Jennifer Truran Rothwell. https://www.cia.gov/static/5fd68956127416735fce722dcdcbe457/McLaughlinMonograph.pdf.

McNeill, William H. 1982. *The Pursuit of Power: Technology, Armed Force, and Society since A.D. 1000*. University of Chicago Press.

Mercer, Jonathan. 2005. "Prospect Theory and Political Science." *Annual Review of Political Science* 8: 1–21.

Mercer, Jonathan. 2010. "Emotional Beliefs." *International Organization* 64 (1): 1–31.

Mercer, Jonathan. 2014. "Feeling Like a State: Social Emotion and Identity." *International Theory* 6 (3): 515–535.

Merel, Ethan R. 2016. "Google's World: The Impact of 'Agnostic Cartographers' on the State-Dominated International Legal System." *Columbia Journal of Transnational Law* 54: 424–453.

Miller, Christopher C. 2006. "A Beast in the Field: The Google Maps Mashups as GIS/2." *Cartographica* 41 (3): 187–199.

Milliken, Jennifer. 1999. "The Study of Discourse in International Relations: A Critique of Research and Methods." *European Journal of International Relations* 5 (2): 225–254.

Mir, Asfandyar. 2018. "What Explains Counterterrorism Effectiveness? Evidence from the U.S. Drone War in Pakistan." *International Security* 43 (2): 45–83.

Mir, Asfandyar, and Dylan Moore. 2019. "Drones, Surveillance, and Violence: Theory and Evidence from a US Drone Program." *International Studies Quarterly* 63 (4): 846–862.

Mitchell, Timothy. 1991. "The Limits of the State: Beyond Statist Approaches and Their Critics." *American Political Science Review* 85 (1): 77–96.

Mitchell, Timothy. 2002. *Rule of Experts: Egypt, Techno-Politics, Modernity*. University of California Press.

Mize, Ramey. 2018. "'Whatever Happens, We Have Got, the Maxim, and They Have Not': The Conspicuous Absence of Machine Guns in British Imperialist Imagery." *Rutgers Art Review* (33/34): 43–65.

Mosco, Vincent. 2004. *The Digital Sublime: Myth, Power, and Cyberspace*. MIT Press.

Mueller, Milton. 2017a. "Is Cybersecurity Eating Internet Governance? Causes and Consequences of Alternative Framings." *Digital Policy, Regulation and Governance* 19 (6): 415–428.

Mueller, Milton. 2017b. *Will the Internet Fragment? Sovereignty, Globalization, and Cyberspace*. Polity.

Mueller, Milton. 2020. "Against Sovereignty in Cyberspace." *International Studies Review* 22 (4): 779–801.

Mukerji, Chandra. 2010. "The Territorial State as a Figured World of Power: Strategics, Logistics, and Impersonal Rule." *Sociological Theory* 28 (4): 402–424.

Müller, Simone M. 2016. "From Cabling the Atlantic to Wiring the World: A Review Essay on the 150th Anniversary of the Atlantic Telegraph Cable of 1866." *Technology and Culture* 57 (3): 507–526.

Mundy, Barbara E. 1996. *The Mapping of New Spain: Indigenous Cartography and the Maps of the Relaciones Geográficas*. University of Chicago Press.

Murphy, Alexander B. 2013. "Territory's Continuing Allure." *Annals of the Association of American Geographers* 103 (5): 1212–1226.

Nakashima, Ellen. 2019. "U.S. Cyber Command Operation Disrupted Internet Access of Russian Troll Factory on Day of 2018 Midterms." *Washington Post*, February 27.

Nakashima, Ellen, and Joby Warrick. 2013. "For NSA Chief, Terrorist Threat Drives Passion to 'Collect It All.'" *Washington Post*, July 14.

Nakasone, Paul M. 2019a. "An Interview with Paul M. Nakasone." *Joint Forces Quarterly* 92 (1): 4–9.

Nakasone, Paul M. 2019b. "A Cyber Force for Persistent Operations." *Joint Forces Quarterly* 92 (1): 10–14.

Nakasone, Paul M., and Michael Sulmeyer. 2020. "How to Compete in Cyberspace: Cyber Command's New Approach." *Foreign Affairs*, August 25. https://www.foreignaffairs.com/articles/united-states/2020-08-25/cybersecurity

Nakayama, Bryan. 2019. "Air, Land, Sea, Space... and Cyberspace? The Development of Military Domains." Unpublished paper.

Naksashima, Ellen, and Missy Ryan. 2016. "U.S. Military Has Launched a New Digital War Against the Islamic State." *Washington Post*, July 15.

National Defense Authorization Act (NDAA) for Fiscal Year 2019, Pub L. No. 115-232 132 Stat. 1636.

National Security Act of 1947, Pub L. No. 80-253 61 Stat. 495.

National Security Agency (NSA). 1995. "SIGINT and INFOSEC in Cyberspace." *Cryptolog*. https://nsarchive2.gwu.edu/NSAEBB/NSAEBB424/docs/Cyber-008.pdf.

Newman, David, and Anssi Paasi. 1998. "Fences and Neighbors in the Postmodern World: Boundary Narratives in Political Geography." *Progress in Human Geography* 22 (2): 186–207.

Nexon, Daniel H., and Vincent Pouliot. 2013. "'Things of Networks': Situating ANT in International Relations." *International Political Sociology* 7 (3): 342–345.

Nickles, David Paull. 2003. *Under the Wire: How the Telegraph Changed Diplomacy*. Harvard University Press.

Niva, Steve. 2013. "Disappearing Violence: JSOC and the Pentagon's New Cartography of Networked Warfare." *Security Dialogue* 44 (3): 185–202.

North Atlantic Treaty Organization (NATO). 2014. "Wales Summit Declaration." September 5. https://www.nato.int/cps/ic/natohq/official_texts_112964.htm.

Nye, David E. 2006. *Technology Matters: Questions to Live With*. MIT Press.

Nye, Joseph S. Jr. 2011. "Nuclear Lessons for Cyber Security?" *Strategic Studies Quarterly* 5 (4): 18–38.

O'Neill, Barry. 2018. "International Negotiation: Some Conceptual Developments." *Annual Review of Political Science* 21: 515–533.

Obama, Barack. 2013. "Remarks by the President at the National Defense University." May 23. https://obamawhitehouse.archives.gov/the-press-office/2013/05/23/remarks-president-national-defense-university

Ogle, Vanessa. 2015. *The Global Transformation of Time: 1870–1950*. Harvard University Press.

Olbrich, Philipp and N. Witjes. 2015. "Earth Observation and International Security: The Role of Uncertainty in Satellite Imagery Analysis by Non-State Actors." https://www.academia.edu/15976553/Earth_Observation_and_International_Security_The_Role_of_Uncertainty_in_Satellite_Imagery_Analysis_by_NonState_Actors.

Onuf, Nicholas G. 1989. *World of Our Making: Rules and Rule in Social Theory and International Relations*. University of South Carolina Press.

Onuf, Nicholas G. 2013. *Making Sense, Making Worlds: Constructivism in social theory and international relations*. Routledge.

Open-ended Working Group on Developments in the Field of Information and Telecommunications in the Context of International Security (OEWG). 2021. "Final Substantive Report." https://front.un-arm.org/wp-content/uploads/2021/03/Final-report-A-AC.290-2021-CRP.2.pdf.

Osenga, Kristen. 2013. "The Internet Is Not a Super Highway: Using Metaphors to Communicate Information and Communications Policy." *Journal of Information Policy* 3: 30–54.

Osiander, Andreas. 2007. *Before the State: Systemic Political Change in the West from the Greeks to the French Revolution.* Oxford University Press.

Otis, Laura. 2001. *Networking: Communicating with Bodies and Machines in the Nineteenth Century.* University of Michigan Press.

Passoth, Jan-Hendrik, and Nicholas J. Rowland. 2010. "Actor-Network State: Integrating Actor-Network Theory and State Theory." *International Sociology* 25 (6): 818–841.

Patriarca, Silvana. 1996. *Numbers and Nationhood: Writing Statistics in Nineteenth-Century Italy.* Cambridge University Press.

Péninou, Jean-Louis. 1998. "The Ethiopian-Eritrean Border Conflict." *IBRU Boundary and Security Bulletin*: 46–50.

Pennsylvania State University (PSU). 2010. "Mapping the Road to Peace." *The Geospatial Revolution*, Episode 3, Chapter 1.

People's Republic of China (PRC). 2015. "China's Military Strategy." http://english.gov.cn/archive/white_paper/2015/05/27/content_281475115610833.htm.

Perkins, Chris, and Martin Dodge. 2009. "Satellite Imagery and the Spectacle of Secret Spaces." *Geoforum* 40 (4): 546–560.

Perkovich, George, and Ariel E. Levite, eds. 2017. *Understanding Cyber Conflict: 14 Analogies.* Georgetown University Press.

Phillips, Andrew, and J. C. Sharman. 2015. *International Order in Diversity: War, Trade and Rule in the Indian Ocean.* Cambridge University Press.

Pickles, John. 2004. *A History of Spaces: Cartographic Reason, Mapping, and the Geo-Coded World.* Routledge.

Pigman, Geoffrey Allen. 2010. *Contemporary Diplomacy: Representation and Communication in a Globalized World.* Polity.

Pinfari, Marco. 2013. *Peace Negotiations and Time: Deadline Diplomacy in Territorial Disputes.* Routledge.

Powell, Robert. 2002. "Bargaining Theory and International Conflict." *Annual Review of Political Science* 5: 1–30.

Purdy, Jill M., Pete Nye, and P. V. Balakrishnan. 2000. "The Impact of Communication Media on Negotiation Outcomes." *International Journal of Conflict Management* 11 (2): 162–187.

Quadrennial Defense Review (QDR). 1997–2014. Historical Office, Office of the Secretary of Defense. http://history.defense.gov/Historical-Sources/Quadrennial-Defense-Review/.

Quiquivix, Linda. 2014. "Art of War, Art of Resistance: Palestinian Counter-Cartography on Google Earth." *Annals of the Association of American Geographers* 104 (3): 444–459.

Rajnovic, Damir. 2012. "Cyberspace—What Is It?" *Cisco Blogs*, July 26. https://blogs.cisco.com/security/cyberspace-what-is-it/.

Rankin, William. 2015. "Global Positioning System (GPS)." In *The History of Cartography, Volume Six: Cartography in the Twentieth Century*, edited by Mark Monmonier. University of Chicago Press.

Rankin, William. 2016. *After the Map: Cartography, Navigation, and the Transformation of Territory in the Twentieth Century*. University of Chicago Press.

Raymond, Mark. 2019. *Social Practices of Rule-Making in World Politics*. Oxford University Press.

Raymond, Mark. 2020. "Social Practices of Rule-Making for International Law in the Cyber Domain." *Journal of Global Security Studies* 6 (2). doi:10.1093/jogss/ogz065.

Raymond, Mark, and Laura DeNardis. 2015. "Multistakeholderism: anatomy of an inchoate global institution." *International Theory* 7 (3): 572–616.

Rid, Thomas. 2012. "Cyber War Will Not Take Place." *Journal of Strategic Studies* 35 (1): 5–32.

Rid, Thomas. 2013. *Cyber War Will Not Take Place*. Oxford University Press.

Rid, Thomas. 2016. *Rise of the Machines: A Cybernetic History*. Norton.

Rid, Thomas, and Ben Buchanan. 2018. "Hacking Democracy." *SAIS Review of International Affairs* 38 (1): 3–16.

Risse, Thomas. 2000. "'Let's Argue!': Communicative Action in World Politics." *International Organization* 54 (1): 1–39.

Risse, Thomas, and Eric Stollenwerk. 2018. "Legitimacy in Areas of Limited Statehood." *Annual Review of Political Science* 21, 403–418.

Roff, Heather M. 2014. "The Strategic Robot Problem: Lethal Autonomous Weapons in War." *Journal of Military Ethics* 13 (3): 211–227.

Roff, Heather M., and Richard Moyes. 2016. "Meaningful Human Control, Artificial Intelligence and Autonomous Weapons." Briefing paper prepared for the Informal Meeting of Experts on Lethal Autonomous Weapons Systems, UN Convention on Certain Conventional Weapons, April.

Rogers, Ann, and John Hill. 2014. *Unmanned: Drone Warfare and Global Security*. Pluto Press.

Ross, Lee, and Constance Stillinger. 1991. "Barriers to Conflict Resolution." *Negotiation Journal* 7 (4): 389–404.

Rothe, Delf, and David Shim. 2018. "Sensing the Ground: On the Global Politics of Satellite-Based Activism." *Review of International Studies* 44 (3): 414–437.

Rowland, Nicholas J., and Jan-Hendrik Passoth. 2015. "Infrastructure and the State in Science and Technology Studies." *Social Studies of Science* 45 (1): 137–145.

Sahlins, Peter. 1989. *Boundaries: The Making of France and Spain in the Pyrenees.* University of California Press.

Sandholtz, Wayne. 2008. "Dynamics of International Norm Change: Rules against Wartime Plunder." *European Journal of International Relations* 14 (1): 101–131.

Sanger, David E. 2018. "Pentagon Puts Cyberwarriors on the Offensive, Increasing the Risk of Conflict." *New York Times*, June 17. https://www.nytimes.com/2018/06/17/us/politics/cyber-command-trump.html

Sanger, David E., and Nicole Perlroth. 2019. "U.S. Escalates Online Attacks on Russia's Power Grid." *New York Times*, June 15. https://www.nytimes.com/2019/06/15/us/politics/trump-cyber-russia-grid.html.

Sasley, Brent E. 2010. "Affective Attachments and Foreign Policy: Israel and the 1993 Oslo Accords." *European Journal of International Relations* 16 (4): 687–709.

Sasley, Brent E. 2011. "Theorizing States' Emotions." *International Studies Review* 13 (3): 452–476.

Sauter, Molly. 2015. "Show Me on the Map Where They Hacked You: Cyberwar and the Geospatial Internet Doctrine." *Case Western Reserve Journal of International Law* 47, 63–78.

Sawhney, Harmeet. 1996. "Information Superhighway: Metaphors as Midwives." *Media, Culture and Society* 18 (2): 291–315.

Schelling, Thomas C. 1960. *The Strategy of Conflict.* Harvard University Press.

Schmitt, Michael N., ed. 2013. *Tallinn Manual on the International Law Applicable to Cyber Warfare.* Cambridge University Press.

Schmitt, Michael N., ed. 2017. *Tallinn Manual 2.0 on the International Law Applicable to Cyber Operations.* Cambridge University Press.

Schneider, Jacquelyn G. 2019. "Persistent Engagement: Foundation, Evolution and Evaluation of a strategy." *Lawfare*, May 10. https://www.lawfareblog.com/persistent-engagement-foundation-evolution-and-evaluation-strategy.

Schneider, Jacquelyn G. 2021. "The Cyber Apocalypse Never Came. Here's What We Got Instead." *Politico*, July 27. https://www.politico.com/news/magazine/2021/07/27/cyber-apocalypse-russia-china-warfare-500787.

Schön, Donald A. 1993. "Generative Metaphor: A Perspective on Problem-Setting in Social Policy." In *Metaphor and Thought*, 2nd ed., edited by Andrew Ortony. Cambridge University Press.

Schouten, Peer. 2013. "The Materiality of State Failure: Social Contract Theory, Infrastructure and Governmental Power in Congo." *Millennium: Journal of International Studies* 41 (3): 553–574.

Schweller, Randall L. 2014. *Maxwell's Demon and the Golden Apple: Global Discord in the New Millennium.* Johns Hopkins University Press.

Scott, James C. 1998. *Seeing Like a State: How Certain Schemes to Improve the Human Condition Have Failed.* Yale University Press.

Scott, James C. 2017. *Against the Grain: A Deep History of the Earliest States.* Yale University Press.

Secretary of Defense. 2009. "Memorandum: Establishment of a Subordinate Unified U.S. Cyber Command Under U.S. Strategic Command for Military Cyberspace Operations." June 23. https://nsarchive2.gwu.edu/NSAEBB/NSAEBB424/docs/Cyber-029.pdf.

Semino, Elena. 2008. *Metaphor in Discourse.* Cambridge University Press.

Shah, Aqil. 2018. "Do U.S. Drone Strikes Cause Blowback? Evidence from Pakistan and Beyond." *International Security* 42 (4): 47–84.

Shandler, Ryan, Michael L Gross, and Daphna Canetti. 2023. "Cyberattacks, Psychological Distress, and Military Escalation: An Internal Meta-Analysis." *Journal of Global Security Studies* 8 (1): 1–19.

Sharman, J. C. 2019. *Empires of the Weak: The Real Story of European Expansion and the Creation of the New World Order.* Princeton University Press.

Shaw, Ian G. R. 2013. "Predator Empire: The Geopolitics of US Drone Warfare." *Geopolitics* 18 (3): 536–559.

Shaw, Ian G. R. 2016. "Scorched Atmospheres: The Violent Geographies of the Vietnam War and the Rise of Drone Warfare." *Annals of the Association of American Geographers* 106 (3): 688–704.

Shelef, Nadav G. 2016. "Unequal Ground: Homelands and Conflict." *International Organization* 70 (1): 33–63.

Sheniak, Amit. 2014. "The Emergence of the State in the Online Frontier: A Theoretical and Historical Comparison." *Dado Journal for Operational Art* 3: 10–45.

Sheppard, Stephen R. J., and Petr Cizek. 2009. "The Ethics of Google Earth: Crossing Thresholds from Spatial Data to Landscape Visualization." *Journal of Environmental Management* 90 (6): 2102–2117.

Sheppard, Stephen R. J., Alison Shaw, David Flanders, and Sarah Burch. 2008. "Can Visualization Save the World? Lessons for Landscape Architects from Visualizing Local Climate Change." *Digital Design in Landscape Architecture, 9th International Conference on IT in Landscape Architecture.* Anhalt University of Applied Sciences.

Shim, David. 2018. "Satellites." In *Visual Global Politics*, edited by Roland Bleiker. Routledge.

Shires, James. 2019. "Cyber-Noir: Cybersecurity and Popular Culture." *Contemporary Security Policy* 41 (1): 82–107.

Shirk, Mark. 2019. "The Universal Eye: Anarchist 'Propaganda of the Deed' and Development of the Modern Surveillance State." *International Studies Quarterly* 63 (2): 334–345.

Siefert, Marsha. 2020. "The Russian Empire and the International Telegraph Union, 1856–1875." In *History of the International Telecommunication Union (ITU): Transnational techno-diplomacy from the telegraph to the Internet*, edited by Gabriele Balbi and Andreas Fickers. De Gruyter Oldenbourg.

Silverman, Jacob. 2015. "Meet the Man Whose Utopian Vision for the Internet Conquered, and Then Warped, Silicon Valley." *Washington Post*, March 20.

Simmons, Beth A. 2017. "The Built Environment: State Presence at Border Crossings in the Modern World." https://ssrn.com/abstract=3251398.

Singer, Peter W. 2009. *Wired for War*. Penguin Books.

Singh, J. P. 2019. "Science, Technology, and Art in International Relations: Origins and Prospects." In *Science, Technology, and Art in International Relations*, edited by J. P. Singh, Madeline Carr, and Renee Marlin-Bennett. Routledge.

Sismondo, Sergio. 2010. *An Introduction to Science and Technology Studies*. 2nd ed. Blackwell.

Skinner, Quentin. 1978. *The Foundations of Modern Political Thought*. 2 vols. Cambridge University Press.

Skolnikoff, Eugene B. 1992. *The Elusive Transformation: Science, Technology, and the Evolution of International Politics*. Princeton University Press.

Smeets, Max W. E., and Herbert Lin. 2018. "A Strategic Assessment of the U.S. Cyber Command Vision." In *Bytes, Bombs, and Spies: The Strategic Dimensions of Offensive Cyber Operations*, edited by Herbert Lin and Amy Zegart. Brookings Institution Press.

Smith, Merritt Roe, and Leo Marx, eds. 1994. *Does Technology Drive History? The Dilemma of Technological Determinism*. MIT Press.

Soifer, Hillel, and Matthias vom Hau. 2008. "Unpacking the *Strength* of the State: The Utility of State Infrastructural Power." *Studies in Comparative International Development* 43 (3–4): 219–230.

Stahl, Roger. 2013. "What the Drone Saw: The Cultural Optics of the Unmanned War." *Australian Journal of International Affairs* 67 (5): 659–674.

Standage, Tom. 1998. *The Victorian Internet: The Remarkable Story of the Telegraph and the Nineteenth Century's Online Pioneers*. Weidenfeld & Nicolson.

Stanley, Jay. 2013. "'Drones' vs 'UAVs'—What's Behind a Name?" *American Civil Liberties Union*, May 20. https://www.aclu.org/blog/national-security/targeted-killing/drones-vs-uavs-whats-behind-name

Stavridis, James, and David Weinsten. 2014. "Time for a U.S. Cyber Force." *US Naval Institute*: *Proceedings*, January.

Stevens, Tim. 2016. *Cyber Security and the Politics of Time*. Cambridge University Press.

Stimmer, Anette. 2019. "Star Wars or Strategic Defense Initiative: What's in a Name?" *Journal of Global Security Studies* 4 (4): 430–447.

Stone, Allucquere Rosanne. 1991. "Will the Real Body Please Stand Up? Boundary Stories about Virtual Cultures." In *Cyberspace: First Steps*, edited by Michael Benedikt. MIT Press.

Strandsbjerg, Jeppe. 2008. "The Cartographic Production of Territorial Space: Mapping and State Formation in Early Modern Denmark." *Geopolitics* 13 (2): 335–358.

Strawser, Bradley Jay. 2010. "Moral Predators: The Duty to Employ Uninhabited Aerial Vehicles." *Journal of Military Ethics* 9 (4): 342–368.

Suchman, Lucy. 2015. "Situational Awareness: Deadly Bioconvergence at the Boundaries of Bodies and Machines." *Media Tropes* 5 (1): 1–24.

Sullivan, J. M. 2006. "Evolution or Revolution? The Rise of UAVs." *IEEE Technology and Society Magazine* 25 (3): 43–49.

Sulmeyer, Michael. 2017. "Much Ado About Nothing? Cyber Command and the NSA." *War on the Rocks*, July 19. https://warontherocks.com/2017/07/much-ado-about-nothing-cyber-command-and-the-nsa/.

Swan, Ryan. 2019. "Drone Strikes: An Overview, Articulation and Assessment of the United States' Position Under International Law." Center for Global Security Research, Lawrence Livermore National Laboratory.

Thomas, Sue. 2013. *Technobiophilia: Nature and Cyberspace*. Bloomsbury.

Thongchai Winichakul. 1994. *Siam Mapped: A History of the Geo-Body of a Nation*. University of Hawai'i Press.

Tikk, Eneken, and Mika Kerttunen. 2018. "Parabasis: Cyber-Diplomacy in Stalemate." *NUPI Policy Brief*, May.

Tilly, Charles. 1992. *Coercion, Capital, and European States, AD 990–1992*. Wiley-Blackwell Publisher.

Toft, Monica Duffy. 2003. *The Geography of Ethnic Violence: Identity, Interests, and the Indivisibility of Territory*. Princeton University Press.

Townes, Miles. 2012. "The Spread of TCP/IP: How the Internet Became the Internet." *Millennium: Journal of International Studies* 41 (1): 43–64.

Turnbull, David. 1996. "Cartography and Science in Early Modern Europe: Mapping the Construction of Knowledge Spaces." *Imago Mundi* 48: 5–24.

United Kingdom Cabinet Office. 2009. "Cyber Security Strategy of the United Kingdom." https://www.gov.uk/government/uploads/system/uploads/attachment_data/file/228841/7642.pdf.

United Nations General Assembly (UNGA). 2013. "Report of the Group of Governmental Experts on Developments in the Field of Information and Telecommunications in the Context of International Security." A/68/98. June 24. https://www.un.org/ga/search/view_doc.asp?symbol=A/68/98.

United Nations General Assembly (UNGA). 2015. "Report of the Group of Governmental Experts on Developments in the Field of Information and Telecommunications in the Context of International Security." A/70/174. July 22. https://www.un.org/ga/search/view_doc.asp?symbol=A/70/174.

United Nations Security Council (UNSC). 2008. "Report of the Secretary-General on Ethiopia and Eritrea." S/2008/40. January 23. https://pcacases.com/web/sendAttach/847.

United States Air Force. 1995. "Cornerstones of Information Warfare." https://catalog.hathitrust.org/Record/101681332.

United States Air Force. 2011. "Air Force Doctrine Document 3-12: Cyberspace Operations, Incorporating Change 1." November 30. https://nsarchive2.gwu.edu/NSAEBB/NSAEBB424/docs/Cyber-060.pdf.

United States Army. 2010. "Cyberspace Operations Concept Capability Plan 2016-2028." February 22. https://nsarchive2.gwu.edu/NSAEBB/NSAEBB424/docs/Cyber-033.pdf.

United States Coast Guard. 2015. "United States Coast Guard Cyber Strategy." https://nsarchive2.gwu.edu//dc.html?doc=2692134-Document-26.

United States Cyber Command. 2016. "Order: To Establish Joint Task Force (JTF)-ARES to Counter the Islamic State of Iraq and the Levant (ISIL) in Cyber Space." May 5. https://nsarchive2.gwu.edu//dc.html?doc=3678213-Document-07-USCYBERCOM-to-CDRUSACYBER-Subj.

United States Cyber Command. 2018. "Achieve and Maintain Cyberspace Superiority: Command Vision for US Cyber Command." https://nsarchive2.gwu.edu//dc.html?doc=4421219-United-States-Cyber-Command-Achieve-and-Maintain.

United States Department of State. 1997. *The Road to Dayton: U.S. Diplomacy and the Bosnia Peace Process. May–December 1995.* http://nsarchive.gwu.edu/NSAEBB/NSAEBB171/.

United States Navy. 2012. "Navy Cyber Power 2020." https://nsarchive2.gwu.edu//dc.html?doc=2692124-Document-16.

United States Strategic Command. 2009. "The Cyber Warfare Lexicon." January 5. https://nsarchive2.gwu.edu//dc.html?doc=2692102-Document-1.

Valeriano, Brandon, and Ryan C. Maness. 2015. *Cyber War versus Cyber Realities: Cyber Conflict in the International System.* Oxford University Press.

Vinge, Vernor. 1981. *True Names.* Dell.

Vinge, Vernor. 2001. *True Names and the Opening of the Cyberspace Frontier.* Edited by James Frenkel. Tor Books.

Vitalis, Robert. 2015. *White World Order, Black Power Politics: The Birth of American International Relations.* Cornell University Press.

Wagner, Ben. 2019. "Constructed 'Cyber' Realities and International Relations Theory." In *Science, Technology, and Art in International Relations*, edited by J. P. Singh, Madeline Carr, and Renee Marlin-Bennett. Routledge.

Wallerstein, Immanuel. 1974. *The Modern World System*. Vol. 1. Academic Press.

Walter, Barbara F. 2003. "Explaining the Intractability of Territorial Conflict." *International Studies Review* 5 (4): 137–153.

Waltz, Kenneth N. 1979. *Theory of International Politics*. Addison-Wesley.

Warner, Michael. 2012. "Cybersecurity: A Pre-history." *Intelligence and National Security* 27 (5): 781–799.

Warner, Michael. 2015. "Notes on Military Doctrine for Cyberspace Operations in the United States, 1992–2014." *The Cyber Defense Review*, August 27.

Watters, Ethan. 1996. "Virtual War and Peace." *Wired*, March 1. https://www.wired.com/1996/03/virtual-war-and-peace/.

Weber, Cynthia. 1995. *Simulating Sovereignty: Intervention, the State and Symbolic Exchange*. Cambridge University Press.

Weber, Max. [1919] 1994. "The Profession and Vocation of Politics." In *Political Writings*, edited by Peter Lassman and Ronald Speirs. Cambridge University Press.

Weidmann, Nils B. 2015. "Communication, Technology, and Political Conflict: Introduction to the Special Issue." *Journal of Peace Research* 52 (3): 263–268.

Wenzlhuemer, Roland. 2013. *Connecting the Nineteenth-Century World: The Telegraph and Globalization*. Cambridge University Press.

White House. 1984. "National Security Decision Directive Number 145: National Policy on Telecommunications and Automated Information Systems Security." September 17. https://fas.org/irp/offdocs/nsdd145.htm.

White House. 1997. "Critical Foundations: Protecting America's Infrastructures." https://fas.org/sgp/library/pccip.pdf.

White House. 1998. PDD–63–Critical Infrastructure Protection." https://clinton.presidentiallibraries.us/items/show/12762.

White House. 2012. "Presidential Policy Directive/PPD-20: U.S. Cyber Operations Policy." October 16. https://nsarchive2.gwu.edu/dc.html?doc=2725521-Document-2-9.

Wilcox, Lauren. 2017. "Embodying Algorithmic War: Gender, Race, and the Posthuman in Drone Warfare." *Security Dialogue* 48 (1): 11–28.

Wilcox, Lauren. 2018. "Drones." In *Visual Global Politics*, edited by Roland Bleiker. Routledge.

Wille, Tobias. 2016. "Diplomatic Cable." In *Making Things International 2: Catalysts and Reactions*, edited by Mark B. Salter. University of Minnesota Press.

Williams, Alison. 2007. "*Hakumat al Tayarrat*: The Role of Air Power in the Enforcement of Iraq's Boundaries." *Geopolitics* 12 (3): 505–528.

Williams, Allison J. 2011. "Enabling Persistent Presence? Performing the Embodied Geopolitics of the Unmanned Aerial Vehicle Assemblage." *Political Geography* 30 (7): 381–390.

Williams, John. 2015. "Distant Intimacy: Space, Drones, and Just War." *Ethics & International Affairs* 29 (1): 93–110.

Winner, Langdon. 1977. *Autonomous Technology: Technics-out-of-Control as a Theme in Political Thought*. MIT Press.

Winner, Langdon. 1980. "Do Artifacts Have Politics?" *Daedalus* 109 (1): 121–136.

Winseck, Dwayne R., and Robert M. Pike. 2007. *Communications and Empire: Media, Markets, and Globalization, 1860–1930*. Duke University Press.

Wood, Denis. 2010. *Rethinking the Power of Maps*. Guilford Press.

Wood, William B. 2000. "GIS as a Tool for Territorial Negotiation." *IBRU Boundary and Security Bulletin* 72–79.

Woolgar, Steve, and Geoff Cooper. 1999. "Do Artefacts Have Ambivalence? Moses' Bridges, Winner's Bridges and other Urban Legends in S&TS." *Social Studies of Science* 29 (3): 433–449.

Work, Robert O., and Shawn Brimley. 2014. "20YY: Preparing for War in the Robotic Age." *Center for a New American Security*, January 22. https://www.cnas.org/publications/reports/20yy-preparing-for-war-in-the-robotic-age

Yang, Daqing. 2010. *Technology of Empire: Telecommunications and Japanese Expansion in Asia, 1883–1945*. Harvard University Press.

Yen, Alfred C. 2002. "Western Frontier or Feudal Society? Metaphors and Perceptions of Cyberspace." *Berkeley Technology Law Journal* 17 (4): 1207–1263.

Zandvliet, Kees. 2007. "Mapping the Dutch World Overseas in the Seventeenth Century." In *The History of Cartography, Vol. 3: Cartography in the European Renaissance*, edited by David Woodward. University of Chicago Press.

Zeng, Jinghan, Tim Stevens, and Yaru Chen. 2017. "China's Solution to Global Cyber Governance: Unpacking the Domestic Discourse of 'Internet Sovereignty.'" *Politics & Policy* 45 (3): 432–464.

INDEX

For the benefit of digital users, indexed terms that span two pages (e.g., 52–53) may, on occasion, appear on only one of those pages.

Tables are indicated by _t_ following the page number.